Dimensions of the Modern Novel

Dimensions of the Modern Novel

German Texts and European Contexts

THEODORE ZIOLKOWSKI

Princeton University Press, Princeton, New Jersey

1969

PT
772
.Z5

For my mother
   and
In memory of my father

Preface

THIS book has a twofold aim: to display some of the brilliant diversity that characterizes the modern German novel and, at the same time, to suggest certain common features that unify the genre in theme and in structure. For this reason I have approached the works from two different points of view: textually and contextually, analytically and analogically. Part I examines five representative texts in close detail in an effort to determine the unique brilliance of each, while Part II expands the focus in order to view these same novels within certain broader contexts. The reader is invited to exercise the optics of his imagination to align the two images into what might be called a stereoscopic vision offering both solidity and perspective, both precision and scope.

My approach to the texts of Part I has been by way of structural analysis. It is helpful, when one is reading a literary work, to put certain questions to it. The question that I have found most productive with novels is this: by what process of selection and organization does the work manage to shape an artistic unity from the totality of the world? It is a question that can be asked of any novel, regardless of its theme or style, and it does not preclude other questions of equal importance. In fact, the response in each case alerts us to the problems that most urgently concern the author. Thus the theoretical remarks at the end of Chapter Five are not intended to be restrictive; they merely propose one possible and methodologically consistent access to fiction. And they explain why I chose these five particular texts for detailed analysis. Needless to say, my choice implies a critical bias toward these novels by Rilke, Kafka, Mann, Döblin, and Broch, but no prejudice against the many that I have omitted.

The more general essays of Part II emerge directly from the interpretations of Part I, for the themes and images that

Preface

I singled out for discussion there—time, death, the thirty-year-old hero, criminality, and insanity—play a conspicious role in the five representative novels. In each case I have briefly sketched the historical development of the theme or image in order to highlight more sharply the characteristically modern form that it assumes in the twentieth century. And I have tried to indicate how deeply these problems are rooted in the general moral consciousness of our times.

These topics, of course, are neither restrictive nor exhaustive: modern literature provides an abundance of themes and images that lay claim to our attention. But the five chapters are closely interrelated and constitute, I believe, a unified whole. For time, like Cronus himself, generates many offspring. It turned out to be impossible to discuss time without a consideration of death. The awareness of time and death, in turn, contributes to the crisis of the thirty-year-old hero. The latter's attempt to suspend time in an effort to avoid commitment and death produces the uneasy conscience that sees itself mirrored in the image of the criminal. And the madhouse appears with startling frequency as the symbolic place where time is held in abeyance.

It should be evident by now that this book does not pretend to offer an exhaustive survey of the twentieth-century German novel. The reader looking for a more inclusive catalogue would do well to consult the two systematic treatments: H. M. Waidson, *The Modern German Novel: A Mid-Twentieth Century Survey* (Oxford University Press, 1959); and Werner Welzig, *Der deutsche Roman im 20. Jahrhundert* (Stuttgart: Kröners Taschenausgabe, Bd. 367, 1967). But to the extent that the five texts of Part I delimit the representative potentialities of the genre and the broader contexts of Part II adumbrate its magnitude, the book as a whole suggests certain "dimensions" of the modern novel that are valid, I believe, well beyond the examples that I treat.

Preface

Although many of the works mentioned here are available in English, I have preferred, unless otherwise indicated, to make my own translations. In order to demonstrate similarities in theme and imagery both within individual works and among them, it is necessary to maintain a level of precision and dogged consistency that is not always feasible—or perhaps even desirable—in standard translations. However, I would like to mention the highly readable English versions of the five basic texts, which I have consulted from time to time without relying upon them: Rainer Maria Rilke, *The Notebooks of Malte Laurids Brigge*, trans. M. D. Herter Norton (1949; New York: W. W. Norton, 1964); Franz Kafka, *The Trial*, trans. Willa and Edwin Muir (1937; rev. by E. M. Butler: New York: Modern Library, 1957); Thomas Mann, *The Magic Mountain*, trans. H. T. Lowe-Porter (1927; New York: Modern Library College Edn., 1967); Alfred Döblin, *Alexanderplatz, Berlin: The Story of Franz Biberkopf*, trans. Eugene Jolas (New York: Viking Press, 1931); Hermann Broch, *The Sleepwalkers: A Trilogy*, trans. Willa and Edwin Muir (1932; New York: Pantheon, 1964). All other bibliographical references are given in the footnotes.

The verses by Hilaire Belloc are reprinted with the permission of Alfred A. Knopf, Inc., and those by Ogden Nash with the permission of Little, Brown and Company.

Two chapters of this book have already appeared in print: Chapter Eight in *Comparatists at Work*, ed. Stephen G. Nichols, Jr., and Richard B. Vowles (Waltham, Mass.: Blaisdell, 1968); and Chapter Ten as "Der Blick von der Irrenanstalt: Verrückung der Perspektive in der modernen deutschen Prosa," *Neophilologus*, Vol. 51 (1967). Both essays appear here, in substantially revised and expanded form, with the permission of the editors and publishers.

I wrote several parts of this book with the aid of a grant

Preface

from the John Simon Guggenheim Memorial Foundation, for which I am deeply grateful. Princeton University generously supported my work both through a leave of absence and with a subsidy for preparation of the manuscript.

Here and there in the notes I have been able to acknowledge specific debts of gratitude. More generally, Hermann J. Weigand deserves my special thanks for listening to Chapter Four and for giving me, as so often in the past, the benefit of his experience and knowledge. I am particularly indebted to two friends and former colleagues, Walter Sokel and Victor Brombert, in whom I was fortunate enough to find the perfect readers for my manuscript: their impressive command of modern literature is matched by an urbane sense of style; their incisive critical frankness by a generous readiness to understand an author's intentions.

For the past four years I have worked on various projects with Princeton University Press, and the association has been so thoroughly pleasant that I am eager to express my appreciation to my friends there. In particular, I would like to mention R. Miriam Brokaw, whose gratifying enthusiasm and responsiveness as Associate Director have benefited me and many other authors. And I am especially grateful to Linda Peterson, whose incorruptible editorial acuity has sharpened my text in many passages where I tried to take the easy way out.

The last and most important acknowledgment is at the same time the most difficult to express: it would require a poem rather than a few lines of prose in a preface. Let me merely suggest that if a scholar-critic can be said to have a Muse, it is probably his wife.

Theodore Ziolkowski

Princeton, New Jersey
June 1968

x

Contents

xi

Part I

German Texts

chapter one

Rainer Maria Rilke

The Notebooks of Malte Laurids Brigge

(1)

IN ONE of his entries, the author of Rilke's fictional notebooks recalls the peculiar story of his former neighbor in a St. Petersburg hotel, a minor official named Nikolai Kusmitsch. On an idle Sunday it once occurred to Kusmitsch to calculate how much time was left to him, assuming he should live for fifty years more, in days, hours, and minutes. He even "converted" his time into seconds and was staggered by the immense "capital" with which he was suddenly blessed. Overwhelmed by this unexpected wealth of time, he began to keep his books very carefully, trying to "save" time whenever possible. He got up earlier, "spent" less time washing, and ran everywhere. But when he balanced his books on each successive Sunday, there were never any tangible "savings." He chided himself because he had not demanded his time in large denominations—say, in four ten-year bills, one five-year, and the rest in petty cash—rather than in the "infamous small change" that slips so easily through one's fingers. In his despair he pored over the municipal address book to locate a "Time Bank," a "Bank for Time," or an "Imperial Time Institute" that might advise him in his economies. Eventually Nikolai Kusmitsch awakened to the fact that he had been deceiving himself by thinking of time in terms of finances. Time, after all, was a dimension that affected everyone in the same way, and not simply a personal affront to him.

3

Rainer Maria Rilke

Just as Nikolai Kusmitsch attained this consoling rationalization, a new sensation smote him. Sitting quietly in his dark room, he began to feel a draft: it was time flowing by! (It is probably not unreasonable to conjecture that Rilke is playing, here, with the conception, current in nineteenth-century physics until the experiments of Michelson and Morley, of an ether that surrounds the world.) Thinking of the neuralgic discomfort that this constant draft would cause, he sprang to his feet in annoyance; but at this moment he sensed a motion under his feet: the revolution of the earth! When he recalled that the axis of the earth is set at an oblique angle, his agony was complete. Despairing of standing upright on a tilted earth, Nikolai Kusmitsch remained in a reclining position from that moment forth. He lay on his couch all day long, reciting from memory poems by Pushkin and Nekrassow. "When one repeated a poem slowly, giving the final rhymes equal stress, then there was, so to speak, something stable that one could keep in sight—inwardly, of course."[1]

The story of Nikolai Kusmitsch is one of the longest episodes that Malte interpolates in his notebooks. As if to underline its importance, Malte concludes: "I remember this story in such detail because it consoled me uncommonly." At this point the reader asks himself why this should be so. In technique the story does not differ from many other episodes in the notebooks. Rilke has taken an abstract topic, time, and treated it with a technical vocabulary borrowed from the area of banking and commerce. This produces the same weirdly comic effect that he achieves elsewhere, for instance, by describing death in terms taken from the jargon of tailors and clothing manufacturers. This technique, moreover

[1] Rainer Maria Rilke, *Die Aufzeichnungen des Malte Laurids Brigge*, pp. 863-70; henceforth cited as *Malte*. Quoted here and elsewhere from Vol. VI of Rilke's *Sämtliche Werke*, ed. Ernst Zinn and Ruth Sieber-Rilke (Frankfurt am Main: Insel, 1966), pp. 709-946.

The Notebooks

—the reification of a metaphor ("to save time")—was not uncommon in the literature of the period. Expressionist dramas, for instance, often exploit precisely the same device for their surreal effects.[2] Similarly, Kafka's "Metamorphosis" is sometimes explained as a concretization of his father's metaphoric abuse when he called Kafka a "dung beetle." In the second part of the episode Rilke achieves an equally grotesque effect by describing the reaction of a hypersensitive temperament when it reduces the abstractions of science— the ether and the revolution of the earth—to its own subjective experience.

It is the ending of the anecdote, rather than its technique, that strikes us as important. For despite his anguish over the passing of time, Nikolai Kusmitsch finds tranquillity when he recites poetry to himself. This aesthetic refutation of temporality consoles Malte. The arrow of time is halted by the power of art. When Nikolai Kusmitsch intones the cadences of Pushkin, time is suspended and he is no longer tormented by its flow. In a letter written fifteen years after the publication of *The Notebooks*, Rilke remarked that the many figures evoked in the novel represent "vocables of [Malte's] anguish."[3] If this applies to Nikolai Kusmitsch, as unquestionably it does, then time is one of the sources of Malte's own anguish. But to pursue the analogy further: Malte seeks in

[2] E.g., Oskar Kokoschka's *Job* (*Hiob*, 1917), in which such metaphors as "she turned his head" and "she put horns on him" are actually enacted upon Job, whose head is wrenched awry and who sprouts antlers. See Walter H. Sokel's introduction to his anthology of *German Expressionist Drama* (New York: Anchor Books, 1963).

[3] Letter of November 10, 1925, to Witold von Hulewicz: "Vokabeln seiner Not." Unless otherwise indicated, all Rilke letters can be found in the six-volume edition of *Gesammelte Briefe, 1892-1926* (Leipzig: Insel, 1939), or in the six single volumes of letters published by Insel Verlag from 1930 to 1937. Several of the letters from the early Paris years are not included in the edition of *Briefe* published by Insel in 1950.

the timelessness of art a refuge from his own temporal existence. If we examine the novel as a whole from this point of view, we find that the tension between the temporality of existence and the timelessness of art does indeed constitute one of the main themes—if not the principal one!—of the whole work and that, further, it determines in large measure the structure of the book.

Time, and especially this conflict between the temporality of life and the timelessness of art, emerges as an increasingly dominant theme throughout Rilke's works. In a poem celebrating "L'Ange du Méridien" (1906), Rilke explicitly contrasts the clock time of mortals with the eternity of art, for the angel on the cathedral at Chartres is impervious to the hours that flow across the sundial that he holds in his arms. For the angel, time is suspended "in a profound equilibrium, as though all hours were ripe and rich":

> gewahrst du gar nicht, wie dir unsre Stunden
> abgleiten von der vollen Sonnenuhr,
>
> auf der des Tages ganze Zahl zugleich,
> gleich wirklich, steht in tiefem Gleichgewichte,
> als wären alle Stunden reif und reich.

One of the central themes of the *Duino Elegies* (1922), stated emphatically in the first poem, is time. And one of the last of the *Sonnets to Orpheus* (ii, 27) asks in its opening line: "Giebt es wirklich die Zeit, die zerstörende?" ("Does Time, the destroyer, really exist?")

Rilke's conception of time develops and is refined in the course of the twenty years from his early poems to the *Sonnets to Orpheus*. We are concerned here only with the precipitation of the theme in the novel. It has sometimes been observed that Rilke has a tendency to translate time into spatial metaphors in his poetry; some critics have even denied that he deals at all, properly speaking, with the dimension of time as such. Certainly, few of the poems refer as explicitly as "L'Ange du Méridien" to the contrast between timelessness and the mechanical clock time of man. In *The Notebooks*, however, Rilke explicitly and repeatedly refers to time; the story of Nikolai Kusmitsch is simply the most elaborate example. Elsewhere we hear of people whose lives "run down like a clock in an empty room." A voice is said to have "the even, indifferent cadence of a clock." In another description Malte observes that a person's life, in the intervals between real action, "jerks along like the hand of a clock, like the shadow of its hands, like time." In all of these instances the clock is a negative image symbolizing the mechanical movement of temporality. In one notable passage Malte remarks that his own daily life, "which nothing interrupts, is like a clock-face without hands." The only good clock, in other words, is a broken clock, for this observation occurs in one of the scenes during which Malte manages to forget his present temporality by succumbing to his memories of the past. Such textual hints as these alert us to the fact that Malte's struggle for identity, fought out on the battleground of his notebooks, must constantly be viewed in terms of the tension between temporality and timelessness.[4]

(2)

MALTE Laurids Brigge is a young Danish nobleman of shabby gentility. He grew up on the family estate at Ulsgaard, his childhood punctuated by a succession of deaths of close relatives. During his adolescence he spent an unhappy period at the Academy at Sörö, years lightened only by his gentle love for his cousin Abelone. As the family died out and its fortunes declined, Malte's father sold the estate and moved

---

[4] *Malte*, pp. 727, 734, 900, and 766.

to Copenhagen, while Malte himself went abroad for his travels, to Russia, France, and Italy. After his father's death Malte returned to Denmark to settle the family affairs. At the time he begins to keep his notebook—the first and only dated entry bears the notation "September 11"—he has just arrived for the first time in Paris. He is twenty-eight years old, unattached, and the author of a study of Carpaccio, a drama about marriage, and some verse.

His life and experiences up to this point have hardly prepared Malte for Paris. Here is the first entry in his notebooks:

> So, this is where people come in order to live; I should sooner think that this is a place for dying. I have been out. I have seen: hospitals. I saw a man who staggered and fell down. People gathered around him; that spared me the end. I saw a pregnant woman. She was pushing herself heavily along a high, warm wall, toward which she groped from time to time as though to convince herself that it was still there. Yes, it was still there. Behind it? I looked at my street-map: Maison d'Accouchement. Good. They will deliver her. They know how.

This is an interesting and revealing passage. Its contrapuntal alternation between the first-person singular and "the others" ("people," "they") exemplifies Malte's alienation.[5] Malte's defensive tone is more precisely defined by two further characteristic attitudes: a tendency to retreat from reality ("that spared me the end") and a sense of helplessness ("They know how"). The fact of isolation is intensified to an almost unbearable pitch by the diction: style and meaning complement each other perfectly and establish one of the central

---

[5] The German text with its impersonal constructions ("es stürbe sich hier") brings out this contrast even more sharply than the English translation.

The Notebooks

themes of the work. For Malte is always isolated from the group. We see him alone among a frolicking carnival crowd, alone among the readers in the Bibliothèque Nationale. In fact, several of his entries, as when he speaks of Beethoven and Ibsen ("the loneliest one"), are hymns to solitude. The world that Malte encounters as he looks around is strangely dehumanized. Note, for instance, the impersonality of death in the following passage:

> This distinguished Hôtel is very old; even in King Clodwig's time people died here in a number of beds. Now the dying goes on in 559 beds. Factory-like, of course. Where production is so enormous the individual death is not so well made. But that doesn't really matter. It is quantity that counts. Who cares anything nowadays for a finely tailored death?

This creeping dehumanization, evident wherever Malte turns, is reflected in the style of the narrative. Hands, for instance, are mentioned with notable frequency, but they are always hands that are somehow detached from the human body; they have become independent things, unrelated objects. "Somewhere a withered, flecked hand crept forward and trembled." "But a day will come when my hand will be far from me, and when I tell it to write, it will write words that I do not mean." "The hands looked malicious and angry." "He took Abelone's hands and opened them like a book." The human body has lost its integrity. In a hospital Malte sees, beneath the bandages, "a single eye that belonged to no one" and "a leg in a cast that protruded from the row on the bench, as large as a whole person."[6]

As death and the human body lose their dignity, things become increasingly personalized and dominant. "Electric

[6] *Malte*, pp. 713, 741, 756, 773, 851, and 759-60.

Rainer Maria Rilke

trains tear, clanging, through my room. Automobiles roll over me. A door falls to. Somewhere a window pane clatters down, I hear its big pieces laugh, the little slivers giggle." "In the long beds of the garden single flowers stood up and said: 'Red' with a shocked voice." Stale air creeps out of open windows "with a bad conscience"; the exposed wall of a wrecked house, with its plumbing fixtures, looks like the cross section of a human intestine. Even jars have a personality. "A top like that ought to have no other desire than to be situated on its jar: this ought to be the utmost that it can imagine; a satisfaction not to be exceeded, the fulfillment of all its wishes."[7]

In a world where people are dehumanized and things personalized, man finds himself wholly at the mercy of the objects surrounding him. Twenty-five years before Sartre's *La Nausée*, Malte is oppressed by a sensation closely akin to the existential "viscousness" of things. We hear of "balconies, onto which one is forced by a little door." A little piece of lace can "fence off our sight, as though we were monasteries or prisons." People are even aghast at the very blood that runs in their veins. "Often it frightened him: it might attack him in his sleep and tear him apart." And a mirror can assume more power over man than the cruelest tyrant. Here is the scene. Malte, as a child, has dressed up in some old costumes that he discovered in the attic.

Hot and angry, I rushed to the mirror and peered laboriously through the mask while my hands worked. But it had been waiting just for this moment. The moment of retribution had come. While I exerted myself in measurelessly increasing uneasiness and sought somehow to force myself out of my disguise, it compelled me—I don't know how—to look up and dictated to me an image, no,

[7] *Malte*, pp. 710, 722, 768, 749-50, and 876-77.

a reality—a strange, incomprehensible, monstrous reality—with which I was saturated against my will: for now it was the stronger of us, and I was the mirror.[8]

This, then, is the situation in which Malte finds himself when he begins to write his notebooks. Alienated from the world about him, threatened in the integrity of his own personality, menaced by the intrusion of hostile and powerful objects, Malte has reached the zero point. He is, as he calls himself, "this Nothing"[9]—a terrified Nothing in a world without order or meaning. When he has been in Paris for three weeks, Malte starts to write a letter, but it occurs to him that his experiences have altered him so radically as to make him a wholly new and different person. "Somewhere else, in the country for instance, three weeks could be like a day; here it is years. I don't want to write any more letters. Why should I tell anyone that I am changing? If I change, then I am no longer the same person that I was, and if I am different from before, then it is clear that I have no acquaintances."[10]

Malte's dilemma prefigures that of the heroes of many modern novels: cut off from his family, his friends, his past, he is rootless, a foreigner, a "stranger" in a hostile city. A new group of images characterizing his situation crowds his mind. He notices, for instance, that he seems to attract beggars and other "rejects" (*Fortgeworfene*) of life—those "peelings, husks of men that fate has spit out."[11] Although his suit is frayed, his shoes scuffed, and his beard neglected, Malte insists at first that he has nothing in common with that band of outcasts. But finally, when his illness drives him to the clinic, he finds that the doctors treat him as one of the

[8] *Malte*, pp. 729, 835, 885, and 807-8.
[9] *Malte*, p. 726: "dieses Nichts."
[10] *Malte*, p. 711.   [11] *Malte*, p. 743.

11

"rejects." This exterior change that takes place during his first six months in Paris reflects the total alienation of his inner being. Reduced to a "Nothing," to one of life's "rejects," Malte must find a way out of his dilemma, or perish.

(3)

MALTE'S anguish, and ultimately his redemption, stem directly from the experience that he calls "learning to see." Piercing through the deceptive veil of accepted conceptions, he encounters reality directly and without the mediation of conventional notions. "I am learning to see. I don't know why it is, but everything penetrates more deeply into me and does not stop at the point where it formerly ended."[12] But this new reality is so unaccustomed that he is frightened by each fresh perception. "I am afraid" echoes like a refrain through the opening pages of the book. For Malte's vision has also revealed to him that the conceptions which formerly gave men faith, which formerly held the world together, have also disintegrated, becoming as discrete and random as the dissociated limbs in the hospital. "Is it possible," he thinks, "that nothing real and important has yet been seen, perceived, and said? Is it possible that men have had thousands of years of time to look, to reflect, and to write it down, and that they have allowed the millennia to slip past like a school recess in which one eats a sandwich and an apple?"[13]

The trouble, Malte gradually concludes, is that man has analyzed all meaning to pieces. In his blind search for categories and systems, man has overlooked the essentials. "Is it possible that men, despite inventions and progress, despite culture, religion and philosophy, have remained on the surface of life?" Even God has been conceptualized out of exist-

---

[12] *Malte*, p. 710.   [13] *Malte*, p. 726.

The Notebooks

ence. "Is it possible that there are people who say 'God' and think it is something they have in common?" Things liberated from the controlling restraints of conventional beliefs float freely, in a chaos, like the parts of bodies that Malte sees about him, and assume that threatening aspect that characterizes the external world in his eyes. Malte's fear, then, is directly related to the breakdown of established order, to his inability to accept conventional patterns of reality any longer. In order to escape his anguish, Malte must find a new possibility of order, one within which the things will once again have a place. And this order, in his mind, is linked to the problem of time.

In the first of his *Duino Elegies* (written in 1912, only two years after the publication of *The Notebooks*) Rilke noted that mortals make the mistake of distinguishing too sharply between things, whereas angels are often unaware whether they are walking among the living or the dead.

—Aber Lebendige machen
alle den Fehler, dass sie zu stark unterscheiden.
Engel (sagt man) wüssten oft nicht, ob sie unter
Lebenden gehn oder Toten. Die ewige Strömung
reisst durch beide Bereiche alle Alter
immer mit sich und übertönt sie in beiden.

Yet even in this world it is possible to live like the angels, aware of the "eternal streaming" that unites all realms of being. Quite early in the journal, Malte recalls his grandfather's rather remarkable attitude toward time:

Sequences of time played no role whatsoever for him. Death was a minor incident that he totally ignored. Persons whom he had once taken into his memory existed, and their death could not change that in the least. Several

13

years later, after the old gentleman's death, it was said that he insisted with equal obstinacy that the future was also present.[14]

People who have attained the level of awareness of the angels—or of Grandfather Brahe—never feel threatened by reality, for everything exists in an eternal order of simultaneity. Unlike ordinary men, they have not broken down the patterns of being by making ever greater distinctions and articulations until no meaningful whole is left. For such men even death poses no threat, since it too is absorbed into the whole as a meaningful part.

In the course of his notebooks Malte slowly works his way toward this goal of simultaneous experience of totality, which alone produces true freedom from fear and death. But he begins more modestly. His first response to his anguish, like that of Nikolai Kusmitsch, is an aesthetic one. "I have done something against my fear. I have sat up the whole night and written."[15] Here we see the true instigation for Malte's notebooks. They represent, at first, an attempt to combat his fear of reality as it has been exposed to him through his new sense of seeing, by organizing his sensations into meaningful aesthetic patterns that will replace the disintegrated patterns of conventional belief. If he can succeed in giving an aesthetic meaning to the things and sensations that rush in upon him, he can halt the flow of temporality by suspending it in an aesthetic whole.

The entirety of *The Notebooks*, in the last analysis, gains its structure through Malte's attempts to come to grips, progressively, with different areas of his experience. For the material is organized roughly, though not in any rigorously systematic way, into three successive groups. First, he is obsessed with the immediate present reality of his life in Paris.

[14] *Malte*, p. 735.　　　　[15] *Malte*, p. 721.

The Notebooks

Gradually he moves back, through interpolated memories that are usually catalyzed by experiences in the present, to the reexperiencing of his own family and of his childhood. Finally, in the second part of the novel, his focus expands to embrace the historical past. Malte's quest for meaning, in other words, leads him to search for his identity in three areas: as an individual, within the group, and in the light of history. Ultimately, as we shall see, this progression leads him to search for a new definition of God: his own identity against the background of eternity. Near the end of his notebooks Malte remarks: "Even before we have begun God, we pray to him: let us survive the night. And then illness. And then love."[16] The night, illness, love, and God—these are the stages of Malte's development. The first half of the book reflects his attempts to survive the first terrible nights in Paris and the illness, a hereditary nervous disorder, that drives him into the very hospitals he fears. In the second part he has recovered sufficiently to think about the problem of love, which leads, in the last pages, to his meditations on God.

(4)

UP TO this point we have talked about *The Notebooks* as though it constituted a novel in the conventional sense of the word. It does not, of course. Even though many novelistic elements are included, they must be reconstructed from the work as a whole. We learn, for instance, a great many details of Malte's life before his arrival in Paris, but these facts are not arranged in any narrative or causal sequence; they are scattered seemingly at random through the notebooks and must be reassembled into a chronological pattern. It is this discrepancy that first alerts us to the fact that Rilke's "prose-book," as he customarily designates it, cannot be

16 *Malte*, p. 926.

grasped according to the structural principles of conventional fiction.

We can approach Rilke's method by considering for a moment the genesis of the work. Though it was not published until 1910, Rilke worked on the book sporadically from 1904 on, and most intensively in the years 1908 and 1909. During much of this period he was living in Paris, but Malte's reaction to the city is based almost wholly on Rilke's experiences during his first visit in 1902-1903.

In order to appreciate fully the impact of that year, we must dispel the mystical aura that often surrounds the name Rilke. The young man who arrived in Paris that August was still far from the object of cultish devotion that he was to become even during his later lifetime. Although he had enjoyed a certain mild *succès d'estime*, Rilke had not as yet written any of his major works. A few stories and poetic dramas plus several slender volumes of rather precious verse—that was the extent of his oeuvre. This was no literary lion come to conquer the salons of Paris. Rilke made his trip on commission, in order to write a small monograph on Auguste Rodin for a series of art volumes to which he had already contributed a study of the Worpswede painters in North Germany. He was prepared to be a disciple in the temple of French culture, a worshipful pupil—Rilke felt at home on his knees—of the symbolist heritage, of Baudelaire, of Mallarmé.[17] His first letters to Rodin, whom he addressed as "Cher Maître," bear the mark of his humility. And it was only after reading *The Notebooks* that Gide conceded to Aline Mayrisch that "through this last book Rilke takes his place beside us."[18] The young poet was not surrounded by

[17] See K.A.J. Batterby, *Rilke and France; A Study in Poetic Development* (London: Oxford University Press, 1966).

[18] Letter of January 14, 1911; in Rilke and Gide, *Correspondance, 1909-1926*, ed. Renée Lang (Paris: Corrêa, 1952), p. 53.

friends and admirers; that was still to come. Alone, timid, Rilke set out each day from his room in Rue Toullier (Malte's address as well) to discover the world he knew through the French art and literature that he admired so boundlessly—only to beat a quick retreat before the bustling life of the modern urban monster that Paris had become in his eyes.

In Rilke's letters from this early period we hear the lamenting voice of Malte. "Paris (we tell ourselves daily) is an oppressive, frightening city. And the lovely things that are here, with all their glittering eternity, cannot compensate for all that one must suffer from the brutality and confusion of the streets and the unnaturalness of the gardens, people, and things. For my apprehensive feeling Paris has something unutterably frightening."[19] This passage, with its people and things crowding in upon the writer and its sense of fear, could have come straight out of *The Notebooks*. In another letter he mentions the hospitals that Malte sees in the first lines of the novel. "I now understand why they constantly appear in the works of Verlaine, Baudelaire, and Mallarmé. In every street you see sick people entering and leaving them. . . . You suddenly feel that in this wide city there are troops of the sick, armies of the dying, and races of the dead."[20] This oppressiveness was something that Rilke had experienced in no other city: Prague, Munich, Berlin, St. Petersburg. For him, Paris was "an alien, alien city."

Rilke undertook his novel specifically in order to come to terms with the experiences of that first year. By the time he started, in February of 1904, he was safely in Rome and the threat of Paris lay behind him. As he worked on his novel, his own attitude toward Paris changed. Describing Paris in

[19] Letter of December 31, 1902, to Otto Modersohn.
[20] Letter of August 31, 1902, to his wife Clara.

Rainer Maria Rilke

May 1906, he thinks of Malte, "who would have loved all this as I do if he had been able to survive his great fear."[21] The following year he wrote to a friend that he had never been "so happy and capable and alone" as in Paris.[22] He can barely tolerate the thought that he had had to leave Paris the preceding summer. "It seems to me as though everything, above all my work, depends upon how soon I can get back there."[23] In order to recover the mood of that first year of misery he requested the return of letters he had written to his wife Clara and to his friend Lou Andreas-Salomé during his despair. These letters contain many of the episodes that later made their way, totally reshaped, into his "prose-book." Although almost every important passage in the novel has an autobiographical basis, often recorded in letters and diaries, the fictional form is consciously shaped to meet the requirements of the work.[24]

The terrifying experiences of Paris in 1902 and 1903, then, constitute the emotional basis of *The Notebooks*, the aspect that deals with Malte's quest for his meaning as an individual. It was not until the latter half of 1904 that Rilke made his first trip to Sweden and Denmark, where he absorbed the atmosphere that went into the second area of the novel: Malte's family and childhood. The Scandinavian background was integrated into Rilke's own personal experience of Paris in order to objectify even more his attitude toward his fictional hero.

It is an easy and fascinating task to reconstruct, from Rilke's letters, the chronology of his travels and the sequence of his readings during the years 1904 to 1910, and thus to

[21] Letter of May 13, 1906, to his wife Clara.
[22] Letter of February 9, 1907, to Ellen Key.
[23] Letter of February 5, 1907, to Paula Modersohn-Becker.
[24] See Eva Cassirer-Solmitz, *Rainer Maria Rilke* (Heidelberg: Obermüller, 1957), Chap. 2, which quotes from Rilke's unpublished diaries.

The Notebooks

catalogue the places and events that constitute the third area of Malte's quest: his meaning in history. But when we correlate the biographical material with the events in the novel, we note immediately that Rilke has reshaped the facts of his own life—his travels, his readings, even his personal experiences in Paris—to take their place in Malte's notebooks regardless of chronological or causal sequence. Thus a letter to Lou Andreas-Salomé, written in July of 1903, contains the original form of an episode (the St. Vitus Dancer) that is told well along in the notebooks, in the spring, by Malte. And another passage that comes early in the novel—the Seine tableau discussed below—occurs in a letter to Rilke's wife as late as 1907. The events and experiences of eight years, in other words, are packed into a narrative that ostensibly records the incidents of somewhat less than a year in Malte's life. And within that compact space the incidents are liberated from any causal relation that they had in Rilke's own biography before they are inserted into the fiction.

This is not a particularly profound observation; it can simply serve as a warning to critics who are fond of establishing close parallels between authors and their fictional heroes. But it reveals a characteristic process, for it reflects the way in which Malte deals with the incidents of his own life in his notebooks. Ripping the events of his past out of their context (even the sequence of deaths in the family is altered), Malte seeks to build up his life into a new pattern. This dissolution of sequential time, moreover, has a deeper, more existential significance for Malte. By freeing his past from any causal nexus, he at the same time asserts his own freedom of identity and liberates himself from temporality. The true heir of his grandfather, Malte attempts through the reshaping of the past in his notebooks to escape the threat of time and death.

It is not only his past, however, that Malte subjects to this process of meaningful reshaping. His most immediate need is to escape the threat of the present: to survive the night, as he says. To achieve this he filters all his experience through his controlling aesthetic imagination so that each scene comes out as a meaningful piece of art.

(5)

MALTE'S notebooks contain notes ("Aufzeichnungen"), in contrast to systematic journal entries or organized autobiographical reminiscences. Although the first entry is dated and although there are enough hints for us to establish the sequence of early fall, winter, spring, and summer, external time plays no role at all for Malte. The notes themselves are independent blocks of prose, ranging in length from a paragraph to several pages and tied together by no causal links. Let us examine a typical example that occurs early in the book.

It is astonishing how much a small moon can do. There are days when everything surrounding us is bright, light, scarcely indicated in the clear air and still distinct. Even the nearest object has tones of distance, is carried away and merely shown, not presented to us; and whatever is related to expanse—the river, the bridges, the long streets, and the plazas that expend themselves—these things have collected their expanse behind themselves, are painted upon it as though upon silk. It cannot be described what, at those times, a light-green carriage on the Pont-neuf can be, or some red that is not to be restrained, or even a placard on the fire-wall of a pearl-gray group of houses. Everything is simplified, reduced to a few right, bright planes, like the face in a portrait by Manet. And nothing is trivial or superfluous. The booksellers along the quai open their stands, and the fresh or shabby yellow of the books, the violet brown of the bindings, the larger green of an album: everything harmonizes, counts, participates, and constitutes a fullness in which nothing is missing.[25]

It would be a sacrilege against poetry to attempt to translate this vision back into its empirical reality. But it is clear what Malte has done here. A commonplace scene, the Seine near the Pont-Neuf, has been shaped into a pattern in which "nothing is trivial or superfluous." The objects are not detached or out of context; everything has its place within the structure of the whole. And Rilke-Malte has achieved this effect by converting the scene into the planes of an impressionist painting; the references to Manet and to painting on silk are not gratuitous.

This particular vignette, taken verbatim from a letter of October 12, 1907 to his wife, was written during the days when Rilke was visiting the Salon d'Automne of 1907; this letter and others teem with discussions of Cézanne and with references to Manet, whose palette Rilke particularly admired. The entire scene is rendered almost solely in terms of its colors and their relations. Malte transforms reality into aesthetics: "landscape into art," to use Kenneth Clark's phrase. But by doing so—and this is the central point—he lifts the component elements from the flow of time. The very first sentence contributes to the effect, for contrary to one's first impression, it is not a tableau under moonlight that Malte is describing, but a daytime scene. The reference to the moon, as the full text of the letter makes clear, is meteorological. It is the moon, according to Rilke, that has given the air its clarity after several gray, misty days. But the subtle and unmotivated shift from night to day creates the effect of suspension of time.[26] Captured in his word-picture and

---

[25] *Malte*, pp. 722-23.

[26] In a highly perceptive article, "Zum dichterischen Verfahren in

given a meaningful function there, the objects are timeless and constitute no threat to the viewer. The light-green carriage on the bridge, rendered immobile in this scene, cannot race through his room, terrifying him like the streetcars and automobiles of those first nights in Paris. The river and the books—all have their function and place in the tableau. Malte has given form and meaning to a reality that was previously formless and fortuitous; he has constructed a new vision of unity in accord with his heightened sense of sight. In a letter to Lou Andreas-Salomé Rilke wrote: "Objects are distinct; the object of art must be even more distinct . . . lifted out of time, handed over to space, it has become more enduring, capable of eternity."[27] This is precisely what Rilke has done with the river scene: rendered it capable of eternity.

The very next entry has precisely the same function, but this time the technique is entirely different. Looking out of his fifth-floor room, Malte observes the following scene:

> Down below is the following composition: a small handcart, pushed by a woman; on the front of it a hurdy-gurdy, lengthwise. Behind it, diagonally, a babybasket in which a very small child stands on sturdy legs, content in its bonnet, and refuses to be forced to sit down. From to time the woman cranks the organ. The small child then immediately gets up again, stamping in its basket, and a little girl in a green Sunday-dress dances and shakes her tambourine up toward the windows.

Rilkes *Aufzeichnungen des Malte Laurids Brigge*," Ernst Hoffmann cites this passage as an example of Rilke's tendency to withhold the original causal sequence underlying certain passages and thus to create the effect of suspended causality. I am grateful to Ernst Hoffmann for permitting me to read his manuscript prior to its publication in *Deutsche Vierteljahresschrift für Literaturwissenschaft und Geistesgeschichte*, 42 (1968), 202-30.

[27] Letter of August 8, 1903.

The Notebooks

What has Malte seen? A picture of poverty and despair of the sort that ordinarily would disconcert him, like the similar episode, a few pages later, centering on the blind cauliflower-vendor. But by shaping the scene aesthetically, Malte has made it into a literary cameo. He has done precisely what he attributes (in a letter of October 4, 1907) to Van Gogh, who "in his most anguished days painted the most anguishing objects. How would he otherwise have survived?"[28] Here, however, there is only one color: the scene is not based on principles of painting, as in the preceding paragraph. Instead, Malte describes everything according to geometrical patterns. First, the word "composition" ("Zusammenstellung"), a highly unusual designation for such a random occurrence as a street scene, draws our attention to the conscious construction of the vignette. Then our eye is directed, in strict geometrical motion, from front to back, with a diagonal interruption. This horizontal motion is emphasized by the vertical thrust of the first words ("Down below") and the last words ("up toward the windows"), which frame the linear composition. Once again Malte has succeeded in ripping an ordinary, and this time rather depressing, street incident out of its temporal context and arresting it in a geometrical pattern. It was undoubtedly this conscious aesthetic shaping that Rilke had in mind when he later told his French translator, Maurice Betz, that the separate units of Malte's notebooks constitute *poèmes en prose* after the fashion of Baudelaire.[29]

[28] Letter of October 4, 1907, to his wife Clara.

[29] Maurice Betz, *Rilke in Frankreich*, trans. Willi Reich (Vienna, Leipzig, and Zürich: Herbert Reichner, 1938), p. 113. Regarding the conscious shock-effect of the word "composition," it is perhaps helpful to recall the critics' indignation at Whistler when he displayed the famous portrait of his mother (1871) at the Royal Academy under the original title of "Arrangement in Grey and Black."

Rainer Maria Rilke

These two short paragraphs represent only two of the many types of notes that are to be found in Malte's notebooks. But whether Malte is concerned with a tableau in the streets glimpsed from his window, as here, or with memories of his childhood, or with episodes from the historical past, in every case he shapes the raw material into a coherent and meaningful image. It would be a mistake to look for the significance of these scenes in their content. This is, rather, a quest for meaning through form, for a purely aesthetic meaning. Individually, each of the "notes" represents an attempt to transcend temporality by fashioning reality into a timeless pattern in which things take on a new meaning and hence are no longer free to threaten Malte.

When we move from the separate notes to their arrangement in the pattern of the whole novel, we see that Malte is trying to suspend the events of his own life aesthetically in such a way that they become meaningful. When he turns from experience of the present to recovery of the past, Malte writes: "I have prayed for my childhood, and it has come back, and I feel that it is still as difficult as it was then and that it has not done any good to become older."[30] His own childhood gains a meaningful place in his eyes only after he has succeeded in shaping it aesthetically in precisely the same way he shapes the events of his everyday life in Paris. By arranging the events of past, present, and even future into a pattern, Malte is viewing reality as a whole, like the angels and like his grandfather. "It is not for nothing," Rilke later wrote his Polish translator, "that Malte is the grandson of old Count Brahe, who considered everything—past as well as future—to be simply 'present.' "[31]

[30] *Malte*, p. 767.
[31] Letter of November 10, 1925, to Witold von Hulewicz.

(6)

MALTE's tableaux are linked and related in a variety of ways. There are principles of association and complementarity, as we shall see, that determine the sequence. But overarching these and reaching far in various directions are parallels of language that give the work a texture of poetic density despite the additive arrangement of the episodes. A typical example occurs in the parable of the Prodigal Son, with which the work closes. Some pages earlier, while narrating an incident from the life of Charles VI of France, Malte had described an attempt made upon the life of the leprous king:

> That was in the days when, from time to time, strange men with blackened faces fell upon him in his bed to tear off the shirt, rotted into his ulcers, that he had long considered to be part of himself. It was dark in the room, and they pulled the rotten rags from his rigid arms wherever they happened to lay hold of them. Then one of them held up a lamp, and only then did they discover the pus-infected sore on his chest, into which the iron amulet had sunk because he pressed it against himself every night with all the force of his ardor. Now it rested deep within him, terribly precious in its pearly fringe of pus, like a miraculous relic in the hollow of a reliquary.[32]

This sight, Malte relates, is revolting enough to frighten off even the hardened assassins chosen for the job. After this incident the story goes on for several pages, and the reader might easily forget the passage but for its vivid description of putrefaction. Then, a few pages from the end, when Malte is depicting the tribulations of the Prodigal Son, we find a rather cryptic remark to the effect that all this occurred at a time

[32] *Malte*, p. 906.

25

"when, everywhere on his body, sores opened up like emergency eyes against the blackness of the visitation."[33] Unless the reader recalls—and very literally—the earlier passage, this description defies translation or interpretation. But if we remember that Charles VI's sores acted as a deterrent to the men *with blackened faces* who *attacked* him in the night, it is instantly clear. It is more than clear: the language, establishing a poetic relationship between Charles VI and the Prodigal Son that might otherwise not be apparent, projects the two cases into a timeless realm where such parallels are meaningful.

This is a striking example, but by no means an isolated one. Here the extended description precedes the metaphor that is dependent upon it. There are other examples in which the opposite relationship obtains. Early in the novel, in the fifth note, Malte sees a woman slumped over in the street, with her face in her hands. As he approaches, his step startles the woman, who "pulled away too quickly, too violently, so that her face remained in her two hands. I could see it lying in them, its hollow form."[34] Much later in the book, when Malte is recounting the story of Charles the Bold, this vivid metaphor, reduced to its reality, is reified. For when Charles was slain in the Battle of Nancy, his face "was frozen into the ice, and as they pulled it out, one of the cheeks peeled off, thin and brittle, and it appeared that the other cheek had been torn out by dogs or wolves."[35] In both cases, through the tension of reality and metaphor, a poetic rela-

---

[33] *Malte*, p. 942: ". . . da sich überall an seinem Leibe Geschwüre aufschlugen wie Notaugen gegen die Schwärze der Heimsuchung."

[34] *Malte*, p. 712.

[35] *Malte*, p. 889. Ernst Hoffmann, *op.cit.*, cites this example in his excellent discussion of the associative links between the sections (p. 225), which he had previously defined as "these cyclical-symmetrical correspondences that illuminate each other reciprocally" (p. 222).

The Notebooks

tionship is established between scenes or tableaux that have otherwise very little in common. Yet aesthetically they are related in Malte's notebooks. Connections of the same sort can be detected between notes that occur much closer together. They assure the notebooks a high degree of cohesiveness on the level of language and metaphor regardless of the other links between the separate episodes.

The sequence of the notes, each of which constitutes in itself an aesthetic whole, is determined by very subtle principles of association. Let us examine, by way of example, the ordering of the first eight notes, which are linked almost musically by a series of motifs that gradually crescendo into themes.[36] The first two entries are organized around the five senses, each successively invoked to register Malte's horror upon his first encounter with the city of Paris.[37] The first note catalogues the sights, tactile sensations, smells, and tastes of daytime in the streets, while the second rehearses the litany of noises that Malte hears from his room at night: streetcars, automobiles, breaking glass, voices, barking dogs, crowing roosters. In abrupt counterpoint, the third entry shifts suddenly to the stillness, "which is even more frightening." After this preoccupation with sounds and stillness, the fourth entry reintroduces the sense of sight, now as a major theme: "I am learning to see." Malte mentions the change wrought in his personality by his new sense of sight and then cites specific examples. The fifth note, beginning with a description of the different faces he sees, ends with his fright at what happens when (in the passage cited above) the startled woman

---

[36] Rilke assured Maurice Betz (*op.cit.*, p. 107) that the contrasts and relationships in this opening section were carefully calculated.

[37] I am grateful to my colleague A. W. Litz, Jr., for pointing out that Joyce, in *A Portrait of the Artist as a Young Man*, similarly builds his opening lines around the five senses. This is by no means the only parallel between the two novels.

27

raises her head from her hands: "I was horrified to see a face from the inside." The motif of fright, introduced in the first note and gradually intensified, in several variations, through the fifth, becomes the main theme of the following section. This fear, catalyzed by deaths that he witnesses in the streets of Paris, provides a smooth transition into the seventh section, which discusses the trivialization of death in the modern city and its hospitals. Finally, the long eighth note, modulating from minor to major, describes the death of Malte's grandfather, Chamberlain Brigge; this first intrusion of the past into Malte's present life in Paris has emerged with absolute poetic consistency from a phrase in the very first sentence: "I should sooner think that this is a place for dying."

It is unnecessary to pursue this stream of associations any further. The links between the separate tableaux—there are seventy-one altogether—as well as the principle of organization governing each one become quickly evident to anyone who reads the notes carefully. Beyond the law of association that controls the opening sections, however, another factor comes into play: the same principle of complementarity that governs Rilke's poetic cycles, such as the *New Poems* and the *Duino Elegies*. Rilke's letters and poetry are filled with expressions of faith in what he calls "ordres complémentaires" and the "sainte loi du contraste." His favorite symbol for the *unio mystica* of seeming disparities is the rose, which—as he put it in his own epitaph—is a "pure contradiction" because it is "no one's sleep" despite its "many lids" (petals):

> Rose, oh reiner Widerspruch. Lust
> Niemandes Schlaf zu sein unter soviel
> Lidern.

In his poetry the theme of equilibrium—the moment of delicate balance between opposing forces—is conspicuous, and explains, for instance, his frequent use of acrobats as a metaphor for human existence (e.g., in the fifth elegy).

This principle of complementarity, which implies a resolution of opposites, not only underlies individual poems and whole poetic cycles; it also determines the sequence of many of the tableaux in *The Notebooks*.[38] Especially the complementarity of temporal levels fascinates Malte. A death in contemporary Paris evokes the memory of his grandfather's death by way of contrast. The magnificent tapestries of the Dame à Licorne in the Cluny Museum call to mind his cousin Abelone. On another occasion Malte recalls his father's death (his own past); this, in turn, generates the story of the death of Christian IV of Denmark (historical past); and the latter, finally, returns Malte to his own reflections on death in Paris (present experience). But the ultimate effect of this radical juxtaposition of various levels of time, for Malte as well as for the reader, is to efface the differences, to suspend time in a continuum. We become acutely conscious of the duration underlying the temporal phenomena as patterns repeat themselves, complementing or contrasting with one another.[39]

In the first third of the book, where Malte is concerned primarily with his own existence in Paris, the principles of association and complementarity that determine the organization of the notes operate largely in the present tense. As he delves back into his own childhood in the second section,

[38] See the excellent discussion of this principle in Ulrich Fülleborn, "Form und Sinn der 'Aufzeichnungen des Malte Laurids Brigge,'" in *Unterscheidung und Bewahrung; Festschrift für Hermann Kunisch* (Berlin: Walter de Gruyter, 1961), pp. 147-69.

[39] See the chapter on *Malte* in Fritz Martini, *Das Wagnis der Sprache* (3rd edn.; Stuttgart: Ernst Klett, 1958), esp. p. 170: "a fictive time is formed which is neither the actual past nor the actual present, but rather creates a kind of artificial time-level of narrative between the two." See also Fülleborn, *op.cit.*, p. 159, who emphasizes that present and past together constitute a new temporal dimension.

these principles are complicated, as we have seen, by different levels of time. Toward the end of the book, however, Malte has grown so accustomed to thinking by association and complementarity that he can afford, repeatedly, to suppress half of the process: his own present existence. Figures from the historical past are simply invoked, without reference to himself, as pure metaphors for his own existence, as "vocables of his anguish."[40] It is quite mistaken to assume that the meaning of these episodes lies in their content. Many years later Rilke wrote his Polish translator that it would be misleading to attempt to pin down the "manifold evocations" too precisely. "The reader must communicate not with their historical or imaginary reality but, through them, with Malte's experience."[41] And he admits that he himself has forgotten, in the fifteen intervening years, some of the specific references. Their significance lies in the "tension of these anonymities," which reflects Malte's state of mind metaphorically.

Through the historical figures Malte's own emotions are generalized in the form of a parable. But as soon as the parabolic significance of the historical life becomes evident through its aesthetic telling in the notebooks, his own life assumes a higher meaning. He *is*, metaphorically, John XXII, Charles VI, and all the other figures that he evokes. Through the historical past Malte is rescued again from the threat of temporality: his own experience is externalized and eternalized in the figures whose stories he narrates. He can stand apart and look at his life objectively, just as he can look objectively at the objects captured in his tableaux.

This process of externalization and objectification of his

---

[40] Martini, *op.cit.*, p. 165: "Rilke . . . seeks the sensuous and objective equivalent of the inward experience. Like Nietzsche, he translates from within to without."

[41] Letter of November 10, 1925, to Witold von Hulewicz.

own life is reflected, in turn, in the style of the narrative. We observed above that the notebooks begin with a radical juxtaposition of self and other. The first-person singular that insistently dominates the first part of the book, as though Malte had to assert his own existence grammatically in the face of the threatening world,[42] gradually gives way to third-person narrative, until, at the end, Malte has been absorbed wholly by the metaphors of his own self. It is characteristic that the work, which begins in the first person, should end with the parable of the Prodigal Son. By the end of his notebooks, in other words, Malte has vanished behind the projections of himself. His own private temporal existence has been subsumed in the supratemporal existence of the parable.

The Notebooks as a whole, then, is subject to precisely the same laws of poetic composition as are the individual tableaux. Beyond the general sequence from existence through family to history, we see a distinct pattern of structure and development: from first person to third person, from Malte to the Prodigal Son, from reality to metaphor, from temporality to timelessness. By organizing its material through association and complementarity Malte has succeeded in creating a meaningful aesthetic pattern out of his own life, putting it back into the context of his childhood and the historical past. Each gemlike scene thus becomes a stone in the elaborate mosaic of the whole. And if the mosaic does not reveal a simple picture according to the expectations of conventional narrative, it does present an abstract design of the sort that we have become accustomed to expect from poetry.

[42] The calculated effect of the first-person narrative is all the more evident when we learn that the novel was originally begun in the third person. (See the two fragmentary beginnings of 1904, now published in *Sämtliche Werke*, Vol. vi, pp. 949-66.) Rilke obviously came to realize the advantages of first-person narrative as he saw more clearly the implications of Malte's story.

The work eschews plot for the sake of structure, epic narrative for the sake of lyric significance.[43]

(7)

THE movement from first to third person that we have noted has an important implication for the interpretation of the novel. In Joyce's *A Portrait of the Artist as a Young Man* Stephen Dedalus mentions precisely the same kind of movement.

> The simplest epical form is seen emerging out of lyrical literature when the artist prolongs and broods upon himself as the center of an epical event and the form progresses till the center of emotional gravity is equidistant from the artist himself and from others. The narrative is no longer purely personal. The personality of the artist passes into the narration itself, flowing round and round the persons and the action like a vital sea. The progress you will see easily in that old English ballad *Turpin Hero*, which begins in the first person and ends in the third person.[44]

This progression from lyric to epic constitutes stylistic evidence of the fact that Malte has liberated himself sufficiently from the frightening obsessions of the first pages to write objectively about reality.

We have seen that Malte set out modestly to survive the night and illness, as he put it, before he undertook the greater task of surviving love and God. In the first half of his notebooks, where he was concerned primarily with his present experiences and the recovery of his childhood, he was not nar-

[43] See Ralph Freedman, *The Lyrical Novel* (Princeton: Princeton University Press, 1963), pp. 4-6 and pp. 8-9. For Freedman, *Malte* is "almost purely lyrical" inasmuch as "the world is reduced to a *lyrical point of view*, the equivalent of the poet's 'I': the lyrical Self."

[44] Signet Book edition (New York, 1954), p. 167.

rating with the calm voice of an objective author. Instead, he responded almost frenetically to experience and memory by attempting to shape everything into a poetic tableau. In the middle of the book he observes: "It must have been before my time that people told stories, really told them. I have never heard anyone tell stories. In the days when Abelone spoke to me of Maman's youth, it became apparent that she could not tell them. Old Count Brahe is said to have been able still to do so."[45] The significance of this remark cannot be overemphasized, for the ability to tell stories, to speak with a narrative voice, is emphatically related to the integral vision of a unified reality that Count Brahe still possessed. The inability to narrate is thus another symptom of the breakdown of reality. And the recovery of this ability must point to the reestablishment, in the mind of the narrator at least, of a whole vision. If this is the case, then it must be concluded that Malte has attained a whole vision once again by the end of his notebooks. For in the parable of the Prodigal Son, as Ernst Hoffmann has pointed out, Malte for the first time actually tells a story with the objectivity of epic narrative.[46] The development of the ability to tell stories is directly related, in the second part of the notebooks, to the themes of love and God.

Malte begins his retelling of the parable of the Prodigal Son by saying: "It will be difficult to convince me that the story of the Prodigal Son is not the legend of one who did not want to be loved."[47] This seemingly paradoxical statement has been carefully prepared for by Malte's mention of the many "Great Lovers" in the second half of the book: Heloïse, Sappho, Marianna Alcoforado, Gaspara Stampa, Louïse

[45] *Malte*, p. 844.
[46] Hoffmann, *op.cit.*, p. 230. Hoffmann remarks in this connection that the "I" of the later sections of the novel is no longer personal.
[47] *Malte*, p. 938.

Labé, Julie Lespinasse, and others. The second part, in turn, was anticipated by the description of the tapestries of the Dame à Licorne at the end of part one: for the unicorn, after all, is the animal that can be subdued only by love. Rilke has cunningly revised the sequence of the six tapestries in such a way that the last one shows the lady holding up a mirror to the unicorn.[48] Through love, in other words, the individual attains self-awareness.

If we reduce Rilke's theory of love to its simplest form, we can say that he regards love in the conventional sense as a threat to be survived, because ordinary love tends to focus upon a specific object, demanding that it remain constant. Being loved thus restricts the freedom of the individual to develop in his own direction. To *love,* on the other hand, is a timeless activity, because real love, according to Malte, is only a direction with no specific object or goal. It is, so to speak, the positive aspect of the attitude that Malte grew to know in the first part of his notebooks. "Those who are loved live badly and in danger. Oh, if they could only overcome themselves and become lovers. Those who love are surrounded with nothing but security."[49]

Love, in Malte's vocabulary, is an image for a dispassionate view of reality, which seeks neither to own reality possessively nor to distinguish too sharply between its aspects. Love—like the angels and like Count Brahe—accepts reality on its own terms. Love, by extension, is therefore the prerequisite for what Malte calls narrative, for narrative is im-

---

[48] There can be little doubt that this reordering was conscious. The normal sequence of the tapestries, both in theme and size is quite clear: five scenes, each symbolizing one of the five senses, precede the more general final scene, which occupies the largest of the tapestries. Rilke isolates one of the smaller preliminary scenes—that symbolizing the sense of sight—and describes it as though it were the high point of the entire series.

[49] *Malte,* p. 924.

possible until the author is willing and able to regard the world with the clear eyes of the lover, until the author is sufficiently disengaged from reality to be no longer threatened or frightened by its manifestations. The lover, in other words, has removed himself from the flow of temporality. "Outside much has changed; I don't know how," Malte remarks toward the end of his book. "But within and before You, my God, within and before you, Spectator: are we not without action?"[50] Characteristically, Rilke develops his abstract thought here in concrete terminology drawn from the unrelated area of the theater. But his meaning is clear: by the end of the notebooks Malte has attained a timeless realm "without action" in his own heart. Outside, the temporal flow goes on, but within he is now secure from the fear of time and death that tormented him during his first weeks in Paris.

In the story of the Prodigal Son, then, the style and theme of the notebooks merge. Now, for the first time, he is able to tell a story because he has himself reached the stage of dispassionate love. And the story that he tells describes the very phenomenon that makes its telling possible, for it recapitulates, with the objectivity of the parable, precisely the stages of Malte's own development, from loneliness through love to God.[51]

Malte's Prodigal Son leaves home in order to escape the bondage of love. He is loved so much, even by the dogs and by the windows of the house, that he is not free. Instead, each time he enters his home he is forced back into the role expected of him by all the others. During his years of tribulation, however, he develops such consistency of character and independence that he is ultimately able to go home again with-

[50] *Malte*, pp. 920-21.

[51] See Armand Nivelle, "Sens et structure des *Cahiers de Malte Laurids Brigge*," *Revue d'Esthétique*, 12 (1959), 5-32; esp. pp. 11-12.

out fear of being forced back into a mold by those who attempted to love him. "How little they knew who he was," the novel ends. "He was now terribly difficult to love, and he felt that only One was capable of it. But He was not yet willing." What Malte writes here of the Prodigal Son applies equally to himself, for the Prodigal Son is but another metaphor for or parable of his own existence.[52]

Since the first frightened lines of the notebooks Malte has come a long way. He has survived the night, his illness, and love. Only God remains to be endured, "but He was not yet willing." That was the task that remained for the *Duino Elegies*.

[52] It is noteworthy that the only utterances in which Rilke unequivocally states that Malte perishes are found in the letters up to 1907, before he had worked out the second part of the novel. In later letters (e.g., March 25, 1910) he says quite the opposite: "Poor Malte begins so deep in misery and extends, if one is precise, all the way to eternal bliss; he is a heart that spans a full octave. After him almost all songs are possible." Rilke, *Briefe an seinen Verleger* (Wiesbaden: Insel, 1949), II, 98.

chapter two

Franz Kafka: *The Trial*

(1)

TWO CLOCKS adorn the Jewish Council Hall in Prague, Franz Kafka's birthplace and his home for most of his life. The one at the top of the tower marks the passing hours in the conventional way, its hands sweeping clockwise around its face. But the lower one, a Hebrew clock from the seventeenth century, is different: not only are the hours indicated by Hebrew letters, but the hands move backward. At first it may seem strange that Kafka, who passed the Hall almost daily, never mentions it in his writings. As a symbol, the two clocks are so appropriate that they might well have been invented by Kafka for his own purposes. For his works are full of clocks and watches that go at a different pace, indicating the discrepancy between man's inner time and the mechanical time of the world outside. But Kafka had an aversion for the obvious, and consistently deleted from his works any passages that stated his meaning too bluntly. It was probably for this reason that he avoided any direct reference to the clocks on the Council Hall. Still, it is perhaps a legitimate association, when we read of Kafka's heroes scurrying through the labyrinthine streets of his world, inevitably late for their appointments, to think of those two clocks: the one ticking irrevocably forward in the usual manner; the other, though also keeping perfectly good time in its own way, moving ever in the opposite direction.

Kafka was obsessed as are few other writers with the discongruity between his own inner time and that of the world about him. In 1922 he noted, in his diaries, a feeling of collapse and disintegration in his life. "It's impossible to sleep,

37

impossible to wake, impossible to bear life or, more precisely, the successiveness of life. The clocks don't agree. The inner one rushes along in a devilish or demonic—in any case, inhuman—way while the outer one goes, falteringly, its accustomed pace."[1] Two years earlier, soon after their first meeting, Kafka apologized to Gustav Janouch for coming more than an hour late for an appointment. "I can never keep an appointment exactly. I always come too late. I want to control time, I have the best intentions of keeping the agreed appointment, but the world, or my body, always breaks this will of mine in order to prove my weakness to me. That is probably the basis of my illness."[2]

This discongruity between two orders of time would not be important or even interesting if it did not play such a conspicuous role in Kafka's works. For it becomes a pronounced symbol there for the loss of contact between man and the world. The destiny of the individual who is torn loose from the successiveness of temporality is manifest in many stories. In one of his earliest sketches Kafka outlines the character of the bachelor, a symbolic figure in all his works. Most people, he says, are held together and contained, as it were, by past and future. "He owns only the moment, the ever continued moment of torment which is not followed by a moment of recovery." Most men live "in the stream of time." As soon as we step out of it, like the bachelor, we are lost. "We are outside of the law—nobody knows it, but everybody treats us accordingly."[3] To step out of temporality—Kafka's "stream

---

[1] Franz Kafka, *Tagebücher, 1910-1923* (Frankfurt am Main: S. Fischer, 1951), p. 552.

[2] Gustav Janouch, *Gespräche mit Kafka; Erinnerungen und Aufzeichnungen* (Frankfurt am Main: S. Fischer, 1951), pp. 20-21.

[3] *Tagebücher*, pp. 21-22. Heinz Politzer, *Franz Kafka; Parable and Paradox* (Ithaca, N.Y.: Cornell University Press, 1962), offers a subtle analysis of the symbolic role of the bachelor in Kafka's works. See esp. Chap. II, pp. 23-47.

of time"—does not bring with it the buoyant freedom of time-lessness that we find in Rilke's tableaux or, later, in Hans Castorp's vision in the snow. It involves, rather, a terrifying stasis that has been called a "paralysis of time,"[4] in which there is nothing but meaningless repetition. Thus Kafka's "Country Doctor," who is jerked out of the stream of time when he responds to a nocturnal summons, finds himself, at the end of the story, frozen in a state of perpetual motion without progress, like a squirrel on a treadmill. "I'll never get home like this," he thinks. "My thriving practice is lost."[5] In the second part of "The Metamorphosis," to show how ineluctably Gregor Samsa is caught in his role as an "insect," Kafka lets the alarm clock disappear unexplainedly from the night table. As long as Gregor was in the stream of time, the clock had meaning for him; now it becomes meaningless and, consistently enough, vanishes. As long as "The Hunger Artist" has contact with the world surrounding him, his cage is adorned conspicuously with a clock that marks the passing hours of his fast. But once the heyday of hunger artists is past, not even the sign on the cage, marking the days of the fast, is renewed. Caught in a static state of paralysis as he is, time does not move for him: he has no need of clocks or of placards marking the date.

When Kafka's protagonists are still capable of action, unlike Gregor Samsa or the Hunger Artist, their deeds are out of step with the time of the temporal world, and this realization intensifies their confusion. Thus in the parable "Give it

---

[4] Günther Anders, *Kafka: Pro und Contra* (Munich: C. H. Beck, 1951), p. 36. This conception of "paralyzed time," which is accepted by most of the Kafka critics mentioned in this chapter, differs essentially from the Platonic idea of timelessness attributed to Kafka by Margaret Church, "Kafka and Proust: A Contrast in Time," *Bucknell Review* (1957), pp. 107-12.

[5] Franz Kafka, *Erzählungen* (3rd edn.; New York: Schocken Books, 1946), p. 153.

up!" the narrator hurries through the streets of a town in the early morning. "As I compared the tower clock with my watch I realized it was already much later than I had thought, I had to hurry, the shock of this discovery made me feel uncertain of the way, I was not very well acquainted with the town yet."[6] As one critic has pointed out, Kafka makes use of time only in order to contrast private time with the normal pattern of time.[7] And it is probably a safe generalization to say that every mention of specific time in his works is intended to draw attention to this discongruity, for his heroes are always either too early or too late.

This is conspicuously the case in *The Trial.* Just after he has been summoned to his first hearing, Josef K. tells the Assistant Manager of the bank where he works: "I have just been rung up and asked to go somewhere, but they forgot to tell me when." When the Assistant Manager suggests that he call back to find out at what time he should present himself, K. replies, "It isn't so important as all that." He assumes that it would be reasonable to appear at nine o'clock on the stated morning, "since that was the hour at which all the law courts started their business on weekdays."[8] On the appointed morning, however, K. almost oversleeps. "In a great hurry, without taking time to think or to coordinate the plans that he had drawn up during the week, he got dressed and rushed off, without his breakfast, to the suburb

[6] Franz Kafka, *Beschreibung eines Kampfs; Novellen, Skizzen und Aphorismen aus dem Nachlass* (New York: Schocken Books, 1946), p. 117. For a detailed analysis of this parable, see the opening chapter of Politzer, *Franz Kafka.*

[7] Martin Walser, *Beschreibung einer Form* (Munich: Hanser, 1961), p. 126. Max Bense, *Die Theorie Kafkas* (Cologne and Berlin: Kiepenheuer, 1952), pp. 61-63, regards Kafka's "private time" as "apparent duration" in the sense of Husserl's phenomenology.

[8] Franz Kafka, *Der Prozess* (5th edn.; New York: Schocken Books, 1946), p. 46.

which had been mentioned to him."[9] When he gets to the right street, he notices that it is shortly after nine o'clock, but by the time he finds his way upstairs, "The first thing he saw in the little room was a great pendulum clock which was already pointing to ten."[10] A few minutes later the Examining Magistrate reproaches him, saying twice for emphasis: "You should have been here an hour and five minutes ago."[11] From this moment on, K.'s sense of time is disturbed or out of focus. The very next week, for instance, he goes back to the interrogation room, but on this occasion no one is there: early or late, he comes at the wrong time.

K.'s distortion of time affects even those who are with him. When he goes with his uncle to visit Lawyer Huld, his uncle complains: "Eight o'clock, an unusual time for clients to call. But Huld won't take it amiss from me."[12] At the bank, K.'s whole schedule is upset. Formerly the model of punctuality, he now keeps clients waiting—"in fact, extremely important clients of the Bank who should on no account have been kept waiting at all."[13] They had appeared, K. felt, at "an unsuitable hour," yet during the entire morning he had gotten almost nothing done. "It was eleven o'clock, he had wasted two hours in dreaming, a long stretch of precious time, and he was, of course, even wearier than before."

Conversely, the meetings most important for K. often take place by chance. Thus the crucial scene in the cathedral, in which K. hears the parable of the Man from the Country and discusses it with the priest, is an accident. "It was absurd to think that a sermon was going to be preached at eleven in the morning on a weekday, in such dreadful weather."[14] Indeed, K.'s very presence in the cathedral is quite possibly due to a misunderstanding regarding time. The Manager of the bank had asked K. to escort a visiting colleague from Italy

[9] *Prozess*, p. 46.   [10] *Prozess*, p. 51.   [11] *Prozess*, p. 52.
[12] *Prozess*, p. 121.   [13] *Prozess*, p. 155.   [14] *Prozess*, p. 249.

around the city. Early that morning the two men agree to meet in the cathedral at ten o'clock; but since K. has great difficulty understanding the rapid Italian of the visitor, it is entirely possible—indeed, in the context of the novel, quite probable—that he misunderstands the time specified. In any case, after rushing to get to the cathedral on time, he waits around for an entire hour without finding the Italian visitor. Instead, he hears the parable told by the priest.

Neither Josef K. nor Kafka's other heroes, of course, are born out of step with time. They lose touch with reality by a simple misstep, by an act of sudden awakening that has been so often noted by critics.[15] "The Country Doctor" is doomed to wander eternally without reaching home because he permitted himself to follow the ringing of the night bell, to be jerked out of his normal sphere of daily activities. "The Hunter Gracchus" can never find peace because the barge conveying him to the place of death made a wrong turn and cannot get back on its proper course. Similarly, Josef K. reflects that he was simply caught unawares. "In the Bank, for instance, I am always prepared," he tells his landlady. "Nothing of that kind could possibly happen to me there, I have my own attendant, the general telephone and the office telephone stand before me on my desk, people keep coming in to see me, clients and clerks. And above all, there I am always in the framework of work and have my wits about me; it would actually be a pleasure to be confronted with a situation like that in the Bank."[16]

In *The Trial* the symbolic act of awakening is rendered in reality. Like Gregor Samsa, who awakes one morning to

[15] Wilhelm Emrich, "Franz Kafka," in *Deutsche Literatur im zwanzigsten Jahrhundert*, ed. Hermann Friedmann and Otto Mann (2nd rev. edn.; Heidelberg: Wolfgang Rothe, 1956), p. 328; Joseph Strelka, *Kafka, Musil, Broch* (Vienna, Hannover, and Basel: Forum, 1959), pp. 12-13.

[16] *Prozess*, p. 31.

find himself, as he believes, transformed into a great insect, Josef K. learns that he is under arrest when he wakes up on the morning of his thirtieth birthday—at an hour, in other words, when he is not safe in the context of his everyday life. In one of the passages subsequently cut from the novel, probably because it is too direct, too clear, Kafka analyzed the dangers of awakening:

> As someone said to me—I can't remember now who it was —it is really remarkable that when you wake up in the morning you nearly always find everything in exactly the same place as the evening before. For when asleep and dreaming you are, apparently at least, in an essentially different state from that of wakefulness; and therefore, as that man truly said, it requires enormous presence of mind or rather quickness of wit, when opening your eyes, to seize hold of everything in the room at exactly the same place where you had let it go on the previous evening. That was why, he said, the moment of waking up was the riskiest moment of the day. Once that was well over without dragging you from your place, you could be at ease for the rest of the day.[17]

This obsession with the dangers of awakening can be explained biographically. In his letters and diaries Kafka returns with constant fascination to the problems of sleeping and waking. In 1922, for instance, he noted that "people are purer [in the evening] than in the morning. The time before falling asleep wearily is the real time of freedom from specters. They have all been driven away. They come back only as the night progresses, and in the morning, though perhaps still unrecognizable, they are all there, and for a healthy person the daily process of driving them away begins all over again."[18] This passage of almost reverse Freudianism

[17] *Prozess*, pp. 304-5.   [18] *Tagebücher*, p. 569.

—there is no cathartic release of repressions through the dreams, nor any process of sublimation, but rather an accumulation of subconscious oppressions—might be of tremendous interest to psychoanalytically oriented critics. For our purposes, however, it is important only to the extent that it reveals the vast significance that Kafka attached to the crucial moment of awakening in the morning. We should single out two points. First, as far as the content is concerned, the "specters" can be understood as including the sense of guilt and responsibility that obsessed Kafka constantly. Second, the act of awakening provides Kafka with a symbolic form for the expression of a new awareness that suddenly lifts man out of the reality that he has hitherto known and shows him his world in a new and terrifying light. In both these senses, *The Trial* is paradigmatic among Kafka's works.

(2)

The Trial is a book about guilt and freedom: the inevitability of man's guilt in the world and man's freedom to accept the responsibility for his own guilt. Guilt and freedom are inextricably intertwined. To be free means, for Kafka, to recognize and accept the fact of one's guilt. There is no such thing as a state of innocence. There is only the freedom of the man who recognizes his guilt and the animal state of those who have not reached that level of awareness or, having reached it, refuse to accept the fact of guilt. This is expressed most succinctly in a cryptic note from the sketch "He," in which Kafka avers: "Original sin, the ancient wrong that man has committed, consists in the reproach that man makes and from which he never desists: that a wrong has been done unto him and that original sin has been committed against him."[19] Like most of Kafka's paradoxes, this one defies every-

[19] "Er," *Beschreibung eines Kampfs*, p. 283. Gerhard Kaiser, "Franz Kafkas 'Prozess': Versuch einer Interpretation," *Euphorion*, 52

day logic, but it explains Josef K.'s dilemma. He is guilty from the moment he feels that he has been falsely accused; his sin, in the words of the paradox, resides in the very fact that he insists an injustice has been done unto him. The paradox has further important implications. Man is redeemed in the instant when he accepts the responsibility for his guilt, rather than feeling that he is being wrongly accused by a hostile world. But most men do not accept this freedom. Instead they attempt, by what Kafka calls the process of *motivation,* to project their own guilt onto the world outside and thus to deny it.[20]

In his "Observations on Sin, Suffering, Hope, and the True Way" Kafka argues that men are essentially equal, since the Fall, in their capacity for recognizing good and evil. It is only in their reactions to this recognition that they differ. For no one is satisfied with cognition alone; men feel compelled to act in accordance with their knowledge. Since, however, the strength to carry out these acts is denied him, man runs the risk of destroying himself in attempting them. As a result, he prefers to deny and revoke his knowledge of good and evil. But knowledge cannot be revoked or annulled; it can only be obscured. "For this purpose motivations arise. The whole world is full of them, indeed, the whole visible world is perhaps nothing but a motivation of the man who wants a single moment of peace. An attempt to falsify the fact of cognition, to make cognition itself the goal" results, instead of action based upon this cognition.[21] There is no obscurity

---

(1958), 23-49, stresses the fact that all men are guilty and that K. is thus representative of humanity as a whole.

[20] In this connection, see the highly enlightening discussion by Ingeborg Henel, "Die Türhüterlegende und ihre Bedeutung für Kafkas 'Prozess,'" *Deutsche Vierteljahresschrift,* 37 (1963), 50-70; also Wilhelm Emrich, *Franz Kafka* (Bonn: Athenäum, 1958), pp. 181-82.

[21] In *Hochzeitsvorbereitungen auf dem Lande und andere Prosa aus dem Nachlass,* ed. Max Brod (Frankfurt am Main: S. Fischer, 1966), pp. 49-50.

here. Kafka clearly affirms that men are aware of good and evil, but, since they lack the strength to act accordingly, they attempt to deny their knowledge. The man who realizes that he is guilty does not normally do the single appropriate thing: accept his guilt freely. Instead, by a series of "motivations" he projects his own guilt onto the world around him in an attempt to escape his own responsibility.

This concept of motivation accounts for what has been called the nightmarish quality of Kafka's fiction. What we have in *The Trial*, to put it most simply, is not a *reflection* of reality, but rather a *distortion* of reality brought about by injection into it of the hero's own sense of guilt. Hence the malevolent, threatening atmosphere: K. attributes to everyone else his own guiltiness. Hence the oppressive sense of being watched constantly: for K. knows, after his awakening to guilt, that he deserves to be under observation.[22] Hence the court that comes only when it is summoned: it is a concrete projection of K.'s inner state of mind, which, recognizing its guilt, demands to be judged.

It is this motivation, finally, that underlies the characteristic style of Kafka's narratives. There are textual grounds for assuming that Kafka originally intended to present the entire novel as a dream of Josef K.,[23] but later deleted the passages which established it as such, choosing to represent K.'s world as a parable of reality. He achieves this effect through his use of narrative point of view, which is consistently so

[22] See Beda Allemann, "Kafka: Der Prozess," *Der deutsche Roman vom Barock bis zur Gegenwart*, ed. Benno von Wiese (Düsseldorf: Bagel, 1963), II, 260-62, who stresses the importance of the motif of "being observed" for Kafka. Flaubert uses precisely the same technique in his story of Saint Julian in *Trois Contes*: it is Julian's guilt that causes the animals of the forest to peer at him with bright eyes.

[23] See esp. the rejected chapter "The House," which is analyzed by Friedrich Beissner, *Der Erzähler Franz Kafka* (Stuttgart: Kohlhammer, 1952), pp. 38-40.

close to that of his hero that the reader sees reality, at every instant, only from Josef K.'s point of view and hence distorted by K.'s *motivation* of the world.

It is important to note this fact. In a conventional first-person narrative, such as *The Notebooks of Malte Laurids Brigge*, we make automatic allowances for the subjectivity of the narrator: the world we see there is the world as experienced by the sensibility of Malte. By contrast, when we read a third-person narrative such as *The Magic Mountain* we assume that we are dealing with an objective narrator interposed between ourselves and the consciousness of the hero, a situation which normally assures us a detached view of the fictional world. But Kafka's technique, which is variously labeled "erlebte Rede" or "style indirect libre," lies between these two methods. For Kafka narrates in the third person, thus arousing the expectation of authorial objectivity. Yet he takes up his narrative stance so close to the point of view of his hero that the result actually amounts to a first-person narrative told in the third person. Kafka's own personality is not permitted to intrude by even so much as an occasional adverb or adjective. We begin reading the novel as though it were a conventional report of reality; only gradually do we realize that the entire narrative is colored from first sentence to last by Josef K.'s sense of guilt, which he constantly projects onto the world surrounding him. The effect of this technique must be fully understood. For the third-person narrative suggests, at first, that the voice of the narrator represents the voice of objectivity. In actuality, however, it shows us reality from the standpoint of the one man who, by his awareness, has been cut off from the community and thus stands alone.

For most men never undergo the moment of awakening and thus never become consciously aware of their guilt. Living from day to day in the stream of time, they never step back, like the bachelor mentioned earlier, and pause to reflect on the many ways in which the individual becomes guilty. Caught within the system, they regard everything as perfectly natural. For this reason most of the characters in Kafka's fictional world accept the reality presented there as perfectly natural. This situation is rendered graphically in "The Penal Colony." The narrative point of view is that of a traveler who, coming from outside, is horrified at the travesty of justice that is accepted without question and, indeed, glorified by the inhabitants of the island. Here we have little difficulty, for the structure of the narrative suggests that the world of the Penal Colony is an alien world, and we tend to identify easily with the viewpoint of the traveler, who comes from our own world. In *The Trial* (and in most of Kafka's other stories) the situation is different, for the hero remains within his own world: it is only his inner point of view that has changed. It is only the hero who is perplexed by the new face of reality that has suddenly been exposed to him through his awakening. Thrust somehow out of the context of everyday life, he suddenly views reality from what Kafka once called the "Archimedean point" outside the world—a perspective from which all reality becomes problematic.[24] Hence Josef K. is the only figure in *The Trial* to whom the processes of the Court seem strange; everyone else takes them for granted, just as he himself had, prior to the moment of awakening.

(3)

IT IS NOT legitimate to ask why Josef K. alone, among the characters of the book, has experienced this awakening. That is simply the premise of the novel, the *terminus ab quo* that makes the entire fiction possible. To put it most bluntly: Kafka is not interested in the question of why or how men become aware of their guilt. Rather, his whole rapt atten-

---

[24] In the paralipomena to "Er," *Hochzeitsvorbereitungen*, p. 418.

tion is focused on the behavior of the man who has suddenly acquired this knowledge. Suffice it to say that a man like Josef K., on reaching a certain stage in life, suddenly and for the first time begins to question the meaning of his own life. Up to now he has lived within the system, safe in the security of his job, his clients and office attendants, his friends at his regular restaurant. But on awaking one morning, he suddenly asks himself "Why?" and that question precipitates the novel.

The actual question "Why?" lies outside of the framework of the novel, of course, since it antecedes temporally the first words of the narrative. Projected into the terms of the fiction, it is rendered by the fact that K. is arrested upon awakening, for the Court comes only to those who feel a need for it, who have become aware of their guilt, who *motivate* the world with their own sense of guilt. From the very first sentence of the book, therefore, we know that Josef K. is guilty. "Someone must have betrayed Josef K., for without having done anything wrong, he was arrested one morning." Here we are already seeing the situation from K.'s point of view. According to Kafka's theory of motivation, the very fact that K. tries to project his guilt onto a "someone" who has betrayed him is a sure sign of his guilt.

But we need not look far for evidence of guilt. Every page of the novel leads K. to an increasing awareness of it. Even though the incidents that reveal his guilt are often trifling, their very triviality serves to intensify the inevitability of guilt. Thus, when K. comes home on the evening following his arrest, he finds it necessary to apologize to his landlady for the trouble he has caused her that day. He concludes the interview by exclaiming: "If you want to keep your house respectable you'll have to begin by giving me notice."[25] Shortly afterward he apologizes to his neighbor, Fräulein

[25] *Prozess*, p. 33.

Bürstner, for the fact that her room was used earlier that day for his hearing. "This morning your room was thrown into some slight confusion and the fault was mine in a certain sense; it was done by strangers against my will, and yet as I have said the fault was mine; I want to beg your pardon for this."[26]

From this point on, K., who had rarely if ever had grounds for feeling responsible for misfortunes that befell others, is constantly reminded of his own guilt. After he complains to the Court of the behavior of the two warders on the morning of his arrest, he realizes that he is responsible for the beatings they receive from the Whipper. Still later his uncle warns him that he is harming his whole family by his behavior: "Josef, my dear Josef, think of yourself, think of your relatives, think of our good name. You have been a credit to us until now, you can't become a family disgrace."[27] And he learns that he is responsible for Lawyer Huld's illness. "In all probability you have helped to bring about his complete collapse and thus hastened the death of a man on whose good offices you are dependent."[28] By his attentions he endangers the wife of the Court Usher; at the bank he is negligent regarding the affairs of his clients. Once the consciousness of guilt has been awakened, the individual realizes that he is, in fact, constantly guilty or responsible in almost every human relationship.[29]

At this point K. begins to think back over his entire life.

[26] *Prozess*, p. 36. The German word "Schuld" has a tantalizing ambiguity here and elsewhere in the novel, for it can mean either "guilt" or simply "fault."

[27] *Prozess*, p. 116.

[28] *Prozess*, p. 136.

[29] Walter H. Sokel, *Franz Kafka; Tragik und Ironie* (Munich and Vienna: Albert Langen-Georg Müller, 1964), pp. 140ff., persuasively speaks of Josef K.'s "threefold guilt" and points out parallels to Kafka's other works.

Up to now he had felt no need to justify his behavior or existence. Swept along in the "stream of time," he had acted as circumstances required. Now, however, he begins to rationalize all his deeds.[30] "He had often considered whether it would not be a good idea to draw up a written defense and hand it in to the Court. In this defense he would give a short account of his life and, when he came to an event of any importance, explain for what reasons he had acted as he did, intimate whether he approved or condemned his way of action in retrospect, and adduce grounds for the condemnation or approval."[31] At this moment K. has reached the turning point. Having granted for the first time the possibility of guilt, he is now free to accept full responsibility for his actions—or to disclaim all guilt. Here, roughly halfway through his thirtieth year, K. reaches a decision of principle that determines his behavior throughout the remainder of the novel: "Above all, if he was to achieve anything, it was imperative to banish from his mind once and for all the idea of possible guilt."[32] Rather than accept his guilt and act accordingly, K. henceforth rigorously disclaims any guilt whatsoever, despite all evidence in the first part of the book that he does indeed stand condemned.

For this reason it is rather academic to discuss whether or not K. is guilty. He is guilty from the first sentence on, and he knows it. Virtually every person with whom he has come into contact has suffered, directly or indirectly, through some fault of his. Yet he decides categorically to ignore the possibility of guilt in order to win his case. It is this decision that is horrendous. Up to this point, K. theoretically enjoyed the

---

[30] Allemann, "Kafka: Der Prozess," p. 258, stresses this theme of self-justification.

[31] *Prozess*, p. 137.

[32] *Prozess*, p. 152. Gerhard Kaiser, *op.cit.*, pp. 29-30, discusses the ambiguity of K.'s attitude toward his guilt: he both recognizes and rejects it.

possibility of acting with human dignity. Now, however, he renounces human freedom, which can be obtained only at the cost of assuming one's responsibility as a man. For men have two alternatives. They may either recognize and freely accept the responsibility for their actions, or they may attempt to avoid this responsibility and thus remain unfree.

K.'s decision is prompted by the dreadful anguish of uncertainty. As Fräulein Montag tells K., "The slightest uncertainty even in the most trifling matter is always a worry, and when, as in this case, it can be easily dispelled, it is better that it should be done at once."[33] Most of K.'s uncertainties cannot be disposed of so easily as the simple matter referred to here: whether or not Fräulein Bürstner will grant him a face to face interview. But the principle is valid. If K. should concede for an instant the possibility of guilt, then he would immediately expose himself to the anguish of endless uncertainty. It is precisely this uncertainty, this constant speculation about the meaning of words and actions, that accounts stylistically for long passages of the novel—those passages so typical of Kafka, and of a sort found repeatedly in his diaries and letters, in which a simple word or event is turned around and around, regarded from every possible point of view, exhausted of its implications.

So K. decides simply to exclude the possibility of guilt altogether. Thereby he also shuts out the possibility of freedom, which consists, as we have seen, in the willingness to accept the fact of guilt. As Lawyer Huld tells K.: "It's often better to be in chains than to be free."[34] For a man in chains is not tormented by any uncertainties; his mind is at rest, his conscience at ease. Yet this is at the same time an illusory tranquillity, for "lack of freedom," as Kafka remarked on another occasion, "is always deadly."[35] Josef K. thus commits

---

[33] *Prozess*, p. 100.   [34] *Prozess*, p. 227.
[35] Gustav Janouch, *Gespräche mit Kafka*, p. 61.

moral suicide by denying his human freedom, and that moral suicide soon enough finds its counterpart in outer events when K. is murdered at the end of the novel. But in the meantime, K.'s decision to thrust his responsibility upon others and his abjuration of human freedom have important implications for both the structure and the metaphors of the text.

(4)

SINCE K. is unwilling to accept responsibility and to approach the Law directly, he constantly seeks helpers to aid him in his case. This is a direct parallel to the theme of motivation: just as he thrusts his guilt into the outside world, so too he externalizes his responsibility. He surrounds himself with a variety of mediating figures, who stand, as it were, between him and his own responsibility. This is all the more conspicuous because K. at the beginning feels a distinct reluctance to accept help from outside. As he goes to the first interrogation, for instance, K. decides to walk. "A sort of defiance had kept K. from taking a vehicle to his destination; he loathed the thought of any outside help—even the slightest—in this case of his; also he did not want to make demands upon anyone and thus initiate anyone even remotely in his affairs."[36] But as he becomes more deeply involved and confused, his initial impulse toward independent action gives way to the desire to enlist outside assistance—especially female.

Even in the first chapter he had decided that Fräulein Bürstner might be of assistance to him, for the very remote reason that she was soon to become a secretary in a legal office. Later he appeals not directly to the court usher, but to his wife. And though he rejects the firsthand advice of Lawyer Huld, he hopes to get somewhere with the aid of his maid,

[36] *Prozess*, p. 47.

Leni. "I am recruiting women helpers, he thought almost in surprise: first Fräulein Bürstner, then the wife of the usher, and now this little nurse who appears to have some incomprehensible need for me."[37] Invariably he takes the indirect approach, hoping thereby to put his responsibility on someone else's shoulders. Thus he approaches the painter Titorelli, whose name had been given to him (again, indirectly and by chance) by one of his business associates at the bank. "If the judges could really be so easily influenced by personal connections as the lawyer insisted, then the painter's connections with these vain functionaries were especially important and certainly not to be underestimated. That made the painter an excellent recruit to the ring of helpers which K. was gradually gathering round him."[38] This continues until the scene in the cathedral:

> "What is the next step you propose to take in the matter?" asked the priest. "I'm going to get more help," said K., looking up again to see how the priest took his statement. "There are several possibilities I haven't exhausted yet." "You cast about too much for outside help," said the priest disapprovingly, "especially from women. Don't you see that it isn't the right kind of help?" "In some cases, even in many I could agree with you," said K., "but not always. Women have great influence. If I could persuade some women I know to join forces in working for me, I couldn't help winning through. Especially before this Court, which consists almost entirely of skirt-chasers."[39]

This passage presents various difficulties of interpretation; critics do not agree on the precise competence of the priest

[37] *Prozess*, p. 133.

[38] *Prozess*, p. 182. Note the word "ring" (Kafka's word is "Kreis," which literally means "circle") for future reference in our discussion of the structure of the novel.

[39] *Prozess*, p. 253.

in judging affairs. However, we can safely make two general statements. First, this seeking for helpers determines in large measure the organization of the book. (We shall have more to say in another connection about the structure.) For it is clear that K.'s course is not determined by any attempt to move directly toward the Court or to shoulder his own responsibility in the world. He sidles, instead, from one helper to the next. Instead of developing organically, the plot offers a succession of episodes, each focused on a helper or group of potential helpers.

Second, Kafka makes it absolutely clear that he agrees with the priest in condemning K.'s search for help. For in the parable related a few minutes later, the helpers that the Man from the Country enlists in his campaign against the door-keeper are—the fleas in the doorkeeper's fur collar! Now, it can easily be demonstrated that in Kafka's metaphorical scale of values animal imagery is employed specifically to characterize men who renounce their freedom. Only he who accepts, fully and completely, responsibility for his actions deserves to be called a true man; others are at best animals or lower forms of life. Consistently enough, Kafka illustrates this conviction by employing animal metaphors for people who do not make use of their freedom.[40]

In *The Trial* the use of animal metaphors increases proportionately as K. depends more heavily upon outside assistance. When K. leaves Fräulein Bürstner, shortly after having solicited her future aid, he "seized her, and kissed her first on the mouth, then all over the face, like some thirsty animal

---

[40] Animals, of course, constitute only one element in Kafka's rhetoric of images. Another example is the bed, which is related to the theme of awakening: it represents the cozy security of an unconditionally accepted system. Thus K. is deprived of his bed by his awakening. Conversely, those figures who are tied most closely to the system —Huld and Titorelli—have rooms in which the bed is the most conspicuous item; and they spend most of their time in bed.

lapping greedily at a spring of long-sought fresh water."[41] Just after he has invoked the assistance of the court usher's wife, he tussles with his rival, the student, "laying his hand on the shoulder of the student, who snapped at it with his teeth."[42] During his dalliance with Leni he discovers that the middle and ring fingers of her right hand are webbed: "What a pretty little paw!" he exclaims.[43] (In general, Leni is characterized by actions—scratching, biting, clawing, and pawing—more typical of a cat than of a human being.)

The merchant Block is the most abject symbol, that of a man degraded wholly into animality because of his total abjuration of personal responsibility and his complete reliance on the aid of the lawyer in his case. "So the lawyer's methods, to which K. fortunately had not been long enough exposed, amounted to this: that the client finally forgot the whole world and lived only in hope of toiling along this false path until the end of his case should come in sight. The client ceased to be a client and became the lawyer's dog. If the lawyer had ordered this man to crawl under the bed as if into a kennel and to bark there, he would gladly have done so."[44] This last image, coming quite late in the book, is the most important of all, and so, just in case the reader might have overlooked the significance of earlier animal metaphors, Kafka draws particular attention to it. He stresses the fact that "K. listened to everything with critical detachment, as if he had been commissioned to observe the proceedings closely, to report them to a higher authority. . . ." For the merchant Block is not merely a symbol of human degradation, but a typological anticipation of K.'s own fate.

It is, of course, no accident that K. himself dies "like a dog" in the last sentence of the book. Having refused to the end to accept the responsibility for his actions, he ignores

[41] *Prozess*, p. 42.   [42] *Prozess*, p. 74.   [43] *Prozess*, p. 135.
[44] *Prozess*, p. 233.

the final opportunity for redemption. As the two men pass the butcher knife back and forth over his head, he senses that it is his responsibility to plunge it into his own heart, thus assuming, in the last instant, responsibility for his life. But K. refuses. "The responsibility for this last failure of his lay with the one who had denied him the remnant of strength necessary for the deed."[45] Even here K. continues to project his guilt, to *motivate*. And in the next instant, as he glances up, he catches sight of a figure in the window of a nearby house and this precipitates again the whole quest for outside assistance. "Who was it?" he thinks. "A friend? A good man? Someone who cared? Somebody who wanted to help? Was it a single person? Was it everybody? Was there still help?" During his year of trial K. has not reached the state of human freedom and responsibility. This final scene, which parallels the opening scene to a remarkable degree, merely emphasizes how little he has changed and the extent to which this last scene is but a repetition of the first. K. still clings to futile hopes of delaying his proceedings, of thrusting the responsibility upon others. Hence he dies, appropriately, "like a dog," in the awareness that his shame will survive him.

K.'s failure is the refusal to accept freedom and the burden that it entails in temporal life. For freedom can be exercised only within time, not in a state of meaningless repetition outside of time. After the initial awakening necessary for the recognition of guilt, it is imperative to return to temporal life with this new dimension of awareness and to accept the responsibility that this awareness involves. Ingeborg Henel aptly describes this paralysis as "the stasis of time before the decision."[46] It is a state that is not meant to be permanent. The entire novel is, in this sense, nothing but an extended metaphor for, or parable of, the instant of reflection during which

[45] *Prozess*, p. 271.   [46] Henel, *op.cit.*, p. 69, note 19.

a man assesses his position and decides to act. K. is given the enviable opportunity, through his awakening, to become a free man by accepting the responsibility for his guilt in temporal reality. By refusing, however, he plunges himself even more deeply into shame than had been the case earlier, before his awakening.

For an entire year K. is caught up in the vicious circle of denial. He avoids temporality just as assiduously as does Malte Laurids Brigge, although his reasons are quite different. From the moment of his awakening he exists in a state of paralyzed time, out of step with the flow of temporal reality in which freedom can be exercised. Kafka's great task as a narrator is to render plausible this sense of stasis that characterizes his hero's thirtieth year.

(5)

HEINZ Politzer has elegantly demonstrated that circularity is one of the most pervasive images in Kafka's works.[47] Caught in an ineluctable circle of repetitions, the individual moves neither forward nor backward, but simply marks time constantly within the same periphery, like the hero who, in Kafka's later novel, circles forever around the Castle. Several diary entries make it clear that Kafka visualized life as a circle. As early as 1910 he speaks of "this circle [of past and future] along whose edge we move. It belongs to us as long as we cling to it. . . ."[48] And twelve years later, summarizing what he considered to be the failures of his own life, he remarked: "It was as though I had been given the center of a circle like any other man; as though then, like any other man, I had to move along the decisive radius and draw the lovely circle. But instead I constantly began one radius, but always

[47] *Franz Kafka*, pp. 73, 78, and *passim*.
[48] *Tagebücher*, p. 22.

had to break it off. . . . The center of my imaginary circle is bristling with incipient radii, and there's no room for a new attempt."[49] We should note here, especially, the reference to the many fruitless attempts to complete a given radius—the failure, like that of Josef K., to pierce directly to the heart of the matter and to "draw the lovely circle." This circularity, by which one is never led closer to the center but constantly returned to the starting point, turns out to be the basic structural principle of *The Trial*.

We first become aware that time is standing still in the eerie scene in which K. returns to the room where he had seen Franz and Willem being punished by the Whipper. "What confronted him, instead of the darkness he expected, bewildered him completely. Everything was still the same, exactly as he had found it on opening the door the previous evening."[50] Reality has been taken out of the flow of time and frozen into a terrifying static image. This scene is actually paradigmatic for the other episodes of the book. For although absolute stasis does not occur—the seasons seem to change, a kind of development seems to take place—the scenes are all essentially repetitions of one another.[51] Though the figures change, the basic constellation remains identical in every episode.

This repetition is immediately evident if we consider the patterns of three that recur throughout the book. In almost every scene we seem to be confronted with the same model.

[49] *Tagebücher*, p. 560.

[50] *Prozess*, p. 110. Allemann, "Kafka: Der Prozess," p. 280, emphasizes the terrifying aspect of this repetition.

[51] See Allemann, pp. 264-65; Clemens Heselhaus, "Kafkas Erzählformen," *Deutsche Vierteljahresschrift*, 26 (1952), 368, relates this structure to the technique of isolation in the traditional fairy tale or *Märchen*. Similarly, Helmut Arntzen, *Der moderne deutsche Roman* (Heidelberg: Wolfgang Rothe, 1962), p. 83, speaks of the "juxtaposition" of the chapters in contrast to the normal sequence.

In the opening chapter, K. is interviewed by an Inspector and two warders. The proceedings are observed, through the window, by three neighbors next door. K. is accompanied from his house that morning by three of his subordinates from the bank; and in subsequent scenes the same three reappear. He is surrounded in his rooming house by three women: Frau Grubach, Fräulein Bürstner, and her friend Fräulein Montag. In the first interrogation K. is again involved with three characters: the Examining Magistrate, the usher's wife, and the student. A week later he meets the usher himself, who takes him to the Clerk of Inquiries and his female assistant. In the Whipper scenes the triad is completed by Franz and Willem. When K. goes with his uncle to visit Lawyer Huld, the group consists of his uncle, Huld himself, and the Chief Clerk, who is visiting the lawyer. In the reception room at the bank, three clients wait to see K. When K. visits Titorelli he sees three tinsmiths working in a shop downstairs. In all of these groupings K. is an alien, an outsider, for from the moment of his awakening he is outside the context of time and life. In the last chapter, however, he is no longer the observer. When the two men take him away to his execution, involving him once again in temporality, he himself constitutes the third member of the group.[52]

Wherever we look we encounter this constellation of three, whose comical overtones are not to be denied. Often these groups seem to assume the role of a comedy team such as the Marx Brothers. This association is intensified, in the last chapter, by K.'s reaction to the executioners who come for him. " 'Tenth-rate old actors they send for me,' said K. to himself, glancing round again to confirm the impression. 'They want

[52] I do not impute to the number three the Freudian symbolism of male genitalia that Harry Slochower finds in the final scene: "Franz Kafka: Pre-Fascist Exile," *A Franz Kafka Miscellany* (2nd edn.; New York: Twice a Year Press, 1946), pp. 7-30.

to finish me off cheaply.' He turned abruptly toward the men and asked: 'What theater are you playing at?' "[53] We must not be led by the basically tragic conception of *The Trial* to overlook its comic aspects. Max Brod relates that when Kafka read the first chapter of *The Trial* to a group of friends, he "laughed so much that there were moments when he could not read any further."[54] Surely the frequent constellations of three in the opening chapter contributed to this effect of laughable absurdity.

The most important function of the triads, however, is to heighten the effect of *déjà vu* from scene to scene. We are not experiencing anything new, we feel, but merely witnessing variations on the same basic theme. K. moves, in the course of his year, from one area to the next: his lodgings, the bank, the interrogation rooms, Huld's apartment, Titorelli's studio, the cathedral. But these areas, unrelated to one another, represent no progress at all. Each turns out, instead, to be a circle that revolves back upon itself, bringing K. no closer to his goal. Each is characterized, usually, by a constellation of three figures. And in each K. seeks out a helper, rejects the helper, and moves on to the next ring. We can visualize this structure as a series of concentric circles or, perhaps better, as a pattern of orbits, like those in which electrons sweep equidistant around a central nucleus— the Law—that is never attained.

As though to reinforce some such image, Kafka has inserted it once again, in almost schematic form, in the parable related by the priest near the end of the novel. The parable, of course, is of immense thematic importance, since it recapitulates the theme of guilt and freedom with all its ambiguities. It is a potentialization of the plot of the novel, projecting the

[53] *Prozess*, pp. 266-67.
[54] Max Brod, *Franz Kafka*, trans. G. Humphrey Roberts and Richard Winston (2nd edn.; New York: Schocken Books, 1960), p. 178.

experiences of the individual K. into mythic proportions.[55]
Here, however, we must consider the structure of the situation. The Man from the Country, it will be recalled,
approaches the Law and finds a guard standing at the door.
Like K. himself, the man never takes the direct approach;
he doesn't attempt to go through the door, which, as we subsequently learn, is there for him alone. He does not assume
the responsibility for entering or make use of his freedom to
enter. Instead, taking the guard at his word, he sits down outside the door and remains there until his death, engaging in
interminable discussions with the guard and even imploring
the aid of the fleas in the guard's fur collar.

From these conversations we learn that the guard is responsible only for the first door. "I am merely the lowest
doorkeeper. From hall to hall, keepers stand at every door,
one more powerful than the other. And the sight of the third
man is already more than even I can endure."[56] The guard's
—and the man's—horizon extends no further than the third
door.[57] But if, from these words, we reconstruct the topography of the situation, it seems clear that the Law is an innermost chamber ringed by halls of increasing circumference,
each one watched over by a different guard, each represent-
ing an entity unto itself. As a matter of fact, even if we
visualize the landscape as a series of chambers leading to the
Law rather than as concentric rings surrounding it, this arrangement still illustrates symbolically the structure of the

[55] There have been countless analyses of this parable. I have profited
most from the articles, previously cited, of Ingeborg Henel and Gerhart Kaiser. Kaiser, pp. 44ff., specifically points to parallels between
Josef K. and the Man from the Country.

[56] *Prozess*, p. 256.

[57] I agree emphatically with Kaiser, *op.cit.*, p. 49, who argues that
there are no sufficient grounds for calling Kafka a nihilist. Kafka
limits the horizons of his characters, but never implies that there is no
meaning beyond that horizon.

chapters of the novel. For each chamber, each guard, is a repetition of the preceding one. There is no development and no progress, merely constant repetition. The structure of the parable has, I think, another implication for the organization of the novel as well.

(6)

The Trial, like Kafka's other novels, is a fragment. Kafka wrote most of it during the period 1914 to 1915 and worked on it thereafter only sporadically, if at all. In any case, what he left after his death was not a completed manuscript, but an unorganized heap of chapters, deleted sections, and notes. This raises two questions that have often been discussed: the organization of the extant chapters and the degree to which the novel as a whole is complete. It is generally agreed that the arrangement of chapters in the standard edition published by Max Brod is subject to improvement.[58] It seems indisputable, for instance, that Chapter 1 should be followed immediately by the section entitled "Fräulein Bürstner's Friend" (Brod's Chapter 4). It is specifically stated in the text that this interview takes place only five days after the events of Chapter 1, whereas the first interrogation (Brod's Chapter 2) takes place ten days after the arrest. This minor adjustment has an advantage from our point of view because it keeps together the chapters that constitute individual episodes or circles, thus highlighting K.'s spasmodic motion from one area of helpers to the next.[59] In other words, when

[58] The boldest revisions have been proposed by Herman Uyttersprot, "Zur Struktur von Kafkas *Der Prozess*—Versuch einer Neu-Ordnung," *Revue des langues vivantes*, 19 (1953), 333-76. Uyttersprot's main arguments are recapitulated in an abridgment of his study in *Franz Kafka Today*, ed. Angel Flores and Homer Swados (Madison: University of Wisconsin Press, 1958).

[59] I find it difficult to agree with E. M. Butler when she argues, in her "Translator's Note" to the Modern Library edition of *The*

K. moves out of the circle represented by his rooming house, that episode is completed. Then he moves on to the next circle, and the basic pattern is repeated again with a different configuration of characters.

The second and more controversial suggestion for rearrangement must, from our point of view, be rejected. Uyttersprot argues at length that the cathedral scene (Chapter 9) should be moved from its penultimate position and inserted before the present Chapter 7 ("Lawyer, Manufacturer, Painter"). He advances three arguments. First, the succession of seasons seems to support this disposition. Second, K.'s psychological condition in the seventh and eighth chapters strikes him as more mature than it is in the cathedral scene. And third: he assumes that the figure of Titorelli was to be developed and enlarged as K.'s most important helper, thus dominating the second part of the novel. These arguments have been plausibly refuted by various scholars,[60] and there is no need to recapitulate the reasons here. Instead, I will add only a further argument against this change from the structural standpoint. First, to insert the cathedral scene *between* the present Chapters 6 and 7 would break up one continuous episode or circle: namely the Huld-Leni constellation. But second, and more significant: the novel consists of a series of episodes involving helpers, building up to the priest's flat denial of the efficacy of these helpers. It is therefore in keeping with the fitful motion of the novel from one

Trial, p. 340, that Uyttersprot's rearrangement "makes the novel appear less episodic and more of an organic whole." By way of contrast, Allemann (*op.cit.*, p. 265) specifically mentions the episodic effect brought about by the new position of Chapter 4.

[60] Kaiser, *op.cit.*, pp. 45-48; Henel, *op.cit.*, pp. 67-68; Politzer, *Franz Kafka*, p. 211n.; Klaus Wagenbach, "Jahreszeiten bei Kafka," *Deutsche Vierteljahresschrift*, 33 (1959), 645-47; and others.

episode to the next for the representative helpers to have been tried and rejected *before* this point.

As far as degree of completion is concerned, the parable also reflects the structure of the novel. *The Trial* has an absolute beginning and an absolute end: K.'s arrest on his thirtieth birthday and his death precisely one year later. These two points are fixed, but the time between them is capable of almost infinite expansion. If we project this temporal scheme onto the topography of the parable, we can see that the possibilities are limitless. The Man from the Country is standing at the outermost door of the Law; at the other extreme is the Law itself: this corresponds to the absolute beginning and end of the novel. It is obvious from the parable, however, that the number of circles surrounding the Law, or of chambers leading to it, is infinite. Even if the Man should decide to go past the guard, he would be confronted with a situation like that which holds the Country Doctor, who drives and drives through the snowy landscape without ever reaching home. Likewise, the number of episodes in the novel itself is infinitely expandable. Thus it becomes rather pointless to ask to what degree the novel is actually finished. It is a novel that can never be finished—or one that is complete, in essence, as soon as the first episode has been written. Since K. never makes any progress or undergoes any development, but merely repeats over and over again the same basic pattern of behavior, the possibilities of variation are endless.[61] Kafka might have kept on inventing episodes for years, but none could have brought K. any closer to the resolution of his dilemma, for the only possible resolution, K.'s death "like

[61] In his original postscript Max Brod said that Kafka "regarded the novel as unfinished" and that "in a certain sense the novel could never be terminated—that is to say, it could be prolonged into infinity" (*Prozess*, pp. 322-23).

a dog," is already established in the last chapter. This precludes any development in the preceding chapters.

Even if Kafka had restricted himself to the temporal rhythm of the first unit, the book would have become a *monstrum*. For the first five chapters, which belong more or less together, cover roughly only the first month; at that rate, a novel filling out K.'s whole thirtieth year would have grown to some sixty chapters, or six times the length of the present fragment. It was probably a realization of this sort that caused Kafka to put the novel aside, leaving it incomplete and disorganized. As Beda Allemann has observed, Kafka strove in all his works to produce the effect of uninterrupted continuity.[62] This is obviously impossible in a work whose structure requires the temporal extent of a calendar year. (In *The Castle* Kafka reduced the external time to a period of seven days and managed, thereby, to maintain an uninterrupted continuity of narrative.) Ultimately the completion, and even the disposition of the chapters, are irrelevant to the meaning of the book. For the instant K. moves out of the ring of paralyzed time into the flow of temporality, he must be executed. By his refusal to accept his guilt, he has committed moral suicide; and this metaphorical death is enacted in reality once he reenters the world of time and action.

In *The Trial* as in few other works of literature, the structure reflects its author's preoccupation with the vicious circle of time. Man can realize himself as free only in temporality; but temporality also involves inevitable guilt and death. The attempt to escape guilt by remaining ensnared in the concentric circles of static contemplation protects man from death; but it also prevents the individual from exercising his freedom. In *The Trial* we find the same basic dilemma that confronts all the writers of Kafka's generation, but his reaction is different. Unlike Malte Laurids Brigge, Josef K. achieves

[62] Allemann, "Kafka: Der Prozess," p. 263: "Lückenlosigkeit."

no freedom or release by freezing time. To be sure, as long as he remains within the static circles of repetition, he avoids death. But this brings no satisfaction, since it also prevents him from achieving the humanity of freedom and reduces him, ultimately, to animality. At the same time, Kafka must not be accused of nihilism. To be sure, Josef K. is not redeemed. But this is his own fault: he does not accept the burden of his freedom. Moreover, the fact that neither he nor his creator ever comes face to face with the Law does not mean that there is no Law, but simply that we cannot know the Law.

It is a mistake, of course, to identify Kafka with his hero. For Kafka, as an artist, actually achieves to some degree the release denied Josef K. In a diary note from the period immediately preceding the composition of *The Trial* Kafka notes that he feels "helpless and alienated"—like Josef K. "But the steadfastness vouchsafed me by the least bit of writing is beyond any doubt and wonderful."[63] Kafka, in other words, is representative of his own generation, a generation of writers who found at least some respite from temporality in aesthetics. The ultimate paradox in Kafka's works is perhaps the insight that the perfect rendition of hopelessness can itself be a gesture of hope.

[63] *Tagebücher*, p. 336.

chapter three

Thomas Mann

The Magic Mountain

(1)

The Notebooks of Malte Laurids Brigge is about a young
man who comes to Paris and, jolted there by the shock of
reality into a reassessment of all his values, begins to write a
journal in order to bring at least some semblance of aesthetic
order to a threatening, disorderly world. *The Trial* is about a
young man who is awakened by his arrest to a consideration
of the problem of personal guilt and who, after he commits
moral suicide by denying his guilt, is punished by execution.
The Magic Mountain is about a young man who goes to a
tuberculosis sanatorium in Switzerland to visit his cousin for
three weeks and—and what? Remains for seven years? Falls
in love with a Russian woman who reminds him of a childhood friend? Listens to interminable philosophical debates
between an Italian humanist and a Jewish-Jesuit-communist-
terrorist? Studies physiology, botany, astronomy? Makes
friends with an inarticulate Dutch plantation owner with an
imposing personality? Goes skiing in snowstorms? Attends
séances and listens to music?

This simple exercise that can be demanded of any reasonably competent student—the statement of theme—highlights
one of the difficulties involved in any discussion of Thomas
Mann's masterpiece. In the novels by Rilke and Kafka the
theme is roughly reflected in the action: there is a correlation
between substance and content. *The Magic Mountain*, by contrast, is *about* one set of things, but it *says* something quite
different. The entire ideological framework of this perhaps

greatest novel of ideas is, ultimately, irrelevant to the meaning of the novel. This detachability of content is not a shortcoming but rather, as we shall see, is implicit in the meaning of the work. It merely emphasizes the fact that we are dealing here with a symbolic novel par excellence, with an absolute novel, with a hermetic novel. This distinguishes it from such works as *The Trial*, which might be described as an extended metaphor. The symbolic novel, by way of distinction, does not have the referential quality of the metaphorical or parabolic novel. In the symbolic novel it is not the content that matters. To state the case most bluntly, its ingredients are virtually interchangeable; they are not important in themselves. It is the tensions and relations obtaining *between* them that reflect the author's meaning. This can be demonstrated most clearly, perhaps, if we resort to what may strike some readers initially as a rather unsophisticated approach: namely, an old-fashioned distinction between the form, the content, and the substance of *The Magic Mountain*. By these I mean simply the organization and structure of the chapters, the ideological texture of the work, and the development of the hero. These three aspects, it turns out, are in themselves only casually related; their true relationship emerges in a *tertium comparationis*. It is in every case the theme of timelessness that provides the link between otherwise disparate elements.

(2)

CRITICS have sometimes objected to what they call the excessive intellectual baggage of Thomas Mann's novels, and especially of *The Magic Mountain*, maintaining that the ideologies are derivative and that their obtrusion delays the denouement of the action. This is not the proper place to discuss to what extent the intellectual contents of the works of most major writers—from Dante to Sartre—are ultimately derivative. In the case of Thomas Mann, the fact that we learn something or nothing new is largely irrelevant, of course. What matters is the fact that the ideologies constitute the intellectual framework through which and within which the development of the hero takes place. It is not the ideas in themselves that contribute to Hans Castorp's spiritual education, but rather the tensions between them.

For the reader with a taste for erudition and "civilized" conversation—and, it must be conceded, with the time and patience to read at the leisurely pace demanded by Mann's novels—there is nothing more delightful than the scintillating, highly articulate ideological fireworks that explode in the conversations of Settembrini and Naphta. Yet few readers, probably, are capable of recapitulating afterwards the main points of the arguments. Certain general attitudes emerge clearly, of course. Settembrini, the humanist, defends the classics and the Renaissance against the fanatic medievalism of the Jewish-Jesuit Naphta. He upholds reason against Naphta's advocacy of faith and discipline, monism against the latter's dualism, nationalism against a communistic church, and humanism in the face of Naphta's endorsement of blind terrorism. In these intellectual duels the flashing stiletto of Naphta usually wins out over the graceful rapier of Settembrini. Yet the reader is no more convinced by one side or the other than is Hans Castorp, who looks rapidly from one disputant to the other as he follows the debate, "roguishly" interjecting from time to time a seemingly innocent remark that spurs them on to ever greater intellectual bravura. For the whole point of these debates is not to persuade Hans Castorp or the reader; they exist for their own sake, for the sake of the dialectical interplay. Hence the subtleties of argumentation rapidly recede in the reader's mind into a loose rhythm of tensions.

The careful structuring of ideologies becomes most appar-

The Magic Mountain

ent if we disregard fine points and concentrate on the main representatives of these ideologies in the two parts of the novel.[1] The first half of the book is dominated largely by the tension obtaining between the oriental temptations of sleepy-eyed Clawdia Chauchat and the Western rationalism of Settembrini, who turns on the brightest lights when he enters a room and constantly "disturbs" Hans Castorp in his acquiescence to the seductiveness of the East. Here the dialectical positions seem to break down into an opposition of East and West, emotion and reason, passivity and action.

In the second half of the book these elements are reshuffled and complicated, for the characters of Naphta and Mynheer Peeperkorn have been added to the game. Various geometrical alignments become evident; or, to use another analogy, the forces are polarized into different configurations in the electrical field.[2] For before the magnitude of Peeperkorn's imposing gestures (*Kulturgebärde*) and mighty cult of feeling, all the posturings and subtly articulated distinctions of Naphta and Settembrini are lumped together into a position that Peeperkorn jocularly and contemptuously calls "cerebrum, cerebral."[3] The utter irrelevancy of their lucubrations is nowhere more apparent than in the magnificent scene where Mynheer, standing before the thundering waterfall, holds forth in a grandiloquent speech that no one can understand—but which nevertheless, through the force of his

[1] See Hermann J. Weigand, *Thomas Mann's Novel Der Zauberberg* (New York and London: Appleton-Century, 1933), p. 10: "As for the principal characters, they frankly function as representatives." Also Andrew White, *Thomas Mann* (Edinburgh and London: Oliver and Boyd, 1965), p. 40.

[2] See Joseph G. Brennan, *Thomas Mann's World* (New York: Russell and Russell, 1962), p. 169: "During his stay at the sanatorium, Hans Castorp runs a gauntlet of opposing forces."

[3] *Der Zauberberg*, p. 818. Quoted here and elsewhere from the text in Vol. III of the twelve-volume edition of Mann's *Gesammelte Werke* (Frankfurt am Main: S. Fischer, 1960).

personality, is more impressive than all the finesse of the two disputants. The tension that originated as a juxtaposition of East and West, then shifted to a battle between reason and faith, is transmuted finally into an opposition of intellect and feeling. In the face of this rhythm of tensions the details of the ideologies become unimportant.

All these positions hold each other in check or cancel one another out. No ideology is left intact at the end of the novel. Peeperkorn, the advocate of blind feeling who regards himself as "God's marriage organ," commits suicide because his sexual powers have receded. Naphta, the vigilante of terror, faith, and discipline, shoots himself in the head in a fit of frustration and rage. Settembrini, the spokesman for work and progress, is reduced by his illness to a bedridden existence. And Madame Chauchat, whose orientalism results in such passivity that she never acts but only responds to others, simply goes away after Peeperkorn's death.

Much has been written about all these figures. It is fascinating to learn that Settembrini often presents the intellectual position of Mann's brother Heinrich; that Naphta has certain characteristics of the Marxist critic Georg Lukács; that Peeperkorn owes his appearance and behavior in part to Gerhart Hauptmann and Leo Tolstoy. Scholars have carefully documented the ideas and phrases, borrowed from the most varied intellectual sources, that Thomas Mann has shaped into convincing and plausible characters. Hermann J. Weigand has demonstrated, for instance, that Settembrini's conversation is a patchwork of borrowings from Goethe's Mephisto, Schiller, young Nietzsche, Giuseppe Mazzini, and the German enlightenment.[4] To detect and savor these elements is the delight of the scholar and educated reader. They demonstrate more clearly than anything else Thomas Mann's brilliant art of epic integration and characterization.

[4] Weigand, *op.cit.*, p. 11.

The Magic Mountain

But structurally these elements are irrelevant: first, because many of them are cryptic and intended only as tidbits for a few readers; and second, because the intellectual positions tend not only to cancel each other out, but to invalidate themselves. What matters ultimately is not, say, that Naphta wins a certain argument with Settembrini or that Hans Castorp's allegiance, in the "Walpurgis Night" chapter, swerves from Settembrini toward Clawdia Chauchat. As one looks back over the thousand pages of the novel, one becomes aware that there has been no dialectical progress; no true belief has emerged. Instead, we see these various ideological possibilities spread out like constant forces in a magnetic field. Hans Castorp does not, in other words, begin as a *tabula rasa* and progress from Settembrini to Clawdia, past Naphta, to Peeperkorn. Rather, through these symbolic figures he encounters various potentialities of being that exist eternally. They awaken within him an awareness of certain human possibilities; it is an expansion, a heightening, a *Steigerung*, in Mann's own expression, but not a progress in the sense of movement through time.

This notion, as we shall see, is central to the conception of Hans Castorp's *Bildung* in this novel of development. But it also illustrates the difference between Thomas Mann's novel and other novels of ideas. In many such novels—in those of Malraux and Sartre, Hermann Broch or Graham Greene; yes, even in Thomas Mann's later novel *Doctor Faustus*—ideas are presented tendentiously, in order to be demonstrated or proved. Here, by contrast, it is merely their constant presence that is argued or set forth. The ideologies within the book are merely intellectual pawns, to be pushed about for the sake of the composition. They mean nothing as far as Thomas Mann's own beliefs are concerned. And nothing could be more mistaken than to attempt any deductions regarding his own position from the ideas expressed in the book.

Thomas Mann

To illustrate this, let us examine a specific case. Among the many technical tricks that Thomas Mann makes use of with sly virtuosity is that of the quotation and self-quotation. In one of his conversations with Naphta, Settembrini has occasion to defend literature against Naphta's disparaging cynicisms. He eulogizes "the purifying and sanctifying influence of letters, the subduing of the passions through cognition and expression; literature as the way to understanding, forgiveness, and love, the redeeming power of language, literary spirit as the noblest manifestation of the human mind, the writer as the most highly developed of human beings, as saint."[5] It is disconcerting to discover that this same passage —not just its sense, but its exact wording—occurs some twenty years earlier in the tale *Tonio Kröger*.[6] But there, oddly enough, the words are spoken by Lisaweta Ivanovna, the woman of the Orient, with specific reference to what Tonio Kröger calls the "sacred" Russian literature!

The novel contains many other examples of such self-quotation, where passages have been lifted out of one context and used in a wholly different one, but this single instance illustrates the point sufficiently. Thomas Mann is above all a writer, not an ideologist. His *Reflections of a Non-Political Man* (1918) contains a number of observations to this effect. "All truths are time-truths," he says on one occasion.[7] "The intellect is the courtier of the will, and the needs, the requisites of a given time present themselves to this time as 'insights,' as 'truths.'" Mann is not concerned merely with the general relativism of values; his own personal experience, he discovers on going through some of his old papers, demonstrates to him "that at the very same time I was capable

[5] *Zauberberg*, p. 724.
[6] *Gesammelte Werke*, VIII, 300; henceforth cited as *GW*.
[7] In the essay "Vom Glauben"; *GW*, XII, 516.

also of thinking the very opposite."[8] Intellectually, all truths and all beliefs exist simultaneously, side by side, just as Naphta and Settembrini both inhabit the same house in Davos. "I shall never be the slave of my ideas," Mann wrote to his friend Paul Amann, "for I know that nothing which is merely thought and said is true and that only *form* is unassailable."[9] And he continues in the same letter: "I am so remote from pinning myself down intellectually through my *écrits* that the literary disposal of my thoughts is, rather, the only sure way of getting rid of them and striving beyond them to other, new, better and—if possible—quite contrary ideas—*sans remords!*"

This intellectual lability marks a fundamental difference between the writer and other men, Thomas Mann stresses in another essay. "It must be clearly understood that someone who is accustomed not to speaking directly and on his own responsibility but, instead, to causing people and objects to speak—that someone who is accustomed to making *art*, never can take the spirit and intellect in full seriousness since it has always been his affair, rather, to treat them as material and playthings, to represent points of view, to practice dialectics, always to allow the person who is speaking to be right. . . . The intellectual thought in the work of art is not understood if one takes it to be its own purpose . . . it is purposeful with respect to the composition, it affirms itself only with reference to the composition. It can be banal, from an absolute and literary point of view, but brilliant within the composition."[10]

[8] In the essay "Einkehr"; *GW*, xii, 100.

[9] Letter of February 25, 1916; in Thomas Mann, *Briefe an Paul Amann, 1915-1952*, ed. Herbert Wegener (Lübeck: Max Schmidt-Römhild, 1959), p. 40.

[10] In the essay "Politik"; *GW*, xii, 229. Regarding Mann's use of quotation and self-quotation, see Herman Meyer, *Das Zitat in der Erzählkunst* (Stuttgart: Metzler, 1961; 2nd edn., 1967); published in

Thomas Mann

This aesthetic attitude, which Mann, borrowing a term from Strindberg, calls "stereoscopic" vision, constitutes the inherent superiority of art over the merely intellectual. Art vouchsafes a certain spiritual freedom and flexibility not to be enjoyed by the intellectual who is bound to his own unyielding position.[11] It is in this light, then, that we must regard the ideological framework of *The Magic Mountain*. None of the positions represents the author's own point of view, but all of them together symbolize potentialities of his own mind, which exist timelessly as eternal positions. More important, however: the stereoscopic or aesthetic vision also characterizes the hero of the novel, Hans Castorp, who takes cognizance of all the positions thrust upon him by the various figures of the novel but commits himself to none. For the most essential element of his personality is a great sense of freedom.[12] His "development" can be regarded not as the acquisition of new ideas, but rather as a series of liberations. And from the structural point of view, the entire novel is constructed in such a way as to heighten the reader's experience of the freedom which characterizes the state of timeless suspension in which Hans Castorp spends seven years on the Magic Mountain.

English as *The Poetics of Quotation in the European Novel* (Princeton: Princeton University Press, 1968); and Gert E. Bruhn, "Das Selbstzitat bei Thomas Mann" (Dissertation: Princeton University, 1967).

[11] Mann's attitude is a perfect illustration of what Jacques Maritain, in *The Responsibility of the Artist* (New York: Scribner's, 1960), p. 95, calls "the sincerity of merely artistic morality," which "refuses to make any choice or moral decision; for this would risk preventing the potentialities of the Ego from freely developing—both toward God and toward the devil."

[12] Weigand, *op.cit.*, p. 27, lists freedom among Hans Castorp's four *Urerlebnisse*—basic psychic experiences.

The Magic Mountain

(3)

ERICH Heller once remarked that Hans Castorp, should he survive the war, would have no choice but to become a writer.[13] He certainly could not go back to the career as a nautical designer that he left behind when he departed from Hamburg for his little visit to the Magic Mountain. This comment reveals the connection between the ideology, or the content, of the novel and the development of its hero, or its substance. For the point of view with which Hans Castorp emerges from his seven "hermetic" years is essentially the "stereoscopic" view that Thomas Mann claims for the writer. While it is perfectly true, as Weigand demonstrates, that Hans Castorp's development consists in an "exposure" to the world in the concentrated, "escalated" compression of the feverish atmosphere of the sanatorium, it is equally true that the ultimate effect of his ideal education at the hands of various mentors is to liberate him successively from all bonds and ties until he emerges, toward the end of the novel, in perfect freedom. And since this absolute freedom is symbolized by a suspension of time, Hans Castorp's development can be regarded in another sense as a movement from time to timelessness.

In this connection the setting of the novel is of central importance. Isolated from the world "down below," existing almost in a different time system, the sanatorium is a realm which recognizes the month as its smallest unit of time, where popular usage reduces even such a measure as the year (*Jahr*) to a diminutive form (*Jährchen*). It is an "Asiatic style of time-consumption," as Settembrini complains in

[13] Heller, "Conversation on the Magic Mountain," in *Thomas Mann: A Collection of Critical Essays*, ed. Henry Hatfield (Englewood Cliffs, N. J.: Prentice-Hall, 1964), pp. 94-95.

77

a formulation that renders even time in ideological terms.[14] The seasons, virtually indistinguishable, "do not adhere to the calendar."[15] It is a world with laws of its own, where the main concerns, as Mann remarks, are one's temperature and flirtation. The mountain is "magic" not least because it is independent of the rules of everyday life, of the reality which binds the world on the plains below. On his first day Hans Castorp learns from Joachim that the young people in the sanatorium are free. "I mean, they're young people, and time plays no role for them, and then they'll probably die anyway. Why should they make serious faces? Sometimes I think that sickness and dying are actually not serious, but more a kind of dawdling. Strictly speaking, seriousness exists only down below."[16] Only in an atmosphere of this sort can Hans Castorp be liberated in the sense mentioned above. For in the world below, the concerns and responsibilities of everyday life absorb one's time and attention; the individual is caught up in the flow of temporality and rendered incapable of the pure reflection ensured by the hermetically enclosed world of the sanatorium.[17]

From the very start the motif of detachment is sounded, anticipating to a remarkable extent the third volume of Broch's *The Sleepwalkers*, where the action also takes place during a "vacation period" of six months in which the hero, Huguenau, wanders through life "as though under a glass bell." For Hans Castorp, as well, the time on the Magic Mountain is a vacation time, both literally and figuratively. On concluding his studies he has taken off three weeks, be-

---

[14] *Zauberberg*, p. 339.
[15] *Zauberberg*, p. 134.
[16] *Zauberberg*, p. 76.
[17] See Richard Thieberger, *Der Begriff der Zeit bei Thomas Mann* (Baden-Baden: Verlag für Kunst und Wissenschaft, 1952), pp. 25-65: "Die Zeitaspekte im Zauberberg."

fore beginning his practical apprenticeship on the wharves, in order to regain his strength and visit his ailing cousin. It is quite literally a vacation that brings him to the mountain. This circumstance causes the narrator to reflect, on the second page of the novel, that "Two days of journeys remove a man—and especially a young man who is still not firmly rooted in life—from the everyday world, from all that he called duty, interests, worries, prospects. . . . [Space] contains powers that one generally believes are reserved for time."

Even after Hans Castorp has become a resident, long after his imagined "visit" has ended, the motif continues to reappear throughout the novel. The narrator refers to him repeatedly as a "Bildungsreisender," a man traveling for the sake of culture and education. And repeatedly the word "vacation" crops up to remind us of the special "holiday privileges"[18] that Hans Castorp enjoys. At one point, for instance, Hans Castorp considers his whole relationship with Clawdia Chauchat to be a "holiday adventure that could lay no claim to approval before the tribunal of reason—his own rational conscience."[19] On another occasion he senses what it is that permits him to listen to Settembrini's discourses: "that holiday irresponsibility of the traveler and visitor who doesn't close himself off from any impression and who lets everything approach him, in the awareness that tomorrow or the day after tomorrow he will again air his wings and return to his accustomed order."[20] It is this mood of ferial lability, then, that permits Hans Castorp to profit from his experiences on the Magic Mountain. At the same time—and this should be borne in mind—this mood anticipates his precipitate return to the plains and its war at the end of the book. For all

[18] *Zauberberg*, p. 757: *Ferienlizenzen*. The narrator uses this expression to qualify Hans Castorp's freedom of thought in the chapter "Walk on the Beach."

[19] *Zauberberg*, p. 203.   [20] *Zauberberg*, pp. 220-21.

holidays must come to an end, even such a spiritual vacation as Hans Castorp's.

Hans Castorp does not succumb immediately to the "advantages of shame" that he discovers in Davos. Everything in his solid bourgeois upbringing impels him to resist, at first, the laxity of the life that he witnesses during his first days and weeks. On the one hand, he is all that Mme. Chauchat calls him: "un petit bonhomme convenable, de bonne famille, d'une tenue appétissante, disciple docile de ses précepteurs."[21] It is this tension between freedom and the restraint of Hans Castorp's training that produces many of the novel's humorous situations, upon which the narrator comments with delicious irony. On the other hand there exist, deeper in his character, qualities that respond inchoately to the appeal of the Magic Mountain. Weigand speaks in this connection of four *Urerlebnisse*, primal experiences rooted at the core of Hans Castorp's being: continuity, death, freedom, and Eros.[22] Like the ideological content discussed above, these experiences also coexist in a state of tension, of dialectical interplay. The sense of continuity, for instance, is associated in Hans Castorp's mind with the memory of his grandfather holding the family baptismal bowl, murmuring the syllables "great-, great-, great-, great-, great-" to indicate how many generations of the family had been baptized in this same bowl. This sense makes Castorp receptive, on the mountain, to the entire cultural tradition spread out before him through the persons of Settembrini, Naphta, and Peeperkorn; somehow, he feels, it belongs to his own heritage. At the same time, this sense represents a certain loyalty to his specific origins on the "plains" below and his responsibility to life. Certainly, this feeling of continuity and tradition functions as a

[21] *Zauberberg*, p. 475.
[22] Weigand, *op.cit.*, pp. 27ff.

timeless constant, an eternal presence of values that contrasts with the bourgeois obsession with temporality.

The same ambivalence attaches to his sense of death. It should be noted, first, that the fact of death, which made Hans Castorp an orphan at the age of eight, contributes to the rationalization of the plot. Since he has no immediate family and since he is financially independent, he can *afford* to spend seven years on the mountain. There are no immediate claims upon him, as there are on his cousin Joachim or the many other inhabitants of the sanatorium, who long for one reason or another to get back to the reality below. Exposed to death from his earliest years, Hans Castorp is both attracted to death with a romantic morbidity and at the same time imbued with a certain reverence for death. In any case, his attitude does not allow him simply to ignore the fact of death, as do most of the inhabitants of the sanatorium. He even seeks out the "moribundi" in the hope of bringing some comfort to their last days and hours. Death, moreover, is associated in his mind with a state of timelessness. When Naphta, in a discourse on alchemic transmutations, speaks of the grave as the symbol of hermetic purification, Hans Castorp recalls the vacuum jars on the shelves at home in Hamburg, in which fruits and meats are preserved. "They sit there for years and years, and if you open one the contents are quite fresh and unspoiled; neither years nor days have been able to affect them. You can partake of them just as they are. This is not alchemy and purification, to be sure, it is simply preservation, hence the name 'preserves.' But the enchanting thing is, that the preserves were lifted out of time, hermetically sealed off; time passed them by, they had no time but stood outside of it on their shelf. Well, that's enough about the vacuum jars."[23]

[23] *Zauberberg*, p. 706.

Thomas Mann

Even Eros assumes a certain quality of timeless irreality in Hans Castorp's mind. This becomes clear through the terms in which he explains and justifies to Peeperkorn his single night of intimacy with Madame Chauchat. He argues that that particular evening was "an evening that falls out of all order and almost out of the calendar, an *hors d'oeuvre*, so to speak, an extra evening, a leap-year evening, the twenty-ninth of February."[24]

The primal experiences of tradition and death, along with freedom and Eros, act as counter-impulses to the more superficial elements of his training and upbringing, and establish in him a subliminal sympathy for the new experiences that he encounters on the Magic Mountain. At first Hans Castorp attempts to resist this appeal. His gradual acclimatization is marked by a series of trivial "liberations" that cut him off from his own past. Though he is startled, upon his arrival, to discover that Joachim, like all the other inhabitants of the sanatorium, goes about without a hat—that mark of civilization—he himself soon finds it agreeable to go bareheaded. He discovers that it is really quite relaxing and easier to slump at the dinner table than to sit rigidly erect the whole time. Disconcerted at first by the casual generalizations about time used by the patients, he rapidly finds himself uttering such terms as *neulich* ("quite recently") to describe periods lying weeks or months back; toward the end of the novel he has developed such a virtuosity in this vocabulary that he even employs the term to refer to the era of the Chaldeans. Each of these minor liberations is reflected by his own fever chart, which records, at least in the first half of the novel, the fluctuations of his inner state.

All these minor points, however, although they contribute to the texture of the novel and attest to Thomas Mann's mag-

[24] *Zauberberg*, p. 843.

nificent powers of observation and detail, merely reflect on a realistic level the more subtle transformations that are taking place within Hans Castorp. The first definitive liberation occurs in the seventh week of his stay. It is only at this point that he commits himself to an indefinite sojourn in the sanatorium as a patient, and in his third letter to his uncle he makes arrangements to have a certain sum forwarded to him regularly at monthly intervals. The chapter is entitled "Freedom," and this is the word that reverberates in his mind as he writes the fateful lines. Up to this point his future had lain in the balance: he could easily have decided to follow Settembrini's admonishments and return home to his existence in the plains. But the first taste of the freedom of the Magic Mountain has exerted its attraction, and he is determined to remain.

It has often been remarked that in this "hermetic" novel, which delights in references to mystical initiation rites, the number seven and its multiples play a central symbolic role.[25] Hans Castorp comes for three weeks (twenty-one days) and remains for seven years. Four times a day he takes his temperature for seven minutes. He occupies Room 34 (three plus four), and during the course of his stay sits at each of the seven tables in the dining room. The entire novel has seven chapters, and the first part (Chapters 1 through 5) covers a period of seven months. His cousin Joachim dies in the twenty-eighth month of his visit. It is not surprising to find, therefore, that this inner or mystical, symbolic rhythm of the novel is punctuated essentially by intervals of seven. Thus the association of Madame Chauchat with his childhood friend Hippe comes to Hans Castorp in a vision on his seventh day in Davos. At the end of three weeks (twenty-one

[25] See Charles Neider, "The Artist as Bourgeois," in *The Stature of Thomas Mann*, ed. Charles Neider (New York: New Directions, 1947), pp. 340-43.

days) Hans Castorp discovers that he has a fever, and is easily persuaded to stay on and submit to three more weeks of bed rest for the purposes of diagnosis.

At the end of seven weeks, then, Hans Castorp has completed his first liberation. He has cut himself off from his home below and committed himself to the hermetic life of the sanatorium, to a life given over to the motto that Settembrini quotes from Petrarch: *Placet Experiri.* The ideological confrontation presented in the first half of the novel, as we have seen, is that of Settembrini and Madame Chauchat. It is perfectly in keeping with the inner rhythm of the novel that the culmination of this phase occurs at the end of Hans Castorp's seventh month on the Magic Mountain, on the "Walpurgis Night" of the Mardi Gras festivities—that timeless twenty-ninth of February that Hans Castorp later discusses with Peeperkorn. For it is on this occasion that he frees himself from the glib rationalism of his mentor and "tastes the pomegranate" of Eros. Love, he argues in his inspired French, must be "une aventure dans le mal."[26] But it is important to remember that this episode is more one of liberation than of commitment.[27] Clawdia and her morality of sin —"Il nous semble qu'il est plus moral de se perdre et même de se laisser dépérir que de se conserver"[28]—help to free him from the bland humanism of Settembrini. But even though he repeats the same sentence later in the book,[29] it must not be assumed that he accepts it. He quotes it in a subsequent conversation with Clawdia for rhetorical effect, to impress her. As an absolute point of view, it runs directly counter to his own primal experience of continuity and tradition.

[26] *Zauberberg*, p. 475.

[27] See Henry Hatfield, *Thomas Mann* (rev. edn.; Norfolk, Conn.: New Directions, 1962), p. 76. Hatfield's discussion of *The Magic Mountain* stresses the tensions that obtain between the various ideological positions.

[28] *Zauberberg*, p. 473.   [29] *Zauberberg*, p. 772.

The Magic Mountain

During the early part of the second half of the novel, the opposing ideological positions are represented by Naphta and Settembrini. But between their radical antitheses of spirit and nature, life and death, sickness and health, freedom and piety, Hans Castorp works out his own position during his vision in the snow. Though the time element has become less specific by this point in the novel, it is not unlikely that this episode falls in Hans Castorp's twenty-first month on the mountain, in the April of his second year; nothing, in any case, speaks against this assumption, since it is late in the winter snow-season when he finally makes his way up to the mountains on skis. Since this vision is the high point of the entire work, the circumstances should be recalled. It is important, first, that his journey through the snow carries him higher than any other walk during his sojourn, that is, farther away from all past attachments. Moreover, it carries him outside the periphery of the sanatorium as such, to a symbolic spot high above, where he is free of and superior to the ideas represented there. Finally, the vision is akin, symbolically, to fleeting visions at the moment of death, since Hans Castorp is very much in danger of succumbing to exhaustion and dying of exposure at the moment of epiphany.

The vision that Hans Castorp experiences—that of an Apollonian People of the Sun carrying on their serene activities side by side with the enactment of the most bloody Dionysian horror—leads him intuitively to the synthesis that all the lucubrations of Settembrini and Naphta are unable to attain. "I am going to keep faith with them in my soul and not with Naphta—and not with Settembrini either. They are both chatterers."[30] He arrives at a conception of man as "Lord of the Antinomies," capable through his freedom and piety of respecting both death and life, of paying allegiance to both. "Love opposes death; only love and not reason is

[30] *Zauberberg*, p. 685.

85

stronger than death," he concludes. The resolution that emerges from the play of ideologies, then, is love of man. *"Man shall, for the sake of goodness and love, concede to death no power over his thoughts"*[31] is the maxim that Thomas Mann sets in italics as the single position that he endorses in the novel. It is for the sake of this vision that Hans Castorp required the absolute freedom of the Magic Mountain, for this that he needed all the experiences of ideologies, love, and death that have preceded. They have supplied the materials for his own great synthesis. But it is a synthesis that can be reached—and maintained—only in absolute freedom. For as he moves back through the clearing evening toward the sanatorium, the ecstatic vision fades in his memory and he recollects only vaguely the position at which he had arrived. The entire vision took place outside of time. When Hans Castorp looks at his watch, he discovers that the whole experience had lasted barely ten minutes.

In the descending rhythm of the last chapter, however, even the positive factors of love and freedom are canceled out in the dialectics of the book. The dominant figure here is Mynheer Peeperkorn, half-buffoon and half-priest in his curious mixture of Dionysus and Christ, who represents a travesty of the vision in the snow. It is as though the absolute truth that Hans Castorp had experienced were possible only in the complete isolation of the mountaintop, as though such a truth were not tenable in reality, where every absolute is degraded and relativized.

To the extent that he represents the dominance of life and love over pure cerebration, the incorporation of all antinomies within his own person, Peeperkorn is a positive figure. With one mighty gesture of his hamlike fist, he makes irrelevant all the vain subtleties of Naphta and Settembrini. Because

[31] *Zauberberg*, p. 686.

The Magic Mountain

Peeperkorn incorporates his vision in part, Hans Castorp is strongly attracted to this magnificent personality. But in reality the ideal that the vision embodies is not so grand. Irony tends to cancel out the ideal, for the People of the Sun are actually just a little bit stupid and pompous. The despair of Naphta and Settembrini is at least partly justified. For this reason Hans Castorp avoids a total identification even with Peeperkorn. The time of their first real meeting is unspecified, but the encounter takes place in the chapter headed "Vingt et un" (again, three times seven). Only later does Peeperkorn, who recognizes a kindred soul in the young German, offer Hans the brotherly "*du*" of close comradeship. But Hans Castorp goes through the most elaborate and amusing grammatical circumlocutions in order to avoid using that intimate form; he cannot, despite all his admiration for the inarticulate "personality of grand format," bring himself to this final identification.

The final years on the Magic Mountain lose all temporal structure; the events are not clearly articulated. The "eternal sameness" has asserted its full prerogative. But after the apex of the snow vision, even the timeless freedom has lost its charm for the hero. Hans Castorp looks around, "and he knew what he was seeing: life without time, life without cares and hope, life as a stagnating and busybody slovenliness, a dead life."[32]

Hans Castorp has long since given up calendars, and he no longer even carries his watch, which broke one day when it fell from his night table. The vision in the snow was not only a high point, but also a turning point. All that happens afterwards reveals to Hans Castorp the negative side of his most affirmative insights. Now he perceives that even the absolute freedom that he has attained can also be viewed as death and stagnation rather than freedom. The interplay of ideas

[32] *Zauberberg*, p. 872.

has become so complex that it is no longer reduced to simple ideological positions. Instead Mann allows us, toward the end, to sense the hero's feelings by experiencing with him the intricate associations which various pieces of music hold for him. In *Aïda* he hears his own confused emotions echoed: Rhadames has broken his oath to fatherland and king for the sake of love and must now be buried alive with his beloved in a tomb. Through this *mêlée* of associations, we grasp intuitively the conflict between love and duty, between life and death in Hans Castorp's own soul. The haunting harmonies of *L'Après-midi d'un faun* seem to him to justify "the innocence of timelessness," whereas *Carmen* again proclaims the almost criminal irresponsibility of a freedom attained at the cost of honor and duty. In a simple folksong by Schubert, "Unterm Lindenbaum," he hears the appeal of home, fatherland, and death.

It is such blurred associations as these that finally impel Hans Castorp to leave the mountain after seven years and to return to serve his country in the war that has broken out below. All the conflicting ideologies have canceled one another out. Even the ideal of life in the face of chaos and horror has been somehow trivialized by its materialization in the person of Peeperkorn. And the ideal of a timeless freedom has revealed its verso: tedium and criminal irresponsibility. The Hans Castorp who goes back down the mountain is not a whit richer in beliefs than the one who came up: as a matter of fact, he is in a sense poorer, since the convictions of his upbringing, his faith in the simple facts of bourgeois life, have been wiped out. And this is indicated by the author's attitude at the end. He does not venture a prediction regarding the future, but merely asks tentatively: Will love emerge once more from the holocaust now engulfing the world? The novel has shattered every illusion, every conviction, every ideal. It has left only frustrating questions.

The Magic Mountain

But Hans Castorp is immeasurably richer in insights and awareness. He is immensely conscious of the world as it exists around him in all its contradictions. And though he is committed to no one position, he is able to view all these antinomies critically. He emerges from his intellectual adventure much like Franz Biberkopf, who returns to reality "with his eyes open." Or like Huguenau in Broch's *The Sleepwalkers*, he represents a new "objectivity" which rejects all traditional values and views the world with a sober sense of reality.[33] So the substance of the novel, the hero's education, has actually travestied the traditional *Bildungsroman*. For Hans Castorp is not educated to the acceptance of any ideal; rather, he is led to a position of neutral objectivity and awareness beyond any ideological position.[34]

(4)

ALL THAT we have said about the substance and content of *The Magic Mountain* would be mere verbiage, and the objections of the critics to its excessive intellectuality justified, were not the meaning so perfectly realized in the structure of the work. *The Magic Mountain* is *the* time novel of the twentieth century. As Thomas Mann has pointed out,[35] it is a time novel in several senses. It is one in that it reflects its time, the period from 1907 to the outbreak of World War I. It is one in that it contains a mass of reflections about time. But

[33] R. Hinton Thomas, *Thomas Mann; The Mediation of Art* (Oxford: Clarendon Press, 1956), p. 11, suggests that Mann's irony might better be described as an "objectivity" that leaves no single position valid.

[34] See Heller, "Conversation," p. 94: "Wilhelm Meister, the model hero of [a *Bildungsroman*], begins as an *Originalgenie* and ends as a useful member of society. Hans Castorp begins as a useful member of society and ends approaching the state of being an *Originalgenie*."

[35] "Einführung in den *Zauberberg* für Studenten der Universität Princeton" (1939); *GW*, XI, 611-12.

this is less important, since these reflections, which are not really very original, belong to the content of the novel, along with the elaborate ideologies. It is a time novel above all, however, because of the brilliant way in which the author structures his narrative. It is time and time alone that provides the framework within which everything else becomes meaningful. "Time is the element of narrative, just as it is the element of life," the author reflects at the beginning of the extensive digression on time in the chapter "Walk on the Beach." And the narrative requires time for its manifestation, "even if it should attempt to be constantly present at every moment."

This is the principle from which the tension of the structure derives. The action, the substance, progresses through time, through the seven years of Hans Castorp's stay on the mountain. At the same time the author must render the loss of time, the movement toward timelessness; and he does this by attempting to keep the entire novel constantly in the reader's mind as a continual present. Thus in the novel's structure, as well as in its content and substance, there is a tension between temporality and timelessness, between direction and presence. It is this tension that provides the essential link between content, substance, and form. Only the tension between time and timelessness keeps the structure from being more than a matter of mere technical brilliance, more than a literary tour de force.

Through the organization of the novel, the reader is led to experience time in a variety of ways. The principle upon which the organization of chapters is based is anything but profound: it is the simple perception that our attention, when first we enter a new situation, is focused upon myriad details that are gradually, as we adjust to the new surroundings, simplified into an accustomed routine of even texture. In this connection the first two short chapters of the novel are but a

The Magic Mountain

prelude. Chapter 1 relates Hans Castorp's arrival on the Magic Mountain on a Tuesday evening in early August, his reunion with his cousin Joachim, their late supper in the restaurant, and the first signs of our hero's confusion and fever. The second chapter, which recounts Hans Castorp's confused dreams during his first night on the mountain, provides us through a flashback with the necessary information about his background.

The temporal sequence begins with Chapter 3, which contains a detailed account of the first day at the sanatorium. This chapter begins with Hans Castorp's awakening and concludes when he retires that same evening, and is punctuated by the five mealtimes in the main dining room of the Sanatorium Berghof: breakfast at eight o'clock; midmorning lunch at eleven; dinner at one; tea at four; and supper at seven. The intervals are filled, for the most part, with walks and rest periods on the balcony. We see—indeed, since everything is narrated from Hans Castorp's point of view, we *experience* —how the new environment and particularly the many people there first obtrude upon his consciousness as a blurred mass and how, by the meal at the end of the day, a few individuals gradually emerge in sharper outline. At the same time we receive a highly detailed report of the daily routine, which, as we are constantly assured, is invariable. This element is highly important. First, it helps to reduce time to a cycle of perpetual recurrences, beginning the movement toward timelessness. And second, it provides the background for the hundreds of pages that follow. For the reader always knows, after this chapter, precisely what is going on at any given time of day that the author may single out as a context for subsequent scenes.

Whereas the third chapter relates the events of one day in a rhythm of hours, the fourth chapter covers three weeks in a rhythm of days. Yet the number of pages required to describe these three weeks is only twice the number required for the single first day. The events of the individual days are effaced here, as we are exposed to the routine of the week with its Sunday concerts and, in the case of Joachim and Hans Castorp, the Saturday examination. In Chapter 5 the process of temporal leveling is carried even further: here we have the events of the first seven months (exclusive of the first three weeks) related in a rhythm of weeks. Individual days are scarcely mentioned. Instead, Hans Castorp lies in bed for the assigned three weeks; a week later he has a second examination. The scenic description that has been the main technique up to now gives way at this point to frequent chapters of iterative-durative time. A particular scene, for instance that of Hans Castorp reading at night on his balcony, is described as representative, as recurring every night; and then the substance of his reading over the course of a full month is related by the narrator. As the length of time expands, scenic description is replaced more and more by iterative-durative narrative.

Chapter 5 and Part One conclude with leap year, which falls at the end of Hans' first seven months on the Magic Mountain. We have experienced the first day in a rhythm of hours, the first three weeks in a rhythm of days, and the first seven months in a rhythm of weeks. The same pattern continues in the two long chapters of Part Two. Chapter 6 covers the year and nine months from that leap year until the November of Hans Castorp's third year at the sanatorium. Here we experience time in a rhythm of months: Naphta is introduced in June, Uncle James Tienappel arrives in October, and so forth. The sequence of months is kept quite clear until the second winter, when even the articulation of months is blurred in the eternal winter depicted in the chapter entitled "Snow." This blurring of months, finally, leads to the introduction of the rhythm of years in Chapter 7, which covers the last four and a half years before the outbreak of World War I and Hans Castorp's departure.

Thomas Mann has constructed this temporal sequence with supreme artistic consciousness. It is quite apparent how, at the end of each chapter, the rhythm of time (hours, days, weeks, months, years) begins to blur into the rhythm of the succeeding chapter, gradually producing the effect of "eternal sameness" that is mentioned in the various digressions on time. The tendency of the novel "to be constantly present" is enhanced, of course, by Thomas Mann's much-discussed use of leitmotif. Settembrini's checkered trousers, Frau Stöhr's malapropisms and her lip drawn back from her teeth, Hans Castorp's habit of staring openmouthed, his head tilted to one side, and dozens of other set descriptions of this sort recur from start to finish; with each mention they call to mind similar situations earlier in the book and stress the repetitive structure of life at the sanatorium. Against a background of this sort even such an object as Hans Castorp's favorite cigar, a brand called Maria Mancini, becomes symbolic. In its constant reappearance (it is mentioned some sixteen times throughout the novel) the Maria Mancini cigar functions as a leitmotif, recalling earlier situations. But inasmuch as it is also a key to his feelings—sometimes it tastes better, sometimes worse, and finally he gives it up altogether for a local brand—it takes on a symbolic function, paralleling with fair accuracy the curve of his fever chart. (Maria Mancini and the daily temperature are far more important, of course, in the shorter rhythms of the first part of the novel; in Part Two they are mentioned with less frequency.)

On a structural level there are major devices that correspond to the repetitive effect of the leitmotif. The "Attack and Repulse," in which Uncle James Tienappel attempts to persuade Hans Castorp to return to Hamburg, is carefully constructed in such a way as to parallel the events of Chapters 1 and 3, Hans Castorp's arrival and first day at Berghof. Indeed, the whole chapter can be regarded as a brief re- capitulation of the two earlier chapters. The same applies to Joachim's return to the sanatorium a year after his flight. The events are repetitive; but here the mood of the scene is shifted from major to minor, as it were, by the sad circum- stances surrounding Joachim's return. And we have already noted that the entire second part is a complex parallel, on a grand scale, to the first part.

Finally, the effect of timeless suspension and eternal recur- rence is vastly heightened by structural references to broad realms that lie outside the novel altogether. Thus, the Wal- purgis Night scene, carefully constructed around quotations from Goethe's *Faust*, suddenly thrusts the novel into another complex of associations altogether. Similarly, the biblical quo- tations, especially those from the Gethsemane scene, cast a radically new light on the figure of Peeperkorn.[36] The same is true of the initiation rites discussed by Settembrini and Naphta, which make it clear that Hans Castorp belongs, typo- logically at least, to a long line of figures in this respect. All these devices, to which attention has often been called, con- tribute ultimately to the effect of timeless suspension: the actions taking place here, one feels, are not unique actions happening just this once in this specific situation, but rather part of certain patterns which in turn belong to an eternal process of repetition.

In all of this, of course, the role of the narrator is of central importance. An omniscient narrator would regard these seven years on the Magic Mountain as a definite point in time, pre- ceded and followed by other events of history that would lo- cate Hans Castorp's sojourn in a temporal sequence. That is not the case here. Instead, Thomas Mann has created for his

[36] See Meyer, *The Poetics of Quotation*, pp. 224-46.

novel a narrator who very distinctly fills the specific needs of this particular work with its movement toward timelessness. The narrator, to be sure, does not tell us all that he knows; but he does not know everything. His point of view is limited rigorously to the events that come to pass on the mountain. All that he tells us of Hans Castorp's earlier life, especially in Chapter 2, is put in such a way that we must assume that it represents a coherent retelling of Hans Castorp's own confused dreams. Similarly, the other principal excursion into the plains—the episode in the schoolyard with Hippe—is related as a vision of the daydreaming Hans Castorp. By the same token, the narrator loses sight of his hero at the end of the work, when Hans returns to the plains and enters the war. He claims not to know what will happen to his hero, whose "hermetic" story is at an end. In other words, the narrator's omniscience is limited to the hermetic seven years on the Magic Mountain. He is tied to the locale; he is the *genius loci.*

It is precisely this hermetic quality of the narrator that lends credence to the timelessness of the events told there: they are not connected in any way, through the narrator, with events taking place on any other plane of time or life. Yet although the narrator "knows" his story before he begins to tell it, he again carefully restricts his point of view to that of the hero. All that we experience happens within Hans Castorp's sight or hearing. When Joachim has an examination in the basement offices, we do not learn of the results until he comes up and reports to his cousin. Before Hans Castorp participates in the séances conducted by Krokowski, we hear about them only at second hand, through the reports that reach Hans Castorp. This point of view is, of course, essential to the time effects of the story. For if, at any point, the narrator should reach ahead and anticipate events by means of his omniscience, then the carefully structured rhythm of exposure, progressing through hours, days, weeks, months, and years, would be destroyed—not so much for Hans Castorp himself as for the reader. Thus the narrator's position is conceived more with an eye to the reader and the effect of the narrative on him than to Hans Castorp. Through the narrator, so to speak, we are permitted to experience the unfolding of time exactly as Hans Castorp does.

The narrator, at the same time, possesses a conspicuous degree of ironic detachment and objectivity. He criticizes, comments, and (in the chapter "Walk on the Beach") even interposes an entire chapter of his own reflections. But his role changes noticeably in the course of the novel. During the early chapters he rather conspicuously keeps himself in the background. His occasional ironic notes are usually enclosed in parentheses. It is not until Chapter 7 that he emerges in the full glory of his narrative sovereignty. He interjects himself far more boldly into the narrative, dropping the coy parenthetical pose that he had maintained up to this point. In the last chapter, indeed, it is only the figure of the narrator who holds the story together. There are good reasons for this. The temporal framework of the novel begins to collapse in the last chapter, where the rhythm of years, according to the scheme of the work, moves gradually toward a rhythm of indefinite suspension of time. The adequate symbol for this breakdown of structure, by the way, is the "vague" personality of Mynheer Peeperkorn, who is imposing but indistinct in his contours, just as the precise articulation of Settembrini reflects the clear disposition of events in the chapter dominated by him. In order to save the situation, the narrator must assume an ever greater role. He becomes a much more clearly defined figure here than was the case earlier, holding together by the strength of his own personality the structure of the otherwise disintegrating action. It is clear that the role of the narrator is conceived in such a way as to complement, indeed to make possible, the illusion of timeless suspension toward which Thomas Mann moves in the course of a thousand pages; and finally it is the narrator who gives the novel, once it has become timeless, the structure of his own personality.

(5)

CAN WE pat ourselves on the back at this point and feel that we have done justice to the novel by our analysis of its content, substance, and structure, and of their interaction in the movement toward the common goal of timeless suspension? Not at all. For this novel is a more delicately woven fabric than most. If we pull one thread in order to follow it to its end, we merely unravel the entire tissue and are left with a meaningless pile of material instead of the meaningful design of the whole. *The Magic Mountain* is not merely a certain rhythm of development toward a suspension of time, through a magnetic field of polarized ideologies, presented by an ironic storyteller. Frau Stöhr remains. Hofrat Behrens remains. The narrative beauty of the vision in the snow and of Hans Castorp's sight of the sun and moon in the evening sky remains. To put matters most bluntly: after all the ideologies have canceled each other out, after the ideal of love and a reconciliation of life and death has turned out to be trivial in its realization or, at best, of questionable value for the future of Hans Castorp, even after the freedom of timelessness has been unmasked as the mere license of indolence—after all this, the novel remains as the one absolute. This is surely what Thomas Mann had in mind when he wrote that "only form is unassailable."

This is perhaps the final irony of this ironic work: absolutely no position is left intact. Only the work remains. But the work, as a work of art, approaches perfection to a degree rarely achieved on such a monumental scale. In its own way, then, *The Magic Mountain* stands in the same relation to reality as do the various prose poems of Malte Laurids Brigge. Though the world represented within the novel turns out to be ultimately meaningless, *The Magic Mountain* gives meaning to this world by ordering it according to the novel's own principles of organization. In an ideologically meaningless world, only aesthetic order is capable of producing meaning. And so Erich Heller was completely right when he suggested that Hans Castorp could only have become a novelist, for only a writer could come to grips with the reality that he encountered on the Magic Mountain.

We see, then, that this is not merely a symbolic novel; it is also the novel *as a symbol*. For if there is any meaning left intact after we have read the last page and closed the volume, it is the book itself. It exists; its aesthetic meaning is there, hermetically sealed within its covers like the timeless atmosphere of the sanatorium on its isolated mountain top. The book remains as a symbol of the aesthetic attitude that is capable of reconciling the conflicting positions not accessible of resolution by the forces portrayed individually within the novel.[37] For this reason its meaning will never be exhausted by a statement of theme and of plot, or by an analysis of structure or content. The book as a whole is a symbol of the life represented within the book. Like that life, it is hermetic and timeless; like that life, it has an existence independent of reality; like that life, it represents an enhancement and intensification of life itself.

[37] See Andrew White, *Thomas Mann*, p. 38: "His intention was to give the novel by this means [the removal of mechanical time from within the novel] an existence of its own in timeless art rather than in human time." It is this aspect that Francis Bulhof treats as "synchronicity" in his study *Transpersonalismus und Synchronizität; Wiederholung als Strukturelement in Thomas Manns "Zauberberg"* (Groningen: Van Donderen, 1966).

chapter four

Alfred Döblin

Berlin Alexanderplatz

(1)

PERHAPS nothing more effectively brings into sharp relief the key differences between *The Magic Mountain* and *Berlin Alexanderplatz* than the contrast of Hans Castorp's fever chart with the weather reports that Döblin scatters through his novel. In both cases we are dealing with a symbolic device that reflects, by means of physical measurement, the psychic fluctuations of the story. But there are few things more personal than a fever chart: the fever is Hans Castorp's alone, and its rise and fall records the rhythm of his development utterly irrespective of any variations in the general atmosphere in the sanatorium. By the same token, few things are more public than the weather: if the frequent meteorological reports constitute a reliable index of the hero's highs and lows, they also demonstrate implicitly how much a part of the city he is and how closely his life is linked to the surrounding world. Whereas Hans Castorp is sealed off hermetically from the ordinary flow of life and time, like a vacuum jar of preserves on a shelf, Franz Biberkopf is plunged into the most intimate association with the teeming life of the metropolis. And the weather reports remind us throughout the book that Franz Biberkopf can be understood only within the network of tensions that ties him to Berlin during the year 1928.

There is a second characteristic difference as well. The fever chart records what has actually happened, while the weather report is part analysis and part forecast. This distinction has certain implications for the narrators who use these devices. The fever chart exists as a fact: Hans Castorp can discuss it with his cousin, it can be mentioned at table and compared objectively with the fever charts of other patients, it can be considered by Hofrat Behrens in his diagnosis of Hans Castorp's illness, and the narrator can refer to it with as much assurance as, for instance, to X-ray photographs. It is simply there, a matter of historical record. To a certain extent this is also true of the weather report, inasmuch as it charts the present state of the weather, the fever of the world. But the narrator who refers to weather forecasts is in an entirely different position: he is unsure of his ground; the forecast is merely a reasonable prediction based on a set of variables. The forecast, in other words, is a surmise regarding reality *in statu nascendi*, not simply a record of accomplished reality. The fever chart is the prerogative of an author who is in complete control of his material and sees it in historical perspective; the weather forecast is the device of an author who is still, so to speak, as much enmeshed in his environment as are his own characters in theirs, and who sees the action only as it develops. To put it most simply: the fever chart permits the narrative past tense, while the weather report and forecast often require the present and even future tenses.

A third feature needs to be pointed out. From time to time the narrator merely mentions the weather in passing: "Despite all this the month of June has arrived in Berlin. The weather continues to be warm and rainy."[1] More often, however, the narrator withdraws and simply reproduces the text of a weather report as it might be stated in a newspaper or a radio broadcast.

[1] Alfred Döblin, *Berlin Alexanderplatz; Die Geschichte vom Franz Biberkopf*, ed. Walter Muschg (Olten and Freiburg im Breisgau: Walter, 1961), p. 257. This edition will henceforth be cited as *BA*.

Berlin Alexanderplatz

Variable, somewhat milder weather, one degree below zero Celsius. A low pressure area is spreading out across Germany and has ended over its entire extent the previous weather pattern. The slight pressure changes that are taking place indicate a slow extension of the low pressure to the south, so that the weather will continue to remain under this influence. During the day the temperature will probably be somewhat lower than previously. Weather forecast for Berlin and general vicinity.[2]

Instead of filtering his material through a central organizing consciousness (as Thomas Mann does, for instance, in the chapters on Hans Castorp's extensive reading) Döblin allows the facts to speak for themselves, presenting them in the form of a montage or collage.

The weather report, in sum, reveals at least three distinctive characteristics of Döblin's novel. It symbolizes the extent to which the individual is tied to the collective fate of the city and thus reflects one of the central themes of *Berlin Alexanderplatz*. It emphasizes the restricted role of the narrator, who writes essentially out of the present tense and experiences the action of his story as it unfolds. And it epitomizes the technique of montage through which Döblin assembles a composite image of Berlin in 1928.

(2)

DÖBLIN was fascinated by facts, and facts of every conceivable kind have found their way into his novels. His narrator and characters refer to contemporary events—speeches in the Reichstag, international politics, sports events, performances in local theaters; they sing snatches of popular songs, tell current jokes, and mention familiar commercial products. And

[2] *BA*, pp. 51-52.

even beyond this, Döblin has incorporated great unassimilated chunks of factual matter into his text. He lists, for instance, all the stops of various streetcar lines, and his topographical data are so precise that a reader with a detailed map of Berlin can follow the action from street to street at any point in the novel. He cites birth and death statistics for 1928 as well as stock-market quotations. We catch glimpses of advertisements in shop windows, restaurant menus, and newspaper headlines. He includes police reports and official forms; he copies down encyclopedia articles and information from the 1928 telephone directory, as well as detailed figures on the operation of the Berlin slaughterhouses. At the beginning of Book 2 he even reproduces the insignia of the important public agencies of the City of Berlin. And from all these facts and countless others, there emerges an immensely vivid and objective image of Berlin between the two world wars, forming the basis of what critics commonly regard as the finest metropolitan novel in German literature.

Döblin has been obsessed with facts in all his works. "I admit that even today," he wrote in 1929 (the year when *Berlin Alexanderplatz* was published), "the communication of facts and documents delights me. Do you know why? In facts and documents nature, that great writer of epics, speaks to me; and I, the little writer, stand before him and rejoice to see how Big Brother does it. And it has happened, as I was writing some historical work or the other, that I could scarcely restrain myself from simply copying off entire reports. Yes, sometimes I collapsed in admiration in the midst of the documents, saying to myself: I can't do it better . . . that is all so magnificent and its manner is so epic that I am entirely superfluous."[3] The fascination with facts and the montage tech-

[3] "Der Bau des epischen Werks," in Alfred Döblin, *Aufsätze zur Literatur*, ed. Walter Muschg (Olten and Freiburg im Breisgau: Walter, 1963), pp. 113-14.

nique are nothing new, then. Any reader familiar with Döblin's earlier works might have expected to find these same elements in *Berlin Alexanderplatz* as well. In *The Three Leaps of Wang-Lun* (*Die Drei Sprünge des Wang-Lun*, 1915), a novel dealing with a revolt in China in 1774, Döblin had copied out long lists of Chinese names, of jewels, animals, plants, cities; he had included copious excerpts from reference works on the customs, dances, and clothing of that time and place. What is new in *Berlin Alexanderplatz* is not the sheer obsession with facts, but their sources and the manner in which they are used.

Döblin was a prolific writer, but as a result of the great and immediate success of *Berlin Alexanderplatz*—due in large measure to the shock value of the criminal milieu he portrayed—most people think of him as a one-book author. "People pinned me down to *Alexanderplatz*, which was commonly misunderstood as being nothing but a portrayal of the underworld of Berlin," Döblin later had reason to complain.[4] This novel was the first work in a number of years in which he had treated present-day society rather than the historical past or imaginary utopias. "At that time I came, so to speak, right out of India," Döblin recalled in a postscript (1955) to a new edition of his novel, "around the mid-twenties. I came out of India: that is, an Indic theme had been occupying me for a time, and it precipitated itself in the epic poem *Manas*. How odd! Here I had spent my entire life in the eastern section of Berlin, had attended the public elementary schools in Berlin, was an active socialist, had a medical practice treating health-insured patients—and I wrote about China, about Wallenstein and the Thirty Years War, and most recently even about a mythical and mystical India."[5]

In *Berlin Alexanderplatz*, written when he was almost

---

[4] "Epilog," in *Aufsätze zur Literatur*, p. 391.
[5] *BA*, p. 507.

fifty, Döblin turned to the city that he knew and loved so well: here the facts and documents were provided not by libraries and archives but by the city that crowded in upon him from every side. And the people in his novel were not historical or imaginary figures from remote civilizations, but gangsters, pimps, prostitutes, and the entire colorful pageant of the lower-class society with which Döblin was so intimately acquainted. "My medical practice has often brought me together with criminals," Döblin told a group in 1932. "A number of years ago I even had an observation-station for criminals."[6] More must be said in another connection about Döblin's interest in the criminal mind; the point to be made here is simply that *Berlin Alexanderplatz* was written directly out of his own experience. Döblin turned to the everyday reality of contemporary Berlin with precisely the same fascination and objectivity that had motivated him when he was culling information on China and India in the reading rooms of libraries and archives.

Alfred Döblin was born in Stettin in 1878, the son of a tailor. While Döblin was still quite young, his father deserted the family and went to America. Döblin's mother soon moved to Berlin with her five children, and except for brief interruptions Döblin lived in the German capital until his emigration in 1933. After elementary and secondary school in Berlin, he studied medicine and obtained his degree in 1905 in Freiburg im Breisgau. For the next six years he carried on neurological research in various laboratories and interned in the psychiatric hospitals of Buch and Regensburg. But in 1911 he moved back to Berlin and settled down to the double career that lasted for the next twenty-two years.

"At an early age I was obsessed by a compulsion to

[6] "Mein Buch *Berlin Alexanderplatz*," in *BA*, p. 505.

write," Döblin recalled in his autobiographical "Epilogue."[7]
Around 1900 he became acquainted with another writer
from the east side of Berlin, Herwarth Walden, and through
him with many other young writers. They were united, above
all, by their rejection of anything that smacked of classicism,
traditionalism, or of what they regarded as insincerity, particularly the productions of the Big Three of the preceding
literary generation: Gerhart Hauptmann, Stefan George, and
Thomas Mann. Their models were certain older writers whose
works anticipated the new mood of expressionism: the poet
Richard Dehmel and the dramatist Frank Wedekind. Döblin's
earliest publications were an experimental one-act drama,
"Lydia und Mäxchen" (1906), which bears a certain resemblance to the plays of Pirandello, and an essay entitled "Discourses with Calypso on Music and Love" (1910). But he
made his literary mark with a series of stories originally published in Walden's expressionist journal *Der Sturm* and subsequently printed together under the title *The Murder of a
Marigold* (*Die Ermordung einer Butterblume*, 1913). But
Döblin's "expressionist" phase was of no great duration. The
Sturm group was perplexed by his first novel, *The Three
Leaps of Wang-Lun*, and events tended to lead him away
from his literary associates. "We remained bound by friend-
ship. But they developed wholly into word-artists, to artists
in the full sense of the word. I went on other paths. I understood them well, but they didn't understand me."

First there was the physical separation of the war years,
which Döblin spent as a military doctor on the western
front, within hearing of the cannon at Verdun. But more essentially: Döblin was not just a writer; he was a psychiatrist

---

[7] This and the following quotations are from "Epilog," pp. 384-86.
To date there are few studies of Döblin in any language; and even
articles are rare in English.

and neurologist with a busy practice on the proletarian east side of Berlin. Finally, like certain of his contemporaries—Gottfried Benn, Robert Musil, Hermann Broch—he was an intellectual with a serious commitment to science. "Generally speaking, I didn't take literature and art very seriously. It was my idea that one must make use of words and literature for other purposes, for more serious purposes." For Döblin this meant that the novels he turned out during these years were variations on the central theme expressed in "The Self over Nature" (1927), his reflections on the philosophy of nature, in which he examined the increasingly complex situation of the individual threatened by the forces of nature and society. These were problems that thrust themselves upon Döblin daily in his work with the sick and the underprivileged during the inflation years in one of the greatest urban centers of Europe. "I found my patients lying in their wretched rooms; they also brought their rooms into my consulting office. I saw their conditions, their milieu; it all moved into the area of the social, the ethical, the political."[8] These social implications are directly related to Döblin's political activity. After the revolution of 1918-1919 he left the Social Democrat Party and published a volume of political satires (*The German Masquerade Ball*, 1921), in which he pleaded for a socialism free of Marxism and communist regimentation. For Döblin was concerned—as a doctor, as a scientist, as a political being, as a writer—with the individual in the face of the forces and complexities of technological society that threaten to overwhelm him. This was nowhere more apparent than in the Berlin of the twenties. Thus Döblin became ever more firmly convinced of the social responsibility of the writer, whose obligation it is to work toward a better society by unmasking the evils that permeate the present one.

[8] "Arzt und Dichter" (1927), in *Aufsätze zur Literatur*, pp. 364-65.

Berlin Alexanderplatz

(3)

ALL OF these elements went into *Berlin Alexanderplatz*. In his fascination with the city, Döblin reflected in part the trend of the times. The city had played a certain role in a few earlier works: for instance, in *The Notebooks of Malte Laurids Brigge*, where it catalyzed Malte's fear and his subsequent quest for meaning. But *Berlin Alexanderplatz* was the first, and still remains probably the greatest, evocation of the city for its own sake in German literature.[9] The new awareness of the city as a force in the lives of men emerged largely with the artists and writers associated with *Der Sturm* and expressionism: Oskar Kokoschka, Ernst Ludwig Kirchner, George Grosz, and Max Beckmann. It is evident in Brecht's early plays (e.g., *In the Jungle of the Cities*, 1923) and in the poetry of Georg Heym. But for his own presentation of the modern urban pandemonium Döblin evolved a radically new and characteristic style.

Technically, Döblin's novel displays certain parallels with John Dos Passos' *Manhattan Transfer* (1925; German translation, 1927) and with Joyce's *Ulysses*, which Döblin read and reviewed in 1928 when he was already well along in his own novel.[10] The techniques of montage and collage, the device of interior monologue, the concern with the struggle of man against the city, as well as other common themes and methods, put these three works into the same general category. And yet, as we shall see, there are vast differences between them as well. It is more reasonable to accept Döblin's

[9] See Muschg's postscript to his edition of *BA*, pp. 509-10; also Werner Welzig's discussion of "Der Grossstadtroman" in his book *Der deutsche Roman im 20. Jahrhundert* (Stuttgart: Kröner, 1967).

[10] In virtually the only consideration of Döblin by an American critic, Joseph Warren Beach, *The Twentieth Century Novel; Studies in Technique* (New York: Century, 1932), pp. 512-15, discusses what he defines as Döblin's "abstract composition" and mentions his similarity to Dos Passos' "breadthwise cutting."

Alfred Döblin

own indignant disclaimer of the "Joyce imitation" that critics saw in his novel in their first attempts to categorize it. "If I am supposed to be dependent upon and to follow someone, then why must I go to Joyce, the Irishman, when I became acquainted with the manner and the method that he employs (in a magnificent way that I admire) at the same source as he himself: from the expressionists, the Dadaists, and so forth."[11] Indeed, Döblin was more profoundly influenced by nonliterary media: by the montage effects, the short scenes, and rapid shifts of perspective of the film; by the new acoustical effects of radio, in which he was an ardent and early experimenter;[12] and by the dadaist collages of such painters as Kurt Schwitters, which Döblin knew from the pages of *Der Sturm.*[13]

The overwhelming impression that we receive from *Berlin Alexanderplatz* is one of discontinuity. The rapid shifts of focus from section to section, from paragraph to paragraph, indeed, even within the same sentence, represent an attempt to capture the full horizontal scope of the city in all its aspects and to render in its simultaneity the chaos of the city.

This horizontal thrust is complemented by a vertical element. Döblin is not only interested in conveying the simultaneity of all facets of city life; he also believes, mystically, that the present moment necessarily contains within it the past and future. "An age is always a *mêlée* of various ages, . . . bears residues of other forces within itself as well as the seeds of new ones. It is a symbiosis of many souls; the dominant

[11] "Epilog," p. 391.

[12] In 1929 Döblin spoke of the "salutary impact of radio on literature." See Heinz Schwitzke, *Das Hörspiel; Dramaturgie und Geschichte* (Cologne and Berlin: Kiepenheuer und Witsch, 1963), p. 33 and *passim.*

[13] See Albrecht Schöne, "Döblin: *Berlin Alexanderplatz*," in *Der deutsche Roman vom Barock bis zur Gegenwart*, ed. Benno von Wiese (Düsseldorf: Bagel, 1963), II, 315.

one seeks to incorporate the others into itself."[14] As a result, past and future are blended into the present moment along with the simultaneity of all contemporary events. "This simultaneity in the present," Döblin wrote in another place, "is a single truth, a meaningful event."[15] This accounts for such anticipations of the future as the narrator's disquisition on a fourteen-year-old boy who gets into a streetcar. The boy, we learn, will become a plumber, father seven children, and die at the age of fifty-five; we are even provided with the text of the obituary notice that will appear in the newspapers some forty years hence.[16] But more important: Döblin's sense of vertical simultaneity accounts for the frequent passages in which the past is meaningfully incorporated into the present. Thus stories from the Bible as well as from Greek myth are introduced as a specific reflection of the present action. The theme of sacrifice, which must be discussed later, first occurs in a series of sections in which the story of Job alternates with reports of activities in the slaughterhouses of Berlin.

This conception of horizontal and vertical simultaneity has important consequences for the form of the novel. In his revealing essay on "The Structure of the Epic Work" Döblin argues, in opposition to customary aesthetic theory, that the epic does not relate past action; rather, it represents or renders the present. In this connection the tense used is immaterial and can be varied at liberty.[17] (Indeed, Döblin jumps easily from past to present and back in the course of a single paragraph.) The narrator must always write as though the events being portrayed were taking place at that very

[14] "Der Geist des naturalistischen Zeitalters" (1924), in *Aufsätze zur Literatur*, p. 80.

[15] Alfred Döblin, *Unser Dasein* (Berlin, 1933), p. 217.

[16] *BA*, p. 54.

[17] "Der Bau des epischen Werks," in *Aufsätze zur Literatur*, pp. 111-12.

moment; he is not allowed the elevated standpoint of the omniscient narrator of traditional epic, who knows in advance the course of his story and how it is going to end.

This conception has radical implications for the role of the narrator as well. The novel does not have any single unified narrative point of view, but literally dozens of different narrative voices. At times the narrator withdraws behind the reporting of factual statements: weather reports, advertisements, newspaper headlines, et cetera. At other times he politely addresses the reader in standard High German, and in the next breath chats with his hero in dialect. He cites statistics at one moment and in the next parodies the tone of Old Testament lamentations or Greek tragedy. Speaking quite broadly, we can say that while Döblin knows generally what is going on in the novel as a whole, the *narrator* is never aware of anything outside the material he happens to be reporting in a given section. Or to put it another way: each section, with the language necessary for it, produces its own narrative voice. For language is in itself productive, Döblin has noted, and if properly chosen can be a stimulus to the imagination. "The greatest formal danger for the epic author arises if he leaps onto the wrong linguistic niveau."[18] Döblin, then, has implicit faith in language, which produces what he has called a "network of tensions" that extends over the entire work. In contrast to most writers, who find a suitable narrative voice and retain it throughout, Döblin leaps from situation to situation: each is related in the language proper to it —police-court, biblical, lyrical, jargonic—and each language produces, within that particular section, its own narrative voice.

All of this means, of course, that the city presents itself to us as a chaos. It is not ordered by any authorial intelligence that relates and explains matters to us. The reality of the

18 *Ibid.*, p. 130.

work is thrust upon us in its rawest form. The very language and organization of the book reflect the chaos of the city.[19] The rationale underlying this stylistic radicality is one of inviting the reader to experience the city as it is experienced by the hero, Franz Biberkopf. We are not simply told that he feels the threat of chaos; we are given an opportunity to feel this chaos along with him.

(4)

DÖBLIN originally entitled his book simply *Berlin Alexanderplatz*, but his publishers, objecting that this title was incomprehensible (since it was merely the name of a streetcar stop), insisted on the addition of a more conventional subtitle: *The Story of Franz Biberkopf*. Döblin was right, of course. The title he had chosen underlines the fact that his book is a book about a collective existence, not a traditional novel about a single hero. The exemplary nature of Franz Biberkopf is repeatedly stressed, as at the beginning of Book 6: "For the man about whom I am reporting is no ordinary man, but still he's an ordinary man insofar as we understand him precisely and occasionally say: step for step, we could have done and experienced the same as he." At the same time, the full title of the work brings out the tension which keeps the novel taut, for the city exists, and is portrayed here, as Franz Biberkopf's adversary.

It is for this reason that the city must be rendered as such a vital, living force. Indeed, the chaotic, even demonic aspect under which the city is presented makes sense only if we un-

[19] See Fritz Martini's chapter on *Berlin Alexanderplatz* in his book *Das Wagnis der Sprache* (3rd edn.; Stuttgart: Ernst Klett, 1958), pp. 336-72. In his general article on "Alfred Döblin" in *Deutsche Dichter der Moderne*, ed. Benno von Wiese (Berlin: Erich Schmidt, 1965), pp. 321-60, Martini says little about *Berlin Alexanderplatz* and adds nothing to the conclusions of his earlier study.

derstand that this is the way in which the city thrusts itself upon Biberkopf. A hero of different character, of greater analytical intelligence, would not experience the city in this way. We have already seen, for instance, how Malte Laurids Brigge tends to aestheticize the city into ordered images in his own consciousness. No, the style of the book is directly dependent upon the character of the hero, of this specific hero. This fact distinguishes Döblin's novel from those of Dos Passos, which have not one but several leading figures. Dos Passos obtains his breadth by following the various figures along their respective parallel courses through the city. In Döblin the situation is reduced to the basic conflict between Biberkopf and the city of Berlin. His novel, he once remarked, is homophonic, in contrast to Dos Passos' polyphony.[20]

"The question that *Manas* left me with was: How does a good man fare in our society? Let's see how he behaves and how our existence looks from his standpoint." This is how Döblin summarized the problem of his book in his autobiographical "Epilogue" in 1948.[21] The "good man" that Döblin chooses for his literary experiment is named Franz Biberkopf. As a soldier in the German Army during the First World War, Biberkopf fought in the trenches. But during the revolutionary days of November 1918, he deserted along with several of his friends, who subsequently became members of the Communist Party. Biberkopf, a big man of great strength but limited intelligence, got a job as a furniture mover and cement worker. But within a very short time he became associated in some unspecified way with the underworld. One of his friends, Herbert, was the boss of a gang of pimps and con men. Eva, Herbert's mistress at the time the novel opens, was

[20] See Robert Minder's excellent article on Döblin in *Deutsche Literatur im zwanzigsten Jahrhundert*, ed. Hermann Friedmann and Otto Mann (2nd edn.; Heidelberg: Wolfgang Rothe, 1956), p. 302.
[21] "Epilog," *Aufsätze zur Literatur*, p. 390.

Biberkopf's girl friend for a while during those first years after the war. By 1923 Franz had met and seduced a girl named Ida. For a time he lived a contented life on her earnings as a prostitute. But when he suspected that she was going to leave him for another man, he beat her so severely in an access of rage that she died of injuries five weeks later. Biberkopf was sentenced to four years in prison for manslaughter. All of this background can be gathered gradually from various hints in the text. But we first meet Biberkopf in the fall of 1927, on the day of his release from Tegel Prison, and we accompany him, in the first chapter, as he rides the streetcar from the outskirts of Berlin into the heart of the city. Biberkopf is at this point about thirty years old.

Despite his criminal record, Biberkopf is at heart a good man with a touchingly naïve longing for order and security. He is, as Robert Minder has pointed out,[22] a secularized and proletarian "Deutscher Michel"—that prototype of the simple German youth who in various hypostases fills the role of hero in German literature from Parzival to Hans Castorp.

When he is released from prison, Biberkopf resolves to begin a new life. He makes no attempt to get in touch with Herbert, Eva, and his other old friends. He wants to begin anew, and the motto that he constantly repeats is: "Be respectable and independent." But the city, as we have seen, presents itself to Biberkopf as anything but orderly. It is a teeming, seething, dangerous chaos—the "great Whore of Babylon," according to one of the most striking images of the book—and in the first paragraph Biberkopf can barely tear himself away from the red wall of the prison. Even at this early point the prison begins to emerge as one of the symbols of order to which Franz frequently returns in his mind. On two occasions, when things go badly for him, he takes the

---

[22] Minder, *op.cit.*, p. 303.

streetcar out to Tegel and spends a few hours in the comforting shadow of the great building. After four years of order, Franz has to confront the chaos of the city.

The first hours spent with the swarming mobs in the city streets are so shattering that Franz is attacked by a hallucinatory vision: the roofs seem to be sliding off the houses! In desperation he rushes through an open gateway and into the courtyard of a building, where he begins singing verses from "Die Wacht am Rhein." This anthem, which recurs as a leitmotif throughout the novel, has an important function: it too epitomizes his longing for an orderly society.

This basic conflict between chaos and order in turn informs a set of symbolic leitmotifs that are interwoven in an almost infinite variety to produce different textures of meaning. Let us consider a few characteristic examples.[23] To render the naïveté of Franz's vision of order, the author introduces at the beginning of Book 2 two motifs: Adam and Eve in the garden of paradise, and the little refrain from Humperdinck's operetta *Hänsel und Gretel*: "Mit den Händchen klapp, klapp, klapp, mit den Füsschen trapp, trapp, trapp, einmal hin, einmal her, ringsherum, es ist nicht schwer." These two motifs are invoked repeatedly to underline the naïve expectations of Biberkopf when things are going well for him. For instance, Biberkopf decides that he will sell newspapers to make an honest living, and his new girl friend can assist him: "They told him about it, Lina can help, and it's a job for him. Einmal hin, einmal her, ringsherum, es ist nicht schwer."[24] No comment whatsoever is needed here beyond the quotation of the operetta lyric.

[23] For a systematic catalogue of the important symbols and leitmotifs see Erich Hülse, "Alfred Döblin: *Berlin Alexanderplatz*," in *Möglichkeiten des modernen deutschen Romans*, ed. Rolf Geissler (Frankfurt am Main, Berlin, and Bonn: Moritz Diesterweg, 1962), pp. 45-101.

[24] *BA*, p. 72.

Berlin Alexanderplatz

But the various associations often produce an effect of bathos. For Franz first begins dealing in magazines for homosexuals, an absurd counterpoint to the childlike innocence of the Humperdinck libretto. Soon, however, he switches to the more profitable Nazi newspaper, *Der Völkische Beobachter*. "He doesn't have anything against the Jews, but he is for order. For there must be order in paradise; anybody can understand that."[25] Only a simpleminded person would be capable of arriving at the grotesque association of Nazi propaganda with visions of paradise and a child's nursery rhyme. Yet without any lecturing or psychologizing, Döblin has laid his finger here on a profound and pathetic truth: the longing for order expressed in these simple idylls did, in fact, underlie the willingness with which many Germans succumbed to the blandishments of Nazi propaganda.[26] Döblin is exposing by subtle means that naïve craving for order which goes hand in hand with a refusal to look reality in the face and to accept personal responsibility.

Franz is wholly apolitical. He handles the Nazi paper, as he says, not because he is against the Jews, but because he is for order. When his friends from the trenches, now in the Communist Party, reproach him for selling out to the Nazis, Franz is indignant. This possibility had never occurred to him. Yet he cannot respond rationally: instead he sings "Die Wacht am Rhein," which is his irrational answer to a perfect-

[25] *BA*, p. 85.

[26] I can think of no more compelling example in real life than Julius Petersen's *Die Sehnsucht nach dem Dritten Reich in deutscher Sage und Dichtung* (Stuttgart: Metzler, 1934). Petersen was one of Germany's most distinguished literary scholars between the two world wars; and, for the most part, his study of the evolution of the chiliastic myth of redemption from ancient times to the twentieth century is a fascinating and valuable work of reliable scholarship. But Petersen succumbed to the Nazi doctrines, and the final chapter of his book makes an obscene attempt to represent Hitler and National Socialism as the ultimate fulfillment of this beautiful and often sacred myth.

115

ly rational question. His favorite newspaper is *"Die Grüne Post*, which he likes best because there's nothing political in it."[27] When he runs into politically oriented people in the bars he frequents, he refuses to enter into their conversations, because politics does not interest him. His feeling for independence is so extreme that he refuses to acknowledge any feeling of solidarity whatsoever. When he hears a worker arguing for organization of the masses, he chuckles to himself. "No higher being saves us, no God, no Kaiser, no tribunal to redeem us from misery, only we ourselves can do it."[28] And the leitmotif that announces this naïve sense of self-reliance is the cobra-snake. Biberkopf longs for order as a bulwark against chaos; he elevates his own independence over any group solidarity. But the language of the leitmotifs warns us in advance that he himself is the serpent in his own paradise. For it is ultimately his blind insistence on independence that brings about the total collapse of his childish vision of order.

The novel, then, presents us on various levels with the problems of man versus the city, order versus chaos, independence versus solidarity. And most of the leitmotifs and symbols of the work are related in one way or another to this network of tensions. As Franz alternates between success and failure, between the vision of paradise and one of roofs sliding from the houses, his mood shifts from happiness and confidence to despair and back again.

(5)

THE NOVEL, however, is more than a montage of elements of contemporary urban life or a symphony of symbols and leitmotifs. It is also a profound character study that reveals in amazing detail Döblin's technical mastery of the theories

---

[27] *BA*, p. 254.   [28] *BA*, p. 298.

of his day. For Franz Biberkopf's personality can be described quite concisely and precisely by reference to the categories suggested by Ernst Kretschmer in his epoch-making study of *Physique and Character* (1921).[29] Kretschmer's book was not only a landmark in psychiatry in the twenties and thirties; it also rapidly became the most influential work on criminology in Germany. The study would therefore have been of compelling interest to Döblin for at least two reasons, and it is inconceivable that he was not familiar with it in his capacity as neurologist and criminologist. But whether Döblin consciously followed Kretschmer's types, whether they were simply abroad as the accepted theory of the day, or whether he created Biberkopf with no preconceived pattern in mind: Biberkopf displays a striking consistency of character when examined in the light of Kretschmer's theory.

Kretschmer divides people by physique into three principal categories: asthenic or leptosome (skinny); athletic; and pyknic (inclining toward fat). As for character, men fall into two main groups: schizothymic (alternating between sensitivity and coldness) or cyclothymic (alternating between gaiety and sadness). Although Kretschmer made no attempt to set up rigid types, his statistics indicated that pyknic types tend most frequently toward cyclothymic character, while asthenic and athletic types more often display schizothymic

---

[29] *Körperbau und Charakter; Untersuchungen zum Konstitutionsproblem und zur Lehre von den Temperamenten.* I have referred to the fourth edition (Berlin: Springer, 1925). Kretschmer was Professor of Psychiatry and Neurology at Tübingen and later at Marburg. His book has been reprinted repeatedly; the twenty-fifth edition appeared in 1967. The text has been considerably revised and enlarged since the seventeenth and eighteenth editions of 1944, which contain a new chapter on "Konstitution und Verbrechen." Here Kretschmer cites criminal statistics based on the types outlined in earlier editions of the book. Though the theory never made any headway in the United States, its influence on German psychiatry and criminology until quite recently cannot be overemphasized.

personalities. It is immediately apparent that Franz Biberkopf, "a big, coarse man of repulsive appearance,"[30] whose
standing epithets are "der Dicke" (heavy or fat fellow) and
"strong as a cobra-snake," belongs to the category of pyknic
cyclothyme. His rather boisterous and simpleminded confidence and gaiety alternate with states of depression and
withdrawal; when he has been thwarted he retires moodily to
his room.

It is this type that is most susceptible to manic-depressive
insanity, and this diagnosis most appropriately fits Biberkopf, whose acute depression ultimately lands him in the psychiatric ward of the hospital at Buch. During the depressive
state the patient is subject to acute melancholy and finds
himself incapable of effort. He is plagued by hypochon-
driacal ideas and subject to hallucinations. This would help
to account for Franz's frequent reflections on his physical
condition: his fear of impotence at the beginning, his worry
about being underweight, his despair and feeling of insuffi-
ciency after losing his arm, and other similar symptoms. It
would also afford a convincing explanation for the hallucinations from which he suffers throughout the book during his
fits of depression—ranging from the vision of the roofs sliding off the houses to the violent delusions he experiences in
the madhouse, where he lies in a state of complete catatonic
stupor. In sum, Franz Biberkopf represents virtually a textbook case for the pyknic cyclothyme whose emotional state
develops into acute manic-depressive insanity.

Now the criminological statistics that Kretschmer collected
from sources all over the world indicated that less hardened
criminals, those most responsive to rehabilitation, tended to
be pyknic cyclothymes; hardened criminals, by contrast,
were usually of the asthenic schizothyme type. (These con-

[30] *BA*, p. 46.

clusions were not verified, incidentally, by statistics subsequently compiled in United States prisons.) The former commit their crimes in sudden fits of anger and are subsequently subject to deep remorse—precisely as Biberkopf was when he killed Ida. The most hardened criminal in the novel, on the other hand, is in every respect a clear-cut case of asthenic schizothyme: thin to the point of haggardness, coldly hating and plotting, Reinhold plans the abduction of Mieze as an act of revenge against Biberkopf, and after he has murdered her shows not the least sign of remorse, but only a shrewd calculation of his own chances to get out on parole. In the case of these two principal figures, then, there is an astonishingly close correlation between Kretschmer's theoretical types and the physique and character of each fictional creation. Influence would not be the proper word to express the connection between Döblin and Kretschmer. The relationship should be viewed negatively: Döblin seems to have avoided in his characterization any traits, physical or emotional, that would have been incompatible with the leading psychiatric and criminological theory of the day. Biberkopf is too consistent and convincing a figure to be merely the embodiment of a theory; he arises, as it were, out of the book itself, the milieu and language of Berlin. And yet the parallel is so striking, and so helpful in the analysis and understanding of his character and his nervous breakdown, that it seems quite relevant to introduce Kretschmer's terminology.

To return to the novel: we have observed that the inner tension of the book is one between chaos and order. Biberkopf returns to the world from prison resolved to make a new life for himself, to be respectable and independent. "But in the outside world nothing had changed, and he himself had remained the same man. How was any new result supposed to emerge?" Döblin questioned in his postscript to the 1955 edition. "Obviously only if one of the two was destroyed, either Berlin or Franz Biberkopf. And since Berlin remained what it was, it was necessary for the punished man to change. So the inner theme is: It is necessary to sacrifice, to offer oneself as a sacrifice."[31] This theme of sacrifice, as we have already noted, is amply anticipated in certain scenes of the novel: the slaughterhouse, the invocation of Job and his suffering, the references to Abraham and Isaac. All these elements of montage emphasize the necessity for sacrifice long before it becomes clear to Biberkopf himself. But there is another complex of montage elements that is, I believe, far more revealing with regard to what might be called the rhythm of development in the novel.

(6)

QUITE early in the book the notion of classical tragedy is introduced as an ironic contrast to present-day reality. Franz Biberkopf has built a new life for himself. "He is as strong as a cobra-snake and once again a member of an athletic club."[32] Then, rather whimsically, the narrator speculates: "Is he plagued by qualms of conscience out of the past, by Ida and so forth, nightmares, restless sleep, torments, Erinyes from the days of our great-grandmothers? Nothing of the sort! Consider the altered situation." Then the narrator briefly recounts Orestes' murder of Clytemnestra and his pursuit by the Erinyes. "I say that times have changed. Hoi ho hatz, awful beasts, ragged women with snakes, mastiffs without a muzzle, a whole unpleasant menagerie, they snap at him, but can't touch him because he is standing at the altar, that's an antique conception. . . . They don't torment Franz Biberkopf." At this point, in one of the most effective montages of the novel, the narrator recounts the killing of Ida, employing for his purposes a lengthy discussion of Newton's

[31] *BA*, p. 508. [32] *BA*, pp. 103ff.

Berlin Alexanderplatz

laws on motion and rest along with the appropriate symbols of physics. "When you consider matters in a contemporary way like this, you can get by without any Erinyes at all," he concludes smugly.

The reader is amused by the juxtaposition of classical tragedy and the formulae of physics. Döblin is well aware of the humorous effects to be achieved by mixing various kinds of language and by recounting the events of one level of action in a vocabulary borrowed from another level.[33] At the same time the reader wonders: Is it all merely parody? For this juxtaposition of ancient and modern, of tragedy and reality, occurs too often in the course of the novel to be merely gratuitous. Thus, at the beginning of Book 7, the sordid murder of a prostitute—under circumstances not unlike those in which Franz earlier murdered Ida—is explicitly called a "fate tragedy"; and the term (*Schicksalstragödie*) is intended to awaken very specific associations with a group of German romantic dramas written in accordance with an exaggerated misconception of Greek tragedy which saw the hero's downfall as being brought about by an external fate. On another occasion a minor character remarks: "A man must come to grips with the facts and with himself. A guy shouldn't brag about his destiny. I'm an opponent of fate. I'm no Greek, I'm from Berlin."[34]

Yet is this not precisely what Franz Biberkopf does? Whenever something adverse happens to him, he loudly denies his own guilt and responsibility, whining that fate has

[33] We recall, of course, Rilke's description of death, couched in the jargon of tailors, or his discussion of time, conducted in the vocabulary of commerce and banking. This technique, by the way, lends itself easily to parody. Robert Neumann chose a passage like this one for his amusing parody of *Berlin Alexanderplatz*; see his *Die Parodien: Gesamtausgabe* (Vienna, Munich, and Basel: Kurt Desch, 1962), pp. 246-48.

[34] *BA*, p. 57.

dealt him a dirty blow. He wants to be respectable, but he goes through life with his eyes closed, totally unable or unwilling to see reality. He is a complete cyclothyme: an open book for the world to read, jovial, unsuspecting, blind to the character of others. It is only on the last pages of the book, after his release from the neurological clinic, that Franz comes to regard the world like a man "from Berlin." "I'll no longer yell 'fate, fate!' as I used to do. You mustn't venerate such things as fate; you should look at them, seize them, and destroy them."[35] Franz Biberkopf's development, if it is permissible to use the term development to describe a change that comes so suddenly and only at the very end of the book, is one that leads from the Greek conception of destiny to a modern view of reality.

But if Biberkopf's point of view up to the last pages is that of a "Greek" rather than that of a modern urbanite, then the narrator's disclaimers about tragedy no longer hold true. Tragedy in the sense of fate is patently impossible for a man with a soberly realistic view of the world. But from Biberkopf's point of view, such a tragedy is indeed possible because he actually *believes*, until the very end, in a blind destiny. Seen objectively and from the standpoint of character, what happens to Biberkopf is the result of his own naïve, stupid, and arrogant disposition, which is unable to come to grips with the world. But viewed from within, the novel has what might quite aptly be called the rhythm of classical tragedy, and it is this rhythm that seems to sustain both the movement of the novel and the plot. The "network of tensions" of which Döblin speaks is provided by the montage of the city, by the language of its various elements, by the character of Biberkopf. But these are the constants, as it were. The actual movement of the action closely resembles the rhythm of tragedy. It is a tragedy which, to be sure, is

[35] *BA*, p. 501.

disclaimed throughout by the narrator and, at the end, even by the hero. But what is disclaimed is the meaning, not the form, of tragedy. And form without meaning is form nonetheless. *Berlin Alexanderplatz*, I would suggest, is given its unity of action by a conscious travesty of tragedy with all its most characteristic elements. We can see this most clearly if we examine the development of the novel in specific detail.

The novel is divided into nine books, punctuated by the three setbacks that Franz Biberkopf experiences. This inner rhythm is anticipated in the narrator's preliminary remarks. "He becomes involved, though economically he gets along tolerably well, in a regular battle with something that comes from outside, that is incalculable, and that looks rather like Fate. Three times it hurls itself against the man and disturbs him in his life-plan."[36] If we arrange the nine books of the novel according to this threefold rhythm, a definite pattern emerges. Book 1, which records Biberkopf's release from prison and his first efforts to regain his equilibrium (covering a period of about five weeks), is really only an upbeat to the first principal episode. The three main episodes then dispose themselves into pairs of books (2 and 3, 4 and 5, 6 and 7), each of which shows the same rhythm, but with increasing intensity. The first book of each pair depicts Biberkopf's recovery from the preceding blow, while the second builds up to the next blow, which comes regularly at the end of Books 3, 5, and 7. Books 8 and 9 together constitute another group, inasmuch as they depict his recovery from the blow at the end of the seventh book and the turning point, his arrival at a completely new view: the realization that life is not an orderly paradise, and that it behooves a man to go

---

[36] This triadic rhythm, by the way, seems to be basic to Döblin's sense of life, for it dominates the development of some of his other novels, most notably *The Three Leaps of Wang-Lun*, in which each leap signifies a turning point in the hero's life.

through the world with his eyes open, not lamenting any "fate" that has dealt unkindly with him.

In each of the three main episodes the circumstances vary considerably. Yet they also reveal a striking similarity of motivation. At the end of Book 2, Biberkopf is completely recovered: "strong as a cobra-snake," he is determined to be "respectable and independent" in the fairy-tale paradise of his imagination. He has a new girl friend, Lina; he has a comfortable income from his newspapers; and in the bars of Berlin East he is a generally well-regarded customer who can boast with as much assurance as the next man. As Christmas approaches, Franz switches jobs. Along with Lina's uncle, Otto Lüders, he goes from door to door selling notions. One day Biberkopf meets a lonely young widow, to whom he sells a great deal more than his tray full of wares. He comes chuckling back to his regular bar and boasts to Lüders about this promising new affair. But when he returns to his little widow a week later, he learns that Lüders, enticed by his crowing, has been there in the meantime to capitalize on the situation. The widow refuses to admit him. Biberkopf is so disturbed by this deception on the part of Lüders, which does not correspond at all to his naïvely paradisical conception of the world, that he disappears from sight for over a month. "He wanted to be respectable, but there are rascals and crooks and bums, and for that reason Franz Biberkopf no longer wants to see or hear anything about the world."[37]

In this first episode we see Biberkopf's complete swing from his initial state of depression up to the first peak of manic exuberance and back into an even greater depression than before. And in each case his reaction is typical: he withdraws from the world, full of self-pity. In comparison with the following episodes, the provocation here seems quite trivial. Any rational, clear-sighted man would have recog-

[37] *BA*, p. 159.

nized Lüders for a scoundrel at first sight. But what is interesting is this: the entire upset comes about because of Franz's boasting! If he had kept his mouth shut and his affairs to himself, Lüders would never have had the opportunity to swindle him. His fall stems directly from a flaw in his own character: his compulsion to boast and to convince others of his own cleverness.

Precisely this same combination of factors leads to the next, far more serious, blow. As he gradually recovers from the Lüders incident, Franz moves a few blocks east from Rosenthaler Platz to another part of Berlin, the Alexanderplatz of the title. Here he finds a new girl friend and a new group of friends. Without realizing it, Franz has stumbled into a gang of thieves. He is able to look at some of the most hardened criminals in Berlin and honestly believe that they deal, as they tell him, in "fruit." His second fall is due directly to one of the members of this gang, whose character Franz is incapable of assessing.

Reinhold's personality consists of an assortment of seemingly contradictory characteristics which nevertheless fit the type of asthenic schizothyme. A man of cold brutality, he is given to moods of sensitivity, and when these are upon him he attends meetings of the Salvation Army. Normally a teetotaler, sipping only coffee and lemonade, he occasionally drinks himself into a fury in order to get rid of his girl friends. A man with pronounced tendencies toward homosexuality, he needs women from time to time, but cannot tolerate a regular mistress for more than a month.[38]

From the first moment Franz is fascinated by Reinhold,

[38] As a type, Reinhold displays a pronounced similarity to Adolf Hitler—a parallel that may well have been consciously intended—and to Marius Ratti, the mythic dictator figure of Hermann Broch's unfinished novel "Demeter" or "The Bewitchment," published posthumously as *Der Versucher*.

125

and in the psychologically complex relationship between the two men at least three elements stand out clearly. First, Reinhold's pronounced sadism corresponds to certain unconscious masochistic tendencies in Franz's personality: he likes to be able to feel sorry for himself. Second, Reinhold's taut self-discipline appeals to Franz's craving for order: the simple "Deutscher Michel" responds to the "Führer" type. Finally, as Robert Minder has pointed out, there is a clear element of homoerotism in the dubious camaraderie between the two.[39]

But it is specifically Reinhold's problem with women that involves him with Biberkopf, for Franz, in his openhearted manner, has a better touch with women than does Reinhold, who knows only violence. Reinhold suggests a plan: "girl-swapping." Franz will take over Reinhold's girl every month and then pass her along in order to be ready to take over the next girl four weeks later. Franz agrees to this arrangement at first, but by the time the second girl comes to live with him, it begins to disturb him. He becomes fond of Cilly and, more-over, it strikes him as wrong and disorderly to treat girls in this way. So he resolves to "educate" Reinhold. When Reinhold begins to tire of his current girl, Franz and Cilly approach her with their plan; secretly they also explain the situation to the new woman on whom Reinhold has cast his eye. In this way, they manage to maintain the *status quo* for much longer than had ever been the case before. Reinhold is vaguely discomfited by the fact that he has somehow been living with the same girl for much longer than is his custom, yet he does not consciously realize what is happening. But Franz's irrepressible compulsion to boast and to broadcast his principles wrecks the precarious situation. People must admire him and his "respectability." So one evening he roguish-ly teases Reinhold in the presence of their friend Meck. "After

[39] Minder, *op.cit.*, p. 303.

all, that is the object of his education, that is his pupil, he can serve him up now to his friend Meck."[40] Slyly he lets Reinhold suspect what has been going on. "That's what he has done. Who else but me? And beams at his friend Meck, who doesn't withhold his admiration. 'What do you say, Meck. We're going to make some order in the world.' " This braggadocio triggers Reinhold's act of violence against Franz.

One evening Franz accompanies the gang on a job. He is still naïve enough to believe that they are carrying out a legitimate pick up and delivery. It is only at the last minute that he realizes that it is actually a robbery and that he, Franz, has been posted as lookout. When Franz piles into the escape cars with the gang, now closely pursued by another car, he chuckles to himself, thinking that it serves them right to be caught and that he has nothing to do with the affair. Reinhold is enraged by this attitude and recalls Franz's early behavior. "That's Biberkopf, the guy who left him in the lurch, who scares his women away, it's proven, this insolent, fat swine, and I once told him all about myself. Suddenly Reinhold is no longer thinking about the drive."[41] In his fury, Reinhold shoves Franz out of the speeding car. Biberkopf is struck by the pursuing automobile and, as a result of the injury, loses his right arm. That is the second blow. But again he interprets it as an act of fate. When he eventually recovers, through the aid of Eva and Herbert, he refuses to tell them what caused the loss of his arm. "I've never squealed on anybody," he had said in a similar case;[42] his naïve concept of independence comes into conflict with his desire for order in the world. He fails to understand that it was ultimately his own boasting and gloating that motivated Reinhold's act. This blindness enables Reinhold to become the tool of yet a third, more terrible blow.

After the loss of his arm in April, Franz makes a slow

[40] *BA*, p. 213.　　　[41] *BA*, p. 231.　　　[42] *BA*, p. 160.

recovery. Gradually he builds up a new life, for the third time, with the help of his newest girl friend, the prostitute Mieze. But this new life is so fine that Franz, again, cannot keep it to himself. By August he is impelled to seek out his old nemesis, Reinhold, and to boast to him about the wonderful recovery he has made. At this point Döblin inserts an episode so clearly patterned after a famous German tragedy that it virtually announces the underlying plan and rhythm of tragedy.

Since Franz is incapable of enjoying his blessings privately, but must have them publicly acclaimed, he works out a plan by which Reinhold can witness his fairy-tale bliss. Reinhold agrees to accompany Franz to his apartment; there Franz hides him in the curtains of the bed, so that Reinhold can observe the great love that Mieze bears him. As it turns out, the little farce is a disaster. Franz and Mieze have their first quarrel, and Reinhold observes the whole fiasco. But the episode is interesting because it lays the ground for the subsequent action and so clearly travesties the central scene in Friedrich Hebbel's *Gyges and his Ring*, a tragedy based on a legend related by Herodotus. Kandaules, king of the Lydians, suffers from the same needs as Franz. Though his wife is the most beautiful woman in the world, he can find no peace until he has a witness to his good fortune. His words might well be uttered, in dialect, by Biberkopf:

> Ich brauche einen Zeugen, dass ich nicht
> Ein eitler Tor bin, der sich selbst belügt,
> Wenn er sich rühmt, das schönste Weib zu küssen. . . .[43]

With the aid of a ring that makes the wearer invisible, Kandaules admits Gyges to his bedroom so that he can admire

---

[43] *Gyges und sein Ring*, ll. 531-33 (end of Act I): "A witness I require, that I am not / A simple fool who dupes himself when he / Asserts that he embraces the loveliest woman. . . ."

Rhodope's beauty. Both witnesses—Gyges and Reinhold—are smitten by the beauty that they are supposed to admire from afar, and this precipitates the tragic events. As though the parallel were not sufficiently clear in itself, Döblin introduces and orchestrates the scene with references to "Persians and Persian rugs," so that the reference to the Lydian tragedy will not be missed. "And then it's three o'clock in the afternoon, Franz and Reinhold walk through the streets, porcelain signs of every sort, porcelain wares, German and genuine Persian carpets, for twelve monthly payments, carpet-runners, tablecloths and couch covers, quilts, curtains, Leisner & Co., read Fashions for You, otherwise send for our free catalogue by return mail, Caution, Mortal Danger, High Tension."[44]

Once again, Franz's boasting leads directly to his downfall. He is still too blind to recognize Reinhold's malevolence despite all the signposts along the way ("Caution, Mortal Danger, High Tension"). Reinhold determines to attack Biberkopf through his most prized possession, Mieze. But when his plans for seduction misfire, he murders the girl. It is this shock—not only the loss of Mieze, but also the realization, finally, of Reinhold's true character—that plunges Franz into his third and deepest depression. After his arrest on suspicion of murder, he spends weeks in the psychiatric ward of the hospital at Buch, in a state of stupor. But before we consider this final scene, we can recapitulate our findings.

In all three cases, Franz's downfall is brought about by his own blindness to the character of others and by his boasting. If we return to the analogy of classical tragedy, it seems quite clear that Franz's problems are created by what Aristotle would have called his *hamartia*. The same basic situation is repeated, but with each repetition he reaches a higher peak of manic happiness and self-complacency, from which he plummets (peripeteia) to progressively deeper abysses of

44 *BA*, p. 364.

depression (catastrophe). In the temporal structure of the work his first recovery, after the deception by Lüders, takes only about a month (January, 1928); the second period of recovery lasts from April well into July; and the third continues from Mieze's murder at the end of August until the winter of 1928-1929.

This rhythm of development is complicated and obscured by the dual aspect of the book: the presentation of the city itself takes up roughly half the book, and the plot is constantly interrupted and loosened by the intrusion of passages not strictly related to it. As a result, it is easy to lose sight of the tragic rhythm that determines the structure of the plot. But in the much tighter version that Döblin prepared for the radio in 1930, the essentially dramatic outline emerges almost paradigmatically.[45] The montage effect is preserved by the rapid shifts of scene, but the major sections devoted almost wholly to the city as such (e.g., Books 1 and 4) are cut out completely. What is left is the basic action itself, just as we have considered it: a series of tragic setbacks. In the radio version the third episode is moved to the center of this action. Of the thirty-one scenes, only thirteen are devoted to the Lüders incident and the loss of Franz's arm; scenes fourteen through twenty-three deal with Mieze; and the last eight scenes recount Franz's gradual recovery. The emphasis of the plot has been shifted in such a way as to bring out the tragic structure: *hamartia*, peripeteia, catastrophe.

The radio play also gives new prominence to another as-

[45] "Berlin-Alexanderplatz; Hörspiel von Alfred Döblin." There is no extant manuscript of this radio play, which was performed in Berlin on September 30, 1930, but a stenographic copy was made from a recording of the broadcast. This version was published for the first time in Heinz Schwitzke's anthology of radio plays, *Sprich, damit ich dich sehe*, the second volume of which contains *Frühe Hörspiele* (Munich: Listbücher 217, 1962), pp. 21-58.

pect: the chorus-like function of the various narrative voices. In the novel, as we have seen, the narrator assumes many voices, each establishing the style of the passage being rendered. It is only at the end that all these voices—as we have yet to discuss—are subsumed into the single voice of Death. In the radio version, by contrast, most of these same passages are grouped from the beginning into chorus-like statements commenting upon each of the three main setbacks; these passages are spoken explicitly by Death, whose voice provides the narrative continuity between the dialogues. This chorus-like function is, of course, present in the novel as well.[46] But there these passages are obscured somewhat by the variety of voices and by the objectivity of the montage, behind which the narrative voice withdraws. Looked at in this light the various aspects of the novel assume a higher unity, one not apparent before. The preliminary statement of the narrator can now be read as an argumentum preceding the tragic action. The main action consists of a series of three reversals of fortune precipitated by the hero's *hamartia*, that is, by his blindness with regard to human nature and his boastfulness (both, in turn, consistent aspects of his cyclothymic nature). This action is accompanied, finally, by a chorus of voices that reflect on the meaning of Biberkopf's destiny and that see far more clearly than he the greater implications of all he does and experiences. The final shift from romantic belief in fate to a modern awareness of reality is a kind of catharsis, precipitated by a series of scenes that make artistic sense only if they are viewed as a pursuit by the Erinyes, an association implicit in the novel since the author's satirical disclaimers in the early chapters.

[46] Schöne, *op.cit.*, p. 318, characterizes these passages as "forms of collective speech" and distinguishes them sharply from the individual streams of consciousness in Joyce's *Ulysses*.

Alfred Döblin

(7)

BIBERKOPF'S third setback, it will be recalled, produces such severe psychic consequences that he lands in the psychiatric ward of the hospital at Buch (where Döblin served for a time as interne).[47] As far as outer appearances are concerned, he is a textbook case of manic-depressive insanity in its severest form: for weeks he lies in a stupor, fed by a tube in his throat, incapable of communication, and a riddle to the swarm of doctors in attendance. (Döblin takes this occasion to satirize his own profession: there are the conservative old professors who take a dim view of psychogenic explanations and believe in sweatbaths as a cure for catatonic stupor, and the young internes who ascribe to the modern theories of Freudian psychiatry.) The objective description of Biberkopf's behavior and of the therapy he receives during these weeks of manic-depressive insanity is as precise as one would expect, coming as it does from an experienced neurologist who spent many years with patients suffering from the same symptoms. But the poetic rendition of the hallucinations that beset Franz is conditioned wholly by the associations with tragedy that have been gradually built up in the course of the novel. In this difficult scene, myth and psychiatry are interwoven with great virtuosity to produce a compelling and convincing image of a neurotic hallucination.

The reader will immediately note that the various images employed in these passages have been anticipated earlier in the work: for instance, the hacking of the axes was heard in the slaughterhouses, while the crash of the giant drills comes from the excavating of a new subway line on Alexanderplatz. The hallucinations are technically a masterpiece of leitmotif and collage. Before Biberkopf can experience cognition

[47] While interning at Buch in 1906-7, Döblin had published a clinical study of a similar case of "Hysterie mit Dämmerzuständen."

132

through suffering and death, his conscience must be awakened.

Voom hit, voom hit, voom batteringram, voom gatecrash. With pressing and racing, crashing, brandishing the Mighty Stormers assemble and consult. It is night. How can one make Franz awaken? They don't want to break his limbs. But the house is so thick, and he doesn't hear what they call out, and if he were closer to them outside, then he would feel them and would hear Mieze screaming. Then his heart would be opened, his conscience would awaken, and he would arise and all would be well.[48]

Raise high, fall down, hack, raise high, strike down, hack, raise, fall, hack, raise, fall hack, raise hack, raise hack. And in the glitter of the light and while it raises and glitters and hacks, Franz crawls and touches the ladder, screams, screams screams. And doesn't crawl back. Franz screams. Death is there.[49]

These scenes can be explained most satisfactorily, I believe, if we regard them as a modern rendition of the pursuit by the Erinyes of Greek tragedy—by avenging spirits informed by twentieth-century psychiatry and drawing their imagery from the technological world of 1928, but Erinyes nonetheless. The structure of tragedy, in other words, is complete from start to finish, for it is these avenging spirits that finally succeed in making Franz accept the fact of his own guilt and responsibility, in curing him of his *hamartia*. This, in turn, casts new light on the frequent references to the Greeks and especially to the legend of Orestes. For Orestes was hounded by the Erinyes, as Döblin pointed out in the passage cited earlier; but unlike the heroes of most Greek tragedies, he lived to be redeemed and freed from the aveng-

[48] *BA*, p. 463.   [49] *BA*, p. 476.

ing spirits. Although the meaning of classical tragedy is trivialized, its form is preserved to an astonishing degree. In fact, it determines essentially the movement and imagery of the whole novel.

After he has been reduced to a trembling pulp by the pile drivers and axes of the modern Erinyes, Franz is ready for the great dialogue with Death that completes his development. Speaking in Berlin dialect, Death shows Franz how stupid he has been:

> I tell you, you didn't open your eyes, you cringing dog! You whine about crooks and cheating and don't even look at people and don't ask why and how come. What kind of a judge of men do you think you are, and you don't even have any eyes! You've been blind and insolent too, arrogant, Mr. Biberkopf from the fancy part of town, and the world has to be just as he wants it to be. It's different, kid, now you understand.[50]

In a series of visions, Death now unfolds before Franz all the crucial episodes of his past, demonstrating clearly how wrong Franz has been and how foolishly he has behaved. Finally Franz acknowledges his guilt. "In this hour of evening Franz Biberkopf died: former furniture mover, thief, pimp, murderer. A different man lay in the bed. The other one has the same papers as Franz, looks like Franz, but in a different world he bears a new name."[51]

One of the central symbols for the city as a menacing chaos has been the Whore of Babylon. At this point, when Franz has been redeemed, Döblin describes in a scene of vivid imagery the retreat of the Whore of Babylon before the power of Death. For now that Franz has learned to look upon the world with new eyes, he no longer regards the city with the eyes of a Greek, seeing in it a nameless destiny or

[50] *BA*, p. 478.   [51] *BA*, p. 488.

threat. The last few pages of the novel recount the first steps of this "new" Biberkopf, who in distinction to his old self is now called Franz Karl Biberkopf. At the trial his friends, as well as Reinhold, notice the new look in his eyes: shrewd, objective, assessing, Biberkopf has clearly undergone a transformation.

At this point the narrator interjects another little note, in a montage of phrases from the newspaper account, which reminds us once again that we have witnessed a tragic action. "The one-armed man arouses general interest, great excitement, murder of the beloved, lovelife in the underworld, after her death he was mentally ill, stood under suspicion of complicity, tragic fate."[52] Here, of course, the word "tragic" is used with double irony. First, the passage parodies headline style, which tends to use the word "tragic" in a loose and often grotesque sense. At the same time, a second level of irony is attained because the reader knows what the newspaper reporter does not know: namely, that Biberkopf's "fate" was indeed "tragic," but in a far more specific way than the reporter suspects.

The novel, then, has revealed many dimensions of meaning. On the aesthetic level, it represents a modern "tragedy" in strict harmony with the laws of classical Greek tragedy; this determines the rhythm of the plot. On the psychological level, it shows the crisis and cure of a case of manic-depressive insanity; this determines the character of Biberkopf. On the sociological level, it depicts the rehabilitation of a criminal who ends up as gateman of a factory in the spring of 1929; this is related to Döblin's social conscience. On a political level, it represents the disenchantment of a "Deutscher Michel" with a dictatorial leader who, for a time, seems to satisfy his masochistic craving for order and obedience; this aspect, totally vitiated by history, has been most frequently

[52] *BA*, p. 497.

attacked by critics (especially the hymn to solidarity on the last two pages of the book). And the entire human action, with its many levels of meaning, is set against a vivid montage that virtually reproduces the city of Berlin in the pages of the novel.

Biberkopf has learned that "the world is made of sugar and filth"[53] and not simply of sweetness and light, as he had believed in the days when he sang "Die Wacht am Rhein" and craved for an impossible order in the world. His vision of paradise and nursery-rhyme bliss is gone, to be sure; but his hallucinations no longer plague him. With this shift, of course, the depiction of the city must also change. Its demons have been exorcized by Biberkopf's new objectivity. The roofs no longer threaten to slide from the houses; the sidewalks do not glide under his feet; the room no longer whirls around him. As a result, the narrative voice during the final pages is much calmer and less frenetic than the voices that have dominated most of the book. Since Biberkopf now feels himself in harmony with the city and in a state of solidarity with his fellowman, the narrative voice now closely parallels his own feelings. "It is nicer and better to be with others. Then I feel and know everything twice as well. A ship doesn't lie fast without a big anchor, and a man cannot get along without many other men. I shall now know better what is true and false."[54] This does not imply a naïve affirmation of the world: it announces, rather, an attitude of critical detachment toward reality that contrasts with Franz's earlier romantic attempts to force the world into a framework or pattern of his own creation. Through his "tragedy" Biberkopf has learned to deny destiny and to accept reality. Like the voice early in the novel, he could now proclaim: "I'm no Greek, I'm from Berlin."

[53] *BA*, p. 498.   [54] *BA*, p. 500.

Berlin Alexanderplatz

DÖBLIN'S APPROACH to the novel, as revealed in *Berlin Alexanderplatz*, differs radically from that of Thomas Mann. Every novelist is confronted with essentially the same problem: How is he to do justice to the totality of the world and, at the same time, to preserve the aesthetic unity that is the prerequisite of any work of art? *The Magic Mountain* attempts to achieve these aims by isolating certain elements of reality and intensifying them to a point where they become symbolically representative of the world as a whole. Totality is assured by the representative quality of the figures and events; but unity is achieved by the control that the author is able to exercise within the "hermetic" isolation of the work.

Berlin Alexanderplatz, by contrast, lets everything in: we are reminded again of our initial distinction between fever chart and weather report. Döblin, in other words, seeks to render totality by means of inclusion, and not by symbolic selectivity. But in order to achieve any degree of unity within this chaotic multiplicity he is compelled to erect a strong underlying structure. He therefore chooses the framework of classical tragedy to contain everything else. Thomas Mann strives toward a total epic integration in which even the most minute part, like the smallest stone in a mosaic, is related to the whole design. Döblin, by contrast, has loosened the integration of the novel. He has adopted, to be sure, a broad and almost mythic framework to hold his novel together; but within that framework the individual elements are allowed to float freely and at random, as a reflection of reality itself. The final stage in this process of fictional disintegration, however, was already underway: in 1929, when *Berlin Alexanderplatz* was published, Hermann Broch had just begun the composition of *The Sleepwalkers*.

chapter five

Hermann Broch

The Sleepwalkers

(1)

FEW WORKS of literature have been so programmatically conceived and so self-consciously heralded as *The Sleepwalkers*, which was published in three volumes in 1931 and 1932. In dozens of letters to his publisher, his translators, and friends, as well as in the "methodological prospectus" that he wrote for the edification of his editors, Broch recorded the genesis and intentions of what he came to call his "*novum* in the genre of the novel."[1] "The age of the polyhistorical novel has dawned," he proudly announced to his publisher in 1931, half a year before the completion of his manuscript.[2] Conscious from the start of his position in world literature, Broch sought out the Rhein Verlag in Zurich largely because it had recently published the German translation of Joyce's *Ulysses*, which he regarded as a counterpart to his own creation. And he was pleased to have Edwin and Willa Muir translate his novel because they had introduced Kafka to the English-speaking world. Before the printer's ink had dried on the pages, Broch was hoping that his novel would be taken up by the Book of the Month Club in the United States. (Of course, it was not, as any reader can easily understand.) And he entered into a lengthy correspondence with Warner Brothers in an—again, highly unrealistic—attempt to have his work filmed.

[1] Hermann Broch, *Briefe von 1929 bis 1951*, ed. Robert Pick (Zurich: Rhein, 1957), p. 55. This edition henceforth cited as *Briefe*.
[2] *Briefe*, p. 60.

138

The Sleepwalkers

Our initial amusement at the self-confidence of this first-time novelist of forty-five, who had only recently given up industrial management for literature, is tempered by the fact that it has proven, belatedly, in large measure justified. Broch, who died in a New Haven hotel in 1951, did not live to enjoy his success. But in the past five years three books have been written on *The Sleepwalkers* alone, apart from numerous articles and unpublished dissertations.[3] Although Broch's works are not yet to be found on every bookshelf, serious critics no longer hesitate to discuss him in connection with those authors of his generation to whom he himself repeatedly referred and with whom he felt himself most closely akin: Joyce, Kafka, Gide, Dos Passos, and Aldous Huxley.

Until he was forty-two, Broch, who was born in Vienna in 1886, spent most of his life managing the family textile mills in Austria and playing the role of a "captain of industry," as he later called himself with more than a touch of self-irony.[4] He pointed out that he had at least one thing in common with Franz Kafka and Robert Musil: "We all three have no

---

[3] Karl Robert Mandelkow, *Hermann Brochs Romantrilogie "Die Schlafwandler"; Gestaltung und Reflexion im modernen deutschen Roman* (Heidelberg: Carl Winter Universitätsverlag, 1962); Leo Kreutzer, *Erkenntnistheorie und Prophetie; Hermann Brochs Roman-trilogie "Die Schlafwandler"* (Tübingen: Max Niemeyer, 1966); Dorrit Claire Cohn, *The Sleepwalkers; Elucidations of Hermann Broch's Trilogy* (The Hague and Paris: Mouton, 1966).

[4] The most complete and factually reliable biography, including the most extensive bibliography, is that by Manfred Durzak, *Hermann Broch* (Stuttgart: Sammlung Metzler, 1967). In the series Rowohlts Monographien (No. 118), Durzak has also published a biography with many pictures and much documentary material (Reinbek bei Hamburg, 1966). The most readable biography is that of Thomas Koebner, *Hermann Broch; Leben und Werk* (Bern and Munich: Francke, 1965). The only general work in English is still my own *Hermann Broch*, in the series Columbia Essays on Modern Writers (New York: Columbia University Press, 1964).

real biography. We lived and wrote, and that's all."[5] Broch devoted himself to his work as assiduously and conscientiously as Kafka attended to his insurance claims: he took out patents on milling processes; attended an "International Cotton Growers, Buyers and Spinners Conference" in Atlanta, Georgia, in 1907; served on government advisory councils; directed a military hospital during the First World War; and acted as a respected and skillful arbitrator in complicated labor disputes. At the same time, he kept up his passionate intellectual interests by attending courses, especially in mathematics and philosophy, at the University of Vienna and by writing a series of essays and literary reviews for various journals. By 1928, however, this double life became untenable. Convinced that an economic crisis was approaching—and history bore him out—Broch sold the mills and announced to his startled family his intention of becoming a full-time writer.

Broch reached this seemingly rash decision through a soberingly consistent process of reasoning. To be sure, he was already a writer of sorts: apart from the published essays, reviews, and stories, Broch had drawers full of manuscripts of every kind that still lie, largely uncatalogued, in the archives of the Yale University Library.[6] But Broch's decision was motivated primarily by intellectual considerations, not by a romantic desire "to write." The central impulse of his life was "cognition" (*Erkenntnis*)—a word that appears more frequently than any other in his writing. Initially he had sought to attain this cognition, which he understood pri-

[5] *Briefe*, p. 321.

[6] Although the Yale University Library has generously permitted many scholars to use and cite this material, much of it still has not been exhausted. For a preliminary description see Götz Wienold, "Werk und Nachlass Hermann Brochs; Editions- und Forschungsprobleme," *Euphorion*, 60 (1966), 370-82.

marily as a knowledge of human reality and ethical behavior, by the conventional avenues of philosophy. But his studies gradually convinced him that the only possible road to this sort of cognition lay, paradoxically, in literature.

The philosophy of the twenties, particularly the logical positivism that dominated the Viennese school, had discarded metaphysical speculation in favor of problems that could be solved by mathematical demonstration. (The hundreds of pages of exercises in symbolic logic that lie in the archives at Yale bear eloquent testimony to Broch's initial endeavors in this direction.) The redemption of ethics by existential thinkers was not yet underway. In other words, philosophy no longer provided Broch with the framework for treating the problems that most vitally obsessed him; and he had no desire to become a theologian. "Those areas of philosophy that are inaccessible to mathematical treatment—primarily ethics and metaphysics—become 'objective' only in the realm of theology. Otherwise they become relativistic and, ultimately, 'subjective.' It was this realization that forced me into the area where subjectivity is radically legitimate, namely into literature."[7]

If philosophy could not fulfill his needs, then literature would have to be pressed into service. It was in this context that he wrote to his publisher about certain startling aspects of *The Sleepwalkers*: "You know my theory, that the novel and its new form have taken over the responsibility of absorbing those parts of philosophy that, to be sure, correspond to metaphysical needs but that, in accord with the present state of scholarship, are nowadays considered to be 'unscientific' or, as Wittgenstein says, 'mystical.' "[8] For this reason

[7] Letter of December 5, 1948, in which he explains his reasons for writing *The Sleepwalkers; Briefe*, p. 322. Cf. *Briefe*, pp. 413-14.
[8] *Briefe*, pp. 59-60.

141

Hermann Broch

Broch often said that his writing represented "an impatience for cognition."[9] Literature, with its intuitive knowledge, leaps ahead of science, so to speak. Hence literature must become "prophecy" in a very specific sense: it must endeavor to attain a cognition that will later be borne out and verified by the slower-paced science and systematic philosophy.

This attitude justifies Hannah Arendt's phrase when she speaks of Broch as "a writer *malgré lui*."[10] Despite a compelling gift for sheer narrative and despite being capable of some of the most powerful evocations of landscape in German literature, Broch felt nothing but contempt for "art for art's sake," and he strenuously resisted what he called his own "temptation to tell stories."[11] He insisted, rather, that we have reached "the age of ethical art." In his important essay on James Joyce (1936), which is actually a veiled commentary on his own novel, he elucidated this idea further, saying that literature has "the mission toward a cognition that embraces totality."[12]

It was in this spirit that Broch conceived *The Sleepwalkers*. It was to be the first attempt at an "epistemological" novel, in contrast to the psychological novel that was currently fashionable. He sought "a novel that delves back behind psychological motivation to basic epistemological attitudes and to the actual logic and plausibility of values."[13] In order to understand a man, we must first of all understand the values by which he lives. For Broch regards psychological

[9] In the essay on "James Joyce und die Gegenwart," in Hermann Broch, *Dichten und Erkennen, Essays I*, ed. Hannah Arendt (Zurich: Rhein, 1955), p. 205 and elsewhere (e.g., p. 246). This edition henceforth cited as *Essays I*.

[10] See her introduction to *Essays I*, p. 5.

[11] *Briefe*, p. 184.

[12] *Essays I*, p. 204.

[13] Letter of July 16, 1930; *Briefe*, p. 23.

behavior as nothing more than the manifestation of an unconscious metaphysical anguish. In this sense, as we shall see, his
plots themselves represent an attempt to explain certain typical situations by exposing their metaphysical patterns: he
raises life to myth.

(2)

IN ORDER fully to grasp Broch's attitude, we must briefly consider the philosophy of history that he evolved during the
twenties and that subsequently made its way into the third
volume of *The Sleepwalkers* as one of the chapters on "The
Disintegration of Values."[14] Broch is interested, as we have
noted, in establishing a means of determining the essential
reality of any given historical period, including above all that
of our own modern age. In periods of cultural unity this is a
relatively simple matter, for all ethical decisions are referred
to an accepted central authority. Thus, at the height of the
Middle Ages all human activity could be judged as good or
bad, right or wrong, by appeal to the eternal values handed
down by God and interpreted by the infallible authority of
the church. The individual was confronted with no ethical
dilemmas and hence suffered no moral crises; his life was regulated by a supreme set of values that he accepted unques-
tioningly. But "that criminal and rebellious time called the
Renaissance, that time in which the Christian system of values
was split into a Catholic and a Protestant half," precipitated
the disintegration of values by destroying the original cul-

---

[14] For a historian's view see Robert A. Kann, "Hermann Broch
und die Geschichtsphilosophie," in *Historica*, ed. Hantsch, Voegelin,
and Valsecchi (Vienna, Basel and Freiburg: Herder, 1965), pp.
37-50. Broch's philosophy of history is, of course, not unique; essentially the same theory, from a Catholic viewpoint, can be found in
Romano Guardini, *Das Ende der Neuzeit: Ein Versuch zur Orien-
tierung* (Basel: Hess, 1950).

tural unity.[15] It inaugurated "the process of the five-hundred year dissolution of values" that produced, in place of the former single and total system, many partial systems, each clamoring for recognition and acceptance. This process, as Broch sees it, led to the historical situation at the end of the nineteenth century, to an ethical pluralism that he illustrates by citing such commonplaces as "business is business," "war is war," and "*l'art pour l'art.*"

Modern man is experiencing the end of a historical cycle. Caught between an old system of values that is no longer adequate and a future system that has not yet crystallized, he is suspended in a state of frustration, loneliness, and despair. For the partial systems by which men attempt to live are secular ones. The man who lives according to the maxim "business is business" has no recourse to a higher authority if he encounters a situation that transcends his narrow framework of values. Men do not realize, however, that the source of their anguish is ultimately metaphysical, and that it can be solved only by finding a new system of earthly values that will be adequate for the modern world.

Few men are willing to take upon themselves the full burden of their loneliness and despair, following it to its end, where, according to Broch, a new future will be born. Instead of attempting to create new human values, they seek means of escape. Thus, on the one hand, they seize upon scapegoats, attributing the guilt for the breakdown of values to other human beings—a process not unlike Kafka's "motivation." In other words, they reduce a metaphysical dilemma to a psychological problem. (Similarly, in his later essays on mass psychology Broch explained such phenomena as the persecution of the Jews as examples of this translation of

[15] I quote from the standard one-volume edition of *Die Schlafwandler* published as Vol. II of Broch's *Gesammelte Werke* (Zurich: Rhein); here, p. 510.

anguish into guilt.) On the other hand, they seek solace for their anguish, and in the absence of transcendental beliefs attempt to elevate earthly phenomena to the level of absolutes—a process that Broch calls romanticism. They seek divine redemption in earthly love; they look for divine truth in the pitiful sects into which religion has dwindled with the collapse of a central authority. This flight from reality, however, necessarily involves guilt, for it represents an abjuration of man's basic metaphysical responsibility: that of establishing a new set of earthly values to replace those transcendental values that disappeared in the general breakdown of the old system. (Broch, by the way, devoted the last ten years of his life to precisely this task, the establishing of what he called a human Bill of Duties.) In sum, then, modern man's malaise is basically a metaphysical dilemma. Because he attempts to evade his metaphysical responsibility, man is beset on the psychological level by feelings of guilt. And he multiplies this guilt by assigning it to other human beings, who become his scapegoats, or, in a religious sense, his Antichrist.

The "sleepwalkers" to whom the title of the novel refers are just such men, living between two systems of values or cycles of historical reality. Their lives have been upset by that intrusion of the irrational which Broch often calls "the irruption from below": that is, something has happened to disrupt the smooth and seemingly rational pattern in which they have hitherto lived. They can no longer be sustained by the values of the past or by their present partial systems, and they have not yet discovered a satisfactory substitute or equivalent. To use another key phrase of Broch's, they are suffering the dilemma of "no longer and not yet." Literature, as Broch wrote in his "methodological prospectus" of 1930, "embraces the entire realm of irrational experience, specifically in the boundary area where the irrational manifests itself as deed and becomes capable of expression and representation."[16] In the metaphors of the novel this ambivalent situation is characterized both as "a longing for home"—the nostalgia and regret of the man who looks back upon the unified totality of the past—and as "a longing for the promised land"—the anticipation of a new historical reality in the future.[17] Broch's characters are "sleepwalkers" because they are suspended between two ethical systems or cycles of reality, just as the sleepwalker exists between sleeping and waking, partaking of both and dreaming of a lost past or longing for a still uncertain future.

(3)

IF READERS are sometimes wearied by the pages of theory in Broch's works, it is, ironically enough, those very passages that mean most to him, because they reflect most directly the "epistemological" function of the novel. Although, of course, the work cannot be separated from this epistemological intent, as a novel it is far more vivid and alive than Broch's postulating might lead the reader to believe. Broch has devised three independent yet related plots in order to show how four representative men react to the dilemma posed by the disintegration of values. All are confronted with the same situation of disorder in the world, but each responds to it in a different and characteristic way. *Pasenow or Romanticism* takes place in the year 1888 in Berlin and the surrounding province of Brandenburg, and deals primarily with members of the Prussian nobility. With *Esch or Anarchy* the locale moves to Cologne and Mannheim in 1903, and the leading characters represent the urban proletariat. *Huguenau*

---

[16] This "prospectus" has recently been published by Manfred Durzak, "Die Wandlung des Huguenau-Bildes in Hermann Brochs *Schlafwandlern*," *Wirkendes Wort*, 17 (1967), 41-47.

[17] E.g., *Schlafwandler*, p. 326: "die Sehnsucht nach der Heimat" and "die Sehnsucht nach dem gelobten Lande."

or Objectivity, finally, portrays the bourgeois society of a small town on the Mosel River in the months preceding the November Revolution of 1918.

It is impossible to do justice here to the complexities of these three plots, in which Broch, despite his best intentions, indeed yielded to "the temptation to tell stories." But we can isolate in each case the key elements of the "epistemological" situation. Reduced to its simplest outline, *Pasenow* is the story of a young officer who becomes involved in a love affair with a barmaid. When it becomes necessary for him to marry a girl of his own social class, he enlists the aid of an acquaintance, Eduard von Bertrand, who helps him to make provisions for the barmaid Ruzena. Then, after the brief complications of a love triangle involving Eduard, he finally marries Elisabeth. It is a tribute to Broch's narrative genius that he has succeeded in making a captivating story out of this overworked plot. But the real meaning of the book lies neither in the plot nor in the "psychology" of the characters, but in its imagery, which reflects the values by which they live. In the confused minds of Broch's figures, what thinking there is takes place not in the form of rational thought, but in inchoate images.

Joachim von Pasenow is a "romantic," and not really a very bright one at that. Faced by the chaos of the world (actually a mirror of his own confused mind) he seeks a desperate kind of security by elevating into an absolute the only earthly value he acknowledges: the military code, especially as symbolized by his uniform. Whenever he is confronted by a situation that falls outside his "partial system," he nervously fingers the buttons of his jacket to make sure that he is properly enclosed and insulated against the forces of disorder. He regards as the gravest threat to his existence the possibility of being "dragged down," as he puts it, into civilian life, where his military code is not valid, where he is not protected by his uniform.

Pasenow's "sleepwalking" is characterized by a "longing for home," by his attachment to the solid values of the Prussian aristocracy. (At the same time, his estrangement from his father, who finally threatens to disinherit him, shows the extent to which he has become alienated from that very world.) His attitude is reflected by the "emotional lethargy" (*Trägheit des Gefühls*)[18] that is his dominant trait and that lends to his personality a certain old-fashioned quaintness, but renders him totally unfit to deal with any situation that demands resourcefulness or adaptability. This attitude also accounts for the two large groups of images into which the world, in his mind, is divided. Order and the traditional values are associated with the land, with the estate at home, and specifically and in numerous passages with the cow's stall, the epitome of warmth and security. The opposing images are generated by the city, more specifically by Berlin, and above all—here we recall Franz Biberkopf—by Alexanderplatz, which is mentioned several times in the first volume as the sinister heart of the city's chaos. Almost all the other images and values in the book can be traced back to this initial dichotomy of order and disorder, country and city.

Ruzena, the barmaid, is a girl of the city; with her black hair—a symbol of erotic desire—she represents the city with all its chaotic attractions and temptations. Joachim can lose himself in her embraces, but at the same time he realizes that by succumbing to her he is losing touch with everything that he treasures, that he is being "dragged down" into civilian life. The blond Elisabeth, by contrast, becomes in his eyes a symbol of divine womanhood; he always sees her "on her silver cloud," and finds it impossible to contemplate anything

[18] Unfortunately this leitmotif and others are not rendered with any consistency in the English translation.

so gross as sexual intercourse with her. When Joachim abandons Ruzena, he attempts to make amends by setting her up in business in a laceshop. But the language of the images makes it clear that he is really trying to rescue her from the chaos of the city: "lace" is one of the chief symbols attached to Elisabeth and her chaste world of order. The black hair, on the other hand, is the first characteristic of Ruzena that is mentioned in the novel. So when we catch our last glimpse of Joachim—it is on his wedding night—lying fully dressed beside his bride, nervously straightening his *uniform* jacket when it falls open to reveal his *black* trousers, we understand through the symbols why he has become impotent: his code of behavior is simply not flexible enough to handle the intrusion of sex into his world of light and order; he is unable to see through his romantic glorification of Elisabeth and to treat her as a woman. For Joachim the marriage does not signify the union of two individuals, but rather "salvation from the filth and swamp and a promise of devotion on the way to God."[19]

If Joachim's reaction represents a flight from disorder into a naïvely romantic glorification of earthly things, the case is just the opposite with the second major figure in the first volume. Eduard von Bertrand is a former officer who has done the unheard of: he has forsaken his uniform for the world of business. For that reason Joachim regards him with suspicion, distrust, and even hostility; he tends, in Broch's terms, to project the blame for his metaphysical anguish onto Bertrand and hold him somehow responsible for the disorderly state of the world. Joachim's worst suspicions are confirmed when he discovers that one of Bertrand's business representatives has his office on, of all places, Alexanderplatz. But through his knowledge of the world and his shrewd realism, Bertrand is able to be of service to Joachim on various occasions—

[19] *Schlafwandler*, p. 162.

particularly with regard to Ruzena, who belongs to his disorderly world.

Yet Bertrand's position is ultimately as tenuous as Joachim's romanticism. He is not restricted, to be sure, by the bonds of the past; he regards dueling and the whole military code as ridiculous. But in contrast to the later "value-free" man, Bertrand has merely *denied* the values of his world, not destroyed them. He can look at the world with a high degree of objectivity. But because he stands above the world, in a state of aesthetic detachment, rather than in it, because he is not committed to the world, he is equally a victim of the dilemma of the sleepwalkers. Further, because he is too objective to accept the existing values and yet intelligent enough to realize that they have not been replaced by better ones, he is the loneliest figure in the whole novel. For him there is not even the consolation of romantic glorification that remains for Joachim. For this reason Broch wrote, in his "methodological prospectus," that Bertrand must be regarded as the chief symbol and "the actual hero of the entire novel." "If his destiny symbolizes on a higher level the totality of the novel, that is, the fiasco of the old value attitudes, at the same time his person, in its form, is a symbol of the growth of the dark and dreamlike element that permeates the action more clearly in each of the three parts."

Bertrand is the only figure who connects the first part of the trilogy with the second; but although we hear of him in the second volume, he never actually appears in the action. He is the owner of the shipping company that employs August Esch. Esch, at large in the "anarchy" of modern pluralism, no longer clings like Pasenow and the representatives of his generation to outmoded values. In contrast to Pasenow's "emotional lethargy," Esch is a "man of impetuosity" (*ein Mensch impetuoser Haltungen*) whose behavior is not controlled even by the conventions that consoled Pase-

The Sleepwalkers

now. Like Franz Biberkopf, Esch longs above all for order and "decency" in the world. Like Biberkopf also, he constantly seeks to avoid the problems of an unpleasant reality, preferring instead to turn away and ignore them. (It is no accident that he dies, in Volume Three, by being stabbed in the back.) Esch, then, does not turn to the past like Pasenow, but neither does he face reality; looking to the future, he is a sleepwalker with "a longing for the promised land." Appropriately, his symbol is not the military uniform of the past, but a reproduction of the Statue of Liberty which represents in his mind the promise of a new future in America. (Broch has created here one of the most striking literary mythifications of the European emigrant mentality.)

Esch, when we meet him in 1903, has always lived by the down-to-earth motto of "business is business." He is an accountant, and in his profession that partial system of values has always worked quite satisfactorily. Then one day he is fired from his job in a wholesale wine company. Esch knows that he has made no mistakes in his books. He was dismissed, he discovers, in order to cover up the embezzlement of his superior, Nentwig; he has been punished for another man's guilt. Confronted for the first time with an irrational experience that has no place in his system of debits and credits, Esch elevates his bookkeeping to a cosmic level: every wrong must be canceled out by a right if order is to be preserved. The whole motion of the book is generated by Esch's confused attempts to reestablish the cosmic harmony. Thus when he meets Ilona, the partner of a knife-thrower in a burlesque act, he sees her as a symbol of the divine who must suffer crucifixion every night because of the unexpiated guilt in the world. "Without order in the accounts there was also no order in the world, and as long as there was no order, Ilona would continue to be exposed to the knives,

151

Nentwig would continue, insolent and hypocritical, to escape his penance."[20]

Esch, like Pasenow, is torn between two women, but his mind, with its longing for the promised land, forces him to make precisely the opposite choice. In his world it is Ilona, with all her associations with crucifixion, who represents the spiritualization of love and an innocence that must be left unsullied. So Esch turns to Mother Hentjen, who offers simple forgetfulness in erotic union. At the same time, however, he has worked it out in his confused mind that by marrying Mother Hentjen, who is seven years older than he, he will be sacrificing himself in order to redeem Ilona; then he will emigrate with Mother Hentjen to America, his secularized version of the promised land.

Matters stand at this point when Esch learns by chance that Eduard von Bertrand, the owner of the shipping company where he has just gotten a job as paymaster, is a homosexual. Suddenly everything falls into a pattern that Esch's confused religious mind can understand: Bertrand is the Antichrist, and his homosexuality is the initial offense that disrupted the cosmic order. By murdering Bertrand, Esch reasons, he can straighten out the cosmic accounts once again. Esch undertakes a journey to Bertrand's estate but fails to meet him in person: instead, he has a dreamlike interview with Bertrand, in which the latter convinces him that the salvation he seeks cannot proceed from death, but can come about only through birth and new life. This explanation gives Esch a new motive for marrying Mother Hentjen, one that appeals to his mystical mentality. Perhaps, he vaguely speculates, their union will produce the child who will proclaim the new age. And shortly after his return, Esch learns that Bertrand has committed suicide, an act that seemingly sets the cosmic accounts in order.

[20] *Schlafwandler*, p. 231.

The Sleepwalkers

Esch's vision in Bertrand's garden is the high point of the second volume; reality is not so gratifying. Mother Hentjen is sterile and no child is forthcoming, a turn of events as ironic in its implications as the announcement that Joachim, after his impotent wedding night, "nevertheless" has a child after eighteen months. Moreover, a swindler cheats Esch and his friends out of the money with which he had planned to make the trip to America. Realizing sadly that his ideal cannot be actualized in this world, Esch takes a new job as an accountant and settles down with Mother Hentjen—with no redeemer, with no promised land.

In the last volume Esch and Pasenow have both ended up in a little village on the Mosel. Pasenow is military commandant of the town, and Esch has become owner and editor of the local newspaper. Characteristically, the obscure religious impulse that was latent in both men in the earlier volumes has here come to the fore. No longer able to find solace in their respective kinds of love, they find a common meeting ground in a religious sect whose meetings they attend. The harmony of the village is disrupted when Wilhelm Huguenau arrives on the scene. Huguenau's objectivism, his complete break with the values of the past, is symbolized by his desertion from the army. During the six months before the November Revolution he is a totally liberated or "value-free" man, bound in no way by old standards.

Broch does not imply that Huguenau is an admirable man; far from it. Many of his actions are contemptible. Yet Broch calls him "the adequate child of his time,"[21] because he represents, during this six-month suspension of all systems of value that is repeatedly called "a vacation," the approach that is necessary to overcome the useless ideals of the past. For revolutions represent the release of irrational forces when all the restraints of value systems have disappeared, and the

[21] *Briefe*, p. 26: "das adäquate Kind seiner Zeit."

value-free man is its tool. Huguenau thus becomes, in a meta-physical sense, "the avenger of the guilt" of Esch and Pasenow.[22] Both men have become guilty by refusing to establish new earthly values: Pasenow by clinging to the values of the past, and Esch by retreating into eroticism and religious sectarianism. (The more clear-sighted Bertrand, of course, has already conceded the guilt of his aesthetic position by committing suicide in Volume Two.)

Huguenau's freewheeling attitude makes it possible for him to arrive in town a penniless deserter, and within a short time to become a leading citizen. He swindles Esch out of his newspaper, and bullies Pasenow into submission so that the commandant will not report him as a deserter. During the revolution he murders Esch by stabbing him in the back, and rapes Mother Hentjen. When the revolution is over, Pasenow and Esch are dead; irrationalism has swept away all remnants of the past, and the world is ready for the creation of a new society, a new system of values. But Huguenau is not the man for this new world. At the end of the novel he too slips back into a handy partial system of business ethics in another town. He has been as much a "sleepwalker" as the others because he has lived totally without values between two cycles of reality, ruled wholly by the forces of the irrational, or the revolution.

If we pause to look back, we see that Broch has used the same technique in each plot. Broch once wrote that "Either poetry is able to proceed to myth, or it goes bankrupt."[23] By tracing commonplace psychological situations back to their metaphysical origins, Broch has succeeded in raising them to a mythic level. He has done this three times, showing the archetypal structure underlying a young officer's romance and

[22] Letter of April 10, 1930; *Briefe*, p. 18.

[23] In the English essay "The Style of the Mythical Age" (1947); *Essays I*, p. 263.

subsequence impotence; the European emigrant mentality; and the ruthlessness of the military deserter in the postwar revolution.

(4)

OUR SKETCHY outline of the plots of the trilogy has focused exclusively on the "epistemological" meaning of the leading figures, at the expense of the strong narrative and rich poetic texture of the work. Although each of the three parts is an independent and integral whole, the trilogy still constitutes a narrative entity that is unified by a complex variety of parallels, symbols, images, and leitmotifs.

As far as its external structure is concerned, Broch's novel is as scientifically devised as a *roman expérimental* in Zola's strictest sense. For purposes of control his heroes are all the same age—thirty years old—and the action in each part lasts for exactly six months, from spring to fall of the years 1888, 1903, and 1918, respectively. At the beginning of each section the partial system of values by which the hero has lived is disrupted. And each protagonist's position is defined by his attitudes toward two women.

But the conditions in each experiment—historical, geographical, and social—vary considerably. First, there is a fifteen-year lag between episodes. *Pasenow* takes place at a time when, historically, the crisis of values had not yet manifested itself openly; it is set in that period of buoyant self-confidence that the Germans know as the *Gründerzeit*: the successful and energetic youth of the Empire. By contrast, Esch wanders through the confused world of the turn of the century, when workers' revolts and assassinations already marred the apparent peace of the Wilhelmine era. Huguenau, finally, emerges during the revolutionary period that marked the end of World War One in Germany, a time when the old systems were publicly collapsing. Second, the movement in the trilogy from Prussia through the Rhineland to the Mosel valley represents a symbolic progression from Eastern romantic mysticism to Western rationalism—a conceit that would not have been lost upon Thomas Mann, who used a similar geographical symbolism in *The Magic Mountain*. Third, the temporal and geographical development of the trilogy is paralleled by the social shift from the vanishing Prussian aristocracy through the emergent proletariat to the bourgeoisie of the third part.

In all three parts, sex—or, more aptly, sexual inadequacy—functions as a symbol of man's response to reality. Pasenow becomes impotent on his wedding night because he is unable to overcome his romantic glorification of Elisabeth and to confront her realistically as a woman. Esch hurls himself into sexual intercourse with total abandon in an attempt to forget the disorders of the world and his disappointment at the loss of the promised land. The sterility of Bertrand's aesthetic position is represented by his homosexuality: in Volume One he falls in love with Elisabeth because of her "boyish" characteristics, and by the time Esch hears of him, fifteen years later, he is involved in affairs with the sailors on his Rhine yacht. (It is implied, moreover, that his suicide is motivated in part by a threat of blackmail.) Huguenau is equally unable to master sex in a meaningful way. He goes to the brothel once a week for hygienic reasons; his only access to Mother Hentjen is by rape (just as he overcomes Esch by murder); and the only female with whom he has any rapport is the child Marguerite, who is still too young to fulfill any sexual desires. In this consciously structured work it is, of course, no accident that Huguenau is caught between the "no longer and not yet" of two females who are, respectively, twenty-two years older and younger than he: they are representatives of the past that he must violate and of the future that he cannot hope to obtain. (After his six-

The Sleepwalkers

month "vacation" Huguenau does, by the way, get married and have children.)

The three volumes are interrelated by a variety of means. As far as plot is concerned, there is little connection: Ruzena is once mentioned briefly in Volume Two, and Bertrand hovers in the background of the action throughout. In Volume Three both Pasenow and Esch provide links with the past. But the language of imagery and leitmotif supplies many links. Pasenow is consistently characterized by his "emotional lethargy," while Esch is identified by the "impetuosity" with which he responds to the anarchic world about him. Bertrand's disengagement is signified in the first volume by the "deprecatory gesture" with which he tends to dismiss romantic attitudes. This gesture leads a life of its own: Pasenow picks it up from Bertrand; and in Volume Two the vision of Bertrand remains so vivid that even Esch adopts this motion. In Volume Three, though Bertrand is already dead, the gesture lives on until it is assumed, finally, by Huguenau.

The symbol of the uniform, which is central to Volume One, figures in the other parts as well, but it is degraded and "de-romanticized" to correspond to the milieu. Thus the customs inspector, Korn, who is not perturbed by the disorder that so disturbs Esch, struts through Volume Two in the confident authority of his uniform. (Like Pasenow fifteen years before, Korn finds it shocking that Bertrand had given up his officer's uniform.) Similarly, the members of the Salvation Army, who find an illusion of stability in their sectarianism, wear uniforms in Volume Three. Conversely, the shattering of reality is signified by loss of uniform, as in the case of the emotionally troubled patients of the military hospital in Volume Three.

In all three parts, travel is a symbol of escape from present reality and disorder. Pasenow's "longing for home" and for the past is mirrored, in the first volume, by his dreams of India—traditionally the symbol of the mystical Orient in German romanticism. Esch does not travel far, but his vague aspirations toward the promised land are manifested in his specific wish to emigrate to America and are symbolized by the miniature reproduction of the Statue of Liberty that he cherishes. Bertrand's business takes him all over the world, both to India and to America; but in his eyes these places do not have the mystical meaning that they assume for Pasenow and Esch. They represent no more than a promising opportunity for future business investments. Yet because Bertrand never completely succeeds in freeing himself from the past, he returns to Germany and dies there. Huguenau does not undertake any long voyages; he sneers contemptuously at the Statue of Liberty that Esch still retains from his years in Cologne and Mannheim. But his desertion from the army on the western front symbolizes a more extreme inner break with the past than even Bertrand's globe-trotting.

These conspicuous leitmotifs and symbols, along with many others that recur through all three volumes, give the trilogy as a whole a consistent texture and contribute to the effect of totality that Broch was anxious to achieve.[24] But they are enforced even on the stylistic level by an elaborate rhetoric of imagery that reflects the meanings of the book. For instance, images of cold and paralysis are constantly used to express the sense of loneliness that obsesses the characters and the breakdown that epitomizes the modern world. Thus Joachim longs for the warmth of the cow's stall when the icy threat of alienation makes itself most strongly felt. And the theme of a disintegrated world runs through the images of the novel, from the description of Joachim's old father, who hobbles with his cane "a little like a dog running on three legs,"

---

[24] See, for instance, the discussion of park, castle, Cross, etc., in Mandelkow, *op.cit.*, pp. 119ff.

all the way to the wounded veteran in the military hospital in part three, whose left arm has been amputated and who is keenly conscious of his "asymmetry" as a man.[25]

In his "methodological prospectus" Broch spoke of the "choreographic symmetry" that dominates the book: it is expressed "not least in the style, which is determined in turn by the three temporal epochs." *Pasenow* is written in subtle parody of late-nineteenth-century fiction: essentially the same plot occurs in stories and novels by such writers as Arthur Schnitzler and Theodor Fontane, a fact that the first critics, in their attempts to categorize Broch's work, were quick to notice. But the critics failed to realize how cunningly Broch has transformed the style in his work. Through a careful and consistent use of point of view he has excluded himself as narrator from the story, relating the entire action through various shifting focuses. The novel opens with the following description of Joachim's father:

> In the year 1888 Herr von Pasenow was seventy years old, and there were people who felt an extraordinary and inexplicable sense of repulsion when they saw him coming toward them in the streets of Berlin, indeed, who in their dislike actually maintained that he must be an evil old man. . . . When he gazed in the mirror he recognized there the face that had returned his gaze fifty years before. Yet though Herr von Pasenow was not dissatisfied with himself, there are people to whom the looks of this old man are displeasing, and who can also not comprehend how any woman could ever have looked upon him or embraced him with desire in her eyes; and at most they will concede him only the Polish maids on his estate in the be-

[25] Peter Collins, "Hermann Broch's Trilogy *Die Schlafwandler*: A Study of the Concept of Sleepwalking" (Dissertation: University of Sydney, Australia, 1967), contains the finest and most exhaustive analysis of Broch's imagery.

lief that even these he must have approached with that slightly hysterical and yet arrogant aggressiveness which is often characteristic of small men. Whether this was true or not, it was the opinion of his two sons, and it goes without saying that he did not share it.

This passage gives us a large amount of narrative information, but when we examine it closely we find that there is no narrative voice with which we can identify, as in traditional novels.[26] Although the paragraph contains certain statements of simple fact, every statement involving any sort of ethical judgment is conditioned by the intrusion of a limited personal subject: "there were people who"; "when he gazed in the mirror"; "there are people to whom"; "they will concede"; "it was the opinion of his two sons." The figure of the traditional narrator, which we still find present in *The Magic Mountain*, has vanished. But in place of the total objectivity achieved through the montage technique of *Berlin Alexanderplatz*, we are confronted instead with a multiplicity of subjective points of view. These are intended to reflect stylistically the pluralism of values rampant in the age. What we have in this first part, then, is a relatively simple and conventional plot related from many points of view.

In *Esch* the process is reversed. The plot, which in mood, milieu, and character bears such a strong resemblance to *Berlin Alexanderplatz* that it again suggests a conscious parody, is a relatively complicated one (and far more elaborate than our synopsis indicates). But the entire narrative

---

[26] See Richard Brinkmann, "Romanform und Werttheorie bei Hermann Broch: Strukturprobleme moderner Dichtung," *Deutsche Vierteljahresschrift*, 31 (1957), 169-97; and Rolf Geissler, "Hermann Broch: *Die Schlafwandler*," in *Möglichkeiten des modernen Romans*, ed. Rolf Geissler (Frankfurt am Main, Berlin, and Bonn: Moritz Diesterweg, 1962), pp. 102-60, has particularly good interpretations of the first two volumes of the trilogy.

here is filtered, as in Kafka's novels, through the consciousness of the hero. The style ranges from sober narrative through hectic expressionistic prose to high pitches of lyricism; but the vision of the world is carefully controlled by its constant reference to the values which rule the confused mind of August Esch. The style of *Pasenow*, then, reflects emergent pluralism, while *Esch* depicts a pluralism so far advanced that the individual clings desperately to his own limited, partial system of values.

In *Huguenau*, finally, the total disintegration of reality is represented by a radical breakdown of style and form. Since Huguenau, the "value-free" man, has no ethical point of view of his own, we do not see the world through his eyes. Instead, the lyric, dramatic, narrative, and essayistic elements that were still intermingled in the prose of *Esch* have been separated into individual strands and occur in separate chapters. The reality of the world presents itself to us, the readers, in the form in which it occurs, without the intervention of a central filtering intelligence. But in order to understand this development we must consider briefly the genesis of the novel.

(5)

BROCH began work on his novel in 1928. There is much reason to believe that he first wrote *Huguenau*, only subsequently adding *Pasenow* and *Esch* in order to supply backgrounds for the other two main figures of the third volume.[27] (In

---

[27] I first suggested this thesis, after a careful examination of the manuscripts, in my article "Zur Entstehung und Struktur von Hermann Brochs *Schlafwandlern*," *Deutsche Vierteljahresschrift*, 38 (1964), 40-69; and the evidence has been accepted as plausible by many Broch scholars. The point is of interest, but of no great significance for the interpretation of the completed trilogy. However, since Manfred Durzak has repeatedly disagreed with me, I should like to take this opportunity to answer his objections.

It is primarily internal evidence that suggests that a version of

Hermann Broch

1929 Broch still intended to call the whole work *Huguenau*, after its most representative hero.) By the time the Rhein Verlag accepted the work for publication in 1930, it existed in three manuscripts of roughly one hundred and fifty pages each. How are we to explain the fact that the novel as pub-

---

Huguenau was written first. The Yale University Library has manuscripts of all three parts dating from 1930; that of *Huguenau* has 150 pages. In addition, there is another MS of *Huguenau* from a different period of composition; since it is much shorter (101 pages) and since it includes corrections in ink that were incorporated in the 150-page MS, logic would suggest that the shorter, less complete version *preceded* the longer, clean copy. (Durzak argues, for reasons that elude me, that it must follow.) Moreover, there are no extant MSS of *Pasenow* and *Esch* from this same stage of composition. They might have been lost, as Durzak suggests; but in the light of Broch's original intention to call the novel *Huguenau* it does not seem illogical to assume that the extant 101-page MS does indeed represent the original conception.

Durzak chooses to ignore logic and textual evidence. Instead he has assailed me with external "facts." Thus, in an article on "Hermann Broch und James Joyce; Zur Ästhetik des modernen Romans," *Deutsche Vierteljahresschrift*, 40 (1966), 419-20, he quotes a recent letter from Broch's publisher Brody, who calls my theory "nonsense" because the manuscript that he purchased in 1930 contained "only a few typed pages" for *Huguenau*, "which grew during the course of type-setting." Mr. Brody reminds me of the man who denied that the sun was in the East at dawn because it was directly overhead when he got up at noon. Brody had not even heard of Broch until 1930; he has no idea what was going on in 1928, and his evidence is in no way authoritative. Moreover, Brody's memory regarding 1930 is not accurate. On January 14, 1931, when Broch was debating the legality of the situation with Brody (*Briefe*, p. 43), the author conceded that the Rhein Verlag had "bought the book in its old version." He goes on to speak of "its present intermediate stage with the interpolated four new chapters." If we take away these four chapters (which are clearly indicated in the Yale manuscript), we are left not with a brief epilogue of a few pages, but with the 150-page version of *Huguenau*.

In the same place Durzak quotes a recollection of Frank Thiess, written in 1951, in which Thiess says that he had the good fortune to read *Pasenow* in 1929. Why not? But this does not refute the fact

lished in three volumes in 1931 and 1932 comprised some six hundred and fifty pages? *Pasenow* was printed in a form rather close to that of the manuscript handed to the publisher in 1930. *Esch* grew by about fifty pages during the process of revision and polishing—what Broch, with a grim irony that must have enraged his publisher, called "the catastrophic *Esch*-proofs."[28] But the fascinating story is that of the manuscript of *Huguenau*, which grew in only a year from one hundred and fifty to over five hundred pages.

Up to this point we have discussed the novel as it existed before that tumefaction: for the plots of the three parts remained unchanged through all this. In other words, the *epistemological basis* of the novel remained constant from its inception in 1928 to its completion in 1932. But the outer structure of Volume Three was altered radically during the

---

that a letter from Broch to Thiess *in 1929* (*Briefe*, p. 13) clearly indicates that Broch had sent him *Huguenau* for perusal. Finally, I mentioned in my article the fact that one of the pages of what I consider to be the original MS of *Huguenau* is typed on the back of an unfinished letter dated August 16, 1928. Durzak, in his Rowohlt biography, p. 63, informs me that the paper bears the letterhead not of Broch, but of his friend George Saiko. I have eyes; I saw Saiko's name. But the fact of the name strikes me as totally irrelevant. What matters is the incontrovertible fact of the date: August 16, 1928. Again, common sense argues that this sheet of paper was probably used rather soon after the letter was discarded: that is, in 1928. I find it far more difficult to accept Durzak's reasoning that an unfinished letter managed to avoid the wastebasket for more than two years before Broch accidentally used it for writing paper.

In conclusion, Durzak has not succeeded in convincing me of his assessment of the facts that he is so indefatigable in collecting. In the meantime, two persons who were in at least as favorable a position as Thiess and Brody have confirmed my original conjecture. The matter will probably never be settled—certainly not to Mr. Durzak's satisfaction. But there is still much reason to believe, as I suggest here, that Broch first wrote a version of his *Huguenau* before going on—or back—to *Pasenow* and *Esch*.

[28] *Briefe*, p. 46.

final months of composition. In addition to the Huguenau
plot, Volume Three also contains a number of seemingly unrelated elements: parallel plots, essays, poems, and so forth.
Broch's working manuscript of this third part is an incredible
jumble. Entire chapters have been added; pages have been
cut out and fold-in pages attached; there are corrections
and additions in the margins and on the backs of the pages in
inks of various colors. But the manuscript, along with the letters that Broch wrote during those crucial months, tells a fascinating story of the process of artistic integration. It is worth
recounting.[29]

On September 27, 1930, when he had begun revising his
150-page manuscript for publication, Broch wrote: "Now
I've worked my way so completely into Huguenau that I
could make a novel of 300 pages out of it. I must continually
apply the brakes so that it won't get too big."[30] By January
1931, Broch had added only four chapters: the ones dealing
with the child Marguerite and hence belonging more or less
intrinsically to the Huguenau plot. But by June 5 of that
same year the volume had, as Broch wrote in astonishment,
"swollen to 300 pages and become increasingly complicated
in its architecture."[31] In addition to the Huguenau plot, the
manuscript now included a number of parallel plots dealing
with doctors and patients from the military hospital in the
Mosel village and with Hanna Wendling, a young woman
who also lives in the town.

It is easy to understand Broch's reasons for making these
additions, for these subsidiary characters reflect far more
drastically than do the main protagonists the malady of the
age. Thus, one of the independent narrative strands deals

[29] This process is elucidated in greater detail in my essay "Zur Entstehung und Struktur," cited in note 27.

[30] *Briefe*, p. 31.

[31] *Briefe*, p. 54.

with the shell-shocked veteran Ludwig Gödicke, who must laboriously reconstruct his personality out of the disparate elements that he finds in his consciousness when he awakes from his coma. (This particular strand, one of Broch's most powerful narratives, closely resembles the passages in *Berlin Alexanderplatz* dealing with Franz Biberkopf's catatonic stupor in the sanatorium at Buch.) The spiritual imbalance of the age is personified by the wounded Lieutenant Jaretzki, an architect by profession (that is, a symbol of perfect proportion), who has lost an arm and must now get accustomed to an artificial limb, that is, to his own lack of physical symmetry. And the progressive stages of loneliness are shown by the story of Hanna Wendling, who is gradually alienated from her husband while he is away at the eastern front. This subplot, which constitutes an independent novella, was first written in its entirety and then introduced into the Huguenau plot piece by piece. Broch has found here a vivid metaphor for the "irruption of the irrational": an intruder breaks into Hanna Wendling's house at night and precipitates her anxiety.

If we go on to ask why Broch undertook this rather startling revision, we find a clue in that same letter of September 27, 1930 in which he originally announced the temptation to expand his novel: "Have you already read the new Dos Passos? He's no Joyce, but he writes with virtuosity." Indeed, the method used by Dos Passos in his novels (*Manhattan Transfer*, 1925, and *The 42nd Parallel*, 1930) corresponds precisely to "the additive technique"[32] that Broch chose for the expansion of *Huguenau*: in both cases we find a series of independent, parallel narratives that are only occasionally brought together into a loose connection. Later Broch did not think so highly of the novels of the American writer; but the technique he uses at this stage of composition

[32] *Briefe*, p. 67.

is, in fact, nothing more than what he later called "the broad-
ening of the old naturalistic novel through such new techniques as the continental cross-slices of Dos Passos,"[33] and
the result was far closer to *Manhattan Transfer* than was
Berlin Alexanderplatz. During the months when Broch was
adding the parallel episodes to his original plot it is appropriate to speak of literary influence in the most direct sense.

However, his reservations regarding Dos Passos, specifically what he considered his lack of "intellectualization," soon
made themselves felt.[34] On June 18, 1931, Broch thought
that his novel was finished and wrote to his publisher that
"only a few pages are still needed—very difficult ones,
though." He promised the manuscript "in a few days."[35] But
the few days became six months, and the few pages turned
out to be more like two hundred. Just as his publisher was
daring to hope that he might at last begin to print the volume
he had purchased more than a year before, a new tone of
excitement suddenly injects itself into Broch's letters. He begins calling his book "a novum" and now, for the first time,
he is able to describe the work in what we know as its final
form. "The book consists of a series of stories that all represent variations on the same theme, namely, the relegation of
man back into loneliness."[36] This much we know already, of
course. But Broch continues: "they rise out of the totally
irrational (the story of the girl from the Salvation Army)
all the way to the complete rationality of the theoretical (Dis-

[33] In the essay "Das Weltbild des Romans" (1933); *Essays I*, p.
237.

[34] Specifically, Broch says that Dos Passos' novels remain "in the
empirical" and are not "durchgeistigt"; *Briefe*, p. 54. Broch was not
the only German writer to be influenced by the American. The study
of Dos Passos' impact on German fiction, which still remains to be
written, will also have to consider Döblin and the postwar novelist
Wolfgang Koeppen.

[35] *Briefe*, pp. 54-55.   [36] *Briefe*, p. 57.

integration of Values). Between these two poles the other stories take place on graduated intermediate levels of rationality." From this time until the book was finally completed in January 1932, a second stage of revision and expansion took place. But whereas the first stage was suggested by the additive technique of Dos Passos, the second is an attempt to integrate the whole once again by the inclusion of two entirely new elements: ten chapters of an essay on "The Disintegration of Values" and sixteen lyrical chapters of "The Story of the Salvation Army Girl from Berlin."

In order to compensate for the looseness of the additive construction, Broch decided to introduce into his novel the figure of the narrator who is writing the novel: the "I" of "The Story of the Salvation Army Girl." Broch had originally turned from philosophy to literature because he had concluded that literature was the only area in which subjectivity was "radically legitimate." Never a man to shy away from the consequences of consistency, Broch now put this very subjectivity into the novel itself. His narrator, who in the first stages of the manuscript is nameless, later gets the name Bertrand Müller. It is clear that the name is no accident; as one critic has noted, Bertrand is his *fore*name in more than one sense.[37] Like Eduard von Bertrand, this narrator is also an aesthete who suffers intolerably from his inability to come to grips with the reality of the Berlin, where he sits in his lonely room and writes.

In a lyrical language that in five of the sixteen chapters rises to pure poetry (that is, pure subjectivity), Bertrand Müller tells the story of a love affair between Marie, the girl

[37] Cohn, *op.cit.*, p. 63. In Broch criticism one of the main arguments revolves around the question of Bertrand Müller's relationship to Eduard von Bertrand. Are they physically identical? Are they symbolically identical? Or is there really no close connection between the positions that they represent?

from the Salvation Army, and the Jew Nuchem. The disquisition on the philosophy of history makes it clear that the Salvation Army and Judaism represent extreme symbolic positions in Broch's thought. The Jew is "the most progressive man," the most radical example of modern man, because he has most consistently created an absolute from his earthly activity with no reference to transcendental authority. The Salvation Army, by contrast, attempts once more to centralize all values under a higher authority, very much in the fashion of the medieval Catholic Church. The love affair between Nuchem and Marie is doomed to failure because they are unable to overcome their respective positions sufficiently to achieve any lasting unity. Thus they represent, in a narrative strand totally unrelated to the other action of the novel, the most extreme cases of human alienation.

But more: they reveal more clearly than anything else the precarious position of the author, Bertrand Müller. For he had been able to achieve at least the illusion of meaningfulness by rendering the stories of his other characters in an aesthetically and epistemologically satisfying form: Pasenow, Esch, and Huguenau, after all, were his creatures, and he could shape their lives as he wished. But the futility of his position, in reality, is brought home to Bertrand Müller when he finally realizes that he is powerless to help Nuchem and Marie. "For even Nuchem and Marie are alien to me, they to whom my last hope was devoted, the hope that they might be my creations, the unfulfillable sweet hope that I had taken their destiny in hand in order to determine it. Nuchem and Marie, they are not my creations and never were. Illusory hope of being able to form the world!"[38] The high point of Bertrand Müller's own anguish manifests itself in the poem in which he apostrophizes himself and his whole generation

[38] *Schlafwandler,* pp. 590-91.

as spiritual heirs of the accursed wanderer Ahasverus.[39] (This poem is, of course, yet another variation on the theme of escape through travel that we noted above.) Thus Bertrand Müller illustrates in his own person the anguish of his characters and the impossibility of any true understanding in an age that lies between the breakdown of one ethical system and the birth of the next. The sole consolation that he can offer to modern man, suspended between cycles of reality, is the thought of human solidarity implicit in the words of the Apostle Paul with which the novel ends: "Do thyself no harm: for we are all here" (Acts 16:28). Yet despite his disillusionment, Müller still represents the unifying consciousness that connects not only the diversified strands of the *Huguenau* volume but, by implication, all three volumes of the trilogy.

Again we should pause to note the literary source of this device: André Gide.[40] In August 1931, just at the time he was making that crucial change, Broch mentioned Gide several times in his letters. For the organizing principle of *The Counterfeiters*, a novel that Broch read during this period and greatly admired, is also that of an author who integrates the various strands of his narrative by commenting upon and interpreting them as they occur. Broch felt the need for a sovereign subject in Gide's sense, in order to combat the centrifugal tendencies of the many parallel plots. The notion was implicit, of course, in his own theory of literature. But the specific technical means was surely suggested by Gide, of

[39] Cohn, *op.cit.*, pp. 103-36, has the only extensive analysis of this poem, hitherto largely ignored by critics of the novel. Regarding Bertrand Müller's despair see Paul Konrad Kurz, "Hermann Brochs 'Schlafwandler'-Trilogie als zeitkritischer Erlösungsroman," *Über moderne Literatur: Standorte und Deutungen* (Frankfurt am Main: Joseph Knecht, 1967), pp. 129-57.

[40] In this connection see Mandelkow, *op.cit.*, pp. 37ff. and pp. 49ff.

whom Broch had remarked that he was the only writer besides Joyce with whom he felt a real affinity.[41]

But even with the introduction of a fictional subject who organizes the entire narrative, the novel was not yet complete. It still lacked the one element that would round it out completely by balancing the pure subjectivity of the lyric. And so, within a matter of weeks and while he was still writing the chapters of "The Story of the Salvation Army Girl," Broch began incorporating into his novel, as its final element, an example of pure rationality: a series of essays on "The Disintegration of Values," of which Bertrand Müller is likewise said to be the author. The circle has been completed. The failure of philosophy had sent Broch originally to literature; now, at the last stage of composition, literature returned Broch once more to philosophy.

(6)

BROCH had been working on his theory of values for many years by this time;[42] it is important, for proper emphasis, to keep in mind the fact that he continued to think out his theory during the very years in which he was writing his novel. What he had to do, therefore, was to take a mass of material that was already in existence and prepare it in a form suitable for the novel. For the ten chapters on "The Disintegration of Values" are not only written in clear counterpoint to "The Story of the Salvation Army Girl"; they also draw their examples from incidents that occur in the various plots of the novel.

Broch's philosophy of history, which we discussed above, appears as Chapter 7 of "The Disintegration of Values": "Historical Digression." To see, in conclusion, how Broch in-

[41] Letter of October 17, 1930; *Briefe*, p. 35.
[42] See Sidonie Cassirer, "Hermann Broch's Early Writings," *PMLA*, 75 (1960), 453-62.

troduces the theory of his novel into the novel itself, let us examine briefly the three theses of the "Epistemological Digression" that constitutes Chapter 9 of "The Disintegration of Values."[43] According to Broch's first thesis, "history is composed of values, since life can be comprehended only in the category of value—yet these values cannot be introduced into reality as absolutes, but can only be thought of in reference to an ethically-motivated value-positing subject." Through this cumbersome language, so unlike the vigorous style of the narrative, we perceive a theoretical justification of the stylistic technique of Volume One, where every value judgment was linked, as we saw, to a "value-positing subject." The second thesis goes on to define the value-positing subject more closely: it cannot be imagined concretely, but "only in the isolation of its selfhood." At this point Broch is no longer talking about the individual stylistic subjects of the first part, but about the more general "value-positing subject" of the entire novel, Bertrand Müller. In order to determine the precise relationship between these two sets of subjects, we must look at Broch's third thesis, which concludes that the entire world is "a product of the intelligible Self."

We have, in other words, a relative reality that we can experience indirectly and an intelligible self that, existing in its isolation, cannot be experienced. How, then, can we come to know this reality? That is where the value-positing subjects of Volume One come in. The world is what Broch calls "a relative organization," since it is produced not directly but only mediately, by the intelligible self. The intelligible self then posits other value-making subjects (the stylistic subjects of part one, for instance), "which in their turn reflect the structure of the intelligible self and fashion their own value-products, their own world formations." These intermediate

[43] *Schlafwandler*, pp. 592-98. In this connection see Erich Kahler, *Die Philosophie von Hermann Broch* (Tübingen: J.C.B. Mohr, 1962).

value-subjects, then, play an immensely important double role. As we have seen in our analyses, they relativize the reality perceived in the novel, for every value judgment is linked to one of their innumerable points of view. We do not, in other words, see reality directly: we see it only through the eyes of Pasenow, of Esch, of "the people who." And at the same time all these points of view reflect, in their multiplicity, the structure of the intelligible self.

This last function comes rather as a surprise, for up to this moment in the novel—within fifty pages of the end—we had not been aware of the presence of the intelligible self. Only now do we understand fully why Broch found it necessary to introduce the seemingly obtrusive lyrical sections and the theoretical essays into his narrative: Bertrand Müller represents the intelligible self, the ethical center of the novel around which everything else revolves. The three-stage process is now complete. According to Broch's epistemology, the Intelligible Self posits Value-Making Subjects, who in turn fashion their own World Formations. In the terms of the novel: Bertrand Müller posits Stylistic or Structural Points of View, which in turn fashion their own fictional world. The cognition that we achieve through this epistemological novel, then, is ultimately a cognition of Bertrand Müller, who embraces within himself all the potentialities of Pasenow, Esch, Huguenau, and Bertrand.

It is only at the end of three volumes that we realize that there is a supreme narrator uniting the many mediate subject voices. By then, however, we have already become acquainted with the narrator, Bertrand Müller, *within* the fictional world, in "The Story of the Salvation Army Girl." When we finally learn that this figure is, in addition, the narrator of the entire action of the three volumes, we are forced to perform an act of mental translation, to rearrange everything we have learned in the light of this new information.

The Sleepwalkers

Everything that seemed to be stable reality is suddenly relativized by the intrusion of this ideal observer, who has been there all the time without our knowledge. What we have taken for absolute reality is revealed as yet another relative system dependent upon this novel's "intelligible self," Bertrand Müller.[44]

The ten essays on "The Disintegration of Values," then, perform two important functions in the novel as a whole. Epistemologically, they provide the theory upon which the entire novel is based and, in this capacity, constitute the inclusion within the fiction of its own theory. Structurally, their purely rational quality stands in balance and counterpoint to the pure lyricism of "The Story of the Salvation Army Girl." For rationality is as much a part of Bertrand Müller's consciousness as is the subjectivity of "The Story of the Salvation Army Girl." What we have, then, is an absolute novel that represents the full scope of Bertrand's mind, from the rational down to the depths of the irrational, from the analytic mind that clearly sees the causes of its anguish down to the quivering soul that suffers this anguish as intensely as any creature of his imagination. We can visualize the total structure as three concentric circles. The innermost circle embraces the "plots" of all three volumes, the stories that Bertrand Müller writes. The next contains the essays on "The Disintegration of Values," which embrace the stories by referring to them. The outermost circle, finally, is "The Story of the Salvation Army Girl," which contains all else within itself and, as the most subjective strand of the work, is written in a subjective form: lyric utterance.

Broch was particularly proud of this achievement of his

[44] Broch regarded this technique as an explicit application of the theory of relativity to literature. For further details see my article on "Hermann Broch and Relativity in Fiction," *Wisconsin Studies in Contemporary Literature*, 8 (Summer 1967), 365-76.

novel. "The polyhistorization of the novel is making progress on every side," he wrote to Willa Muir on August 3, 1931, with special reference to Joyce, Gide, Thomas Mann, Aldous Huxley, and Robert Musil.[45] But with the exception of Joyce, he continued, the other writers attempted to introduce "cultural elements" into their fiction in chunks and pieces in order to decorate their writing. Only he and Joyce, Broch felt, had "dared" to introduce science into their works "productively," by using it "immanently" as the basis for plot and characterization. This is not the place to discuss Broch's conception of Joyce, with its intuitive grasp of Joyce's technique as well as its subjective misunderstanding of Joyce's aims. But it is safe to say that *The Sleepwalkers* goes further in the "polyhistorization" of fiction than any other novel of the twentieth century. This accounts both for its greatness and, at the same time, for its sometimes tedious presumptuousness. At times Broch runs precisely the danger that he ascribed to naturalism, impressionism, and expressionism. "If in all these forms [art] renders the reality of our time, it does so in fact only as anarchy reflecting anarchy."[46] Broch is at his finest when, succumbing to "the temptation to tell stories," he produces a fictional reality which in fact achieves a Kafkaesque reality by translating psychology into myth.

To write, Broch was fond of saying, means "to attain cognition through form."[47] And this, ultimately, is what Broch hoped to do through his radical revision of the third volume of *The Sleepwalkers*. Not convinced that the basic epistemological pattern of his trilogy sufficed to express his meaning, he went on to create a work in which the form itself

---

[45] Letter of August 3, 1931; in *Die Unbekannte Grösse und frühe Schriften mit den Briefen an Willa Muir*, ed. Ernst Schönwiese (Zurich: Rhein, 1961), pp. 319-20.

[46] "The Style of the Mythic Age"; *Essays I*, p. 260.

[47] *Briefe*, p. 78.

reflected the disintegration that he had detected in the consciousness of modern man. For if our world is disunified, reasoned Broch with characteristic consistency, then any literary work that attempts to represent the world as harmoniously unified must be dishonest. Thus the disparate, seemingly unrelated strands of *The Sleepwalkers* constitute a carefully calculated effort to suggest through aesthetic form the disintegration of reality depicted within the fiction.

Yet this aesthetic ambition reveals an ambiguity inherent in the novel, for Broch was already beset by the nagging doubts that were later to precipitate themselves in such abrupt formulations as "the immorality of the work of art." In a letter of 1947, for instance, he concluded that "the playful element in the work of art is unacceptable in an era of gas chambers."[48] Ten years earlier he had noted that the experience of his arrest and imprisonment by the Nazis and his subsequent flight from Austria were "the final and valid proof of my thesis regarding the superfluousness of all artistic or, more generally, intellectual endeavor."[49] *The Death of Vergil* (1945), written during the years when Broch was witnessing the ravages of Nazi terror from his American exile, is the agonizing record of the writer's growing conviction that a life dedicated to art in what he called "the end of a cultural era" was wasted and even immoral. In fact, Broch never fully resolved in his conscience his doubts about the publication of the novel, whose central theme suggested that literature should not be written and preserved.

These later statements and feelings were not the result of his experiences with the Nazis, but were merely confirmed by them. For precisely this same distrust of literature and philosophy creeps in toward the end of *The Sleepwalkers*, adding a final fascinating dimension to the work. When

[48] *Briefe*, p. 280.　　　[49] *Briefe*, p. 165.

Bertrand Müller, late in his reflections, comes to the conclusion that he is unable to help Nuchem and Marie, this frustration of his efforts by reality forces him to question the validity of the entire novel to which he has devoted his life. "I am trying to write philosophy—but what has happened to the dignity of philosophy? Has it not long since died away? Has not philosophy itself, owing to the collapse of its object, disintegrated to mere words?"[50] This concession, taken literally, vitiates the entire series of essays on "The Disintegration of Values." But Bertrand Müller goes even further. "Even the act of writing philosophy has become an aesthetic game, a game that no longer exists. . . ." Broch seems to be suggesting that the novel's philosophical discourses must be taken as no more and no less than another element of the fiction itself—that, like the ideologies in *The Magic Mountain*, they have no absolute validity. But this amounts to a radical reversal of the attitude with which Broch began his novel. In 1928, as we have noted, he undertook his novel as a vehicle for philosophical speculation because literature was the realm in which subjective thought was still legitimate: literature was a road to cognition. By the end of the novel, however, Bertrand Müller has come to the gloomy conclusion that his philosophy is "merely" aesthetic, and that aesthetics is a rather futile preoccupation in the face of the reality of the world surrounding him. If philosophy has lost its meaning, then there is no longer any justification for the fiction that contains and supports it. Thus Bertrand Müller is exposed as an author who has lost the mainstay of his entire existence: he himself emerges as the most shattering symbol of alienation, loneliness, and despair.

Now it is precisely this ambivalent attitude toward literature, which emerged only gradually during the genesis of the work, that ultimately qualifies our understanding of the

[50] *Schlafwandler,* p. 590.

novel. On the one hand, it becomes more poignantly compelling as a human document. Like Hermann Hesse's *The Glass Bead Game* (1943), it is one of those rare works in which we can observe the author, during the very process of composition, gradually coming to the realization that he must reject the principle of aesthetics upon which the work was initially based.[51] Human sincerity of this sort implies a certain nobility of character that we admire.

On the other hand, this uncertainty regarding the value of aesthetics has unquestionably affected the quality of the novel as a work of art. Unwilling to commit himself with full assurance either to the polyhistorization of Joyce or to the parables of Kafka, Broch created a synthetic form that undeniably partakes of the brilliance of both his models. Hence *The Sleepwalkers* is one of the indisputable masterpieces of twentieth-century fiction. At the same time, his troubling rationality, which questions the legitimacy of art during the very act of writing, denied to Broch the self-centered aesthetic confidence that sustained Joyce and Kafka in their enterprises. And it undermines the reader's faith: we are unable to accept unconditionally a work of art *qua* art if the author infects us with his own doubts. As a result, despite the brilliance of its conception, *The Sleepwalkers* falls short of *Ulysses* and *The Trial* in execution.

AT THE RISK of appearing excessively schematic I would now like to suggest that Broch's novel is the logical outcome, and probably the end point, of a development that began with Rilke and Kafka. With a sure instinct those two geniuses established the limits of the modern novel in their efforts to forge a unified aesthetic whole from the reality that terrified them.

[51] I have suggested this interpretation in my study of *The Novels of Hermann Hesse* (Princeton: Princeton University Press, 1965), esp. pp. 307-20.

Both writers filter the totality of the world through the consciousness of an experiencing subject: they give us a selective totality. But each went to an opposite extreme in presenting this totality and thus achieved a different kind of unity.[52]

Rilke's "prose-book" achieves its unity by taking the elements of the world out of their normal contexts and putting them back together again in meaningful patterns controlled wholly by the imagination of the author: it is the unity of aesthetic design. The language of such a work is, almost of necessity, highly lyrical and in the first person. In Kafka, by contrast, there is no aesthetic shaping of the world. He achieves unity by reducing the world to a pure action whose simplicity is intensified by its repetition: it is the unity of mythic action. Kafka's language, which reproduces as faithfully as possible and with no intrusion of his own subjectivity the reality that his hero experiences, is a sober, third-person speech.

Since it is impossible to go beyond Rilke and Kafka without returning, respectively, to pure poetry and pure myth, subsequent novelists were confronted with the challenge of somehow synthesizing these achievements. Thomas Mann chose to occupy the middle ground. Like both Rilke and Kafka, Thomas Mann contents himself with a selective totality. But though he rises on occasion to a mildly lyrical prose and tends at other times toward essayism, his language itself

[52] It was only during the final revision of my manuscript that I read Frank Trommler, *Roman und Wirklichkeit* (Stuttgart, Berlin, Cologne, and Mainz: Kohlhammer, 1966). Trommler's study of five Austrian novelists (Musil, Broch, Roth, Doderer, and Gütersloh) is concerned, as is the first part of this book, with the fictional representation of reality. But he poses the question in a somewhat different way: "Wie kann sich der Roman als erzählte Welt in einem Zeitalter behaupten, dessen komplizierte gesellschaftliche und technische Prozesse offenbar in den Wissenschaften ihre adäquate Deutung erfahren?" (p. 5). And his answers tend to be more theoretical and less bound to specific analyses.

indicates how instinctively he shies away from the extremes of subjectivity and objectivity. Instead, all reality is filtered through the consciousness of a human narrator who stands between the hero and his world. What we have, then, is neither poetry nor myth, but a realistic novel that achieves its unity by a patterned intensification of the selective totality: it is the unity of a symbolic model.

Whereas Rilke, Kafka, and Thomas Mann suggest totality through selectivity, Broch and Döblin go to the opposite extreme: both attempt to represent totality through multiplicity. The montages of *Berlin Alexanderplatz* constitute a radical attempt to let the world speak for itself, in absolute objectivity. And yet the underlying rhythm of tragedy reveals the author's desire to control and shape his material. The result is a unity of mythic action much like that achieved by Kafka.

Broch, similarly, strives for the totality of multiplicity; in his own way he, too, lets everything in. In the ballads he moves to the wholly lyrical position of Rilke, where the narrative consciousness shapes its own world. In the essays he swings back to the other pole of total objectivity and generalization. The purely narrative passages, by contrast, occupy the symbolic middle ground of Thomas Mann. But if we consider Broch's response to the formal exigencies of the novel, we see that the unity he arrives at is basically that of aesthetic design. For the final structure of *The Sleepwalkers* is that of a consciousness (Bertrand Müller) that reflects, in the disintegration of his own personality, the state of the world as he experiences it.

These five works exemplify, I believe, the basic possibilities for the rendition of totality and the achievement of unity in the modern novel. The novel's limits are pure subjectivity (selective totality and unity of aesthetic design) and pure objectivity (selective totality and unity of mythic action). Between these extremes lies the middle ground of selective totality and unity of the symbolic model. The other two possibilities are: totality through multiplicity within a unity of mythic action; and totality through multiplicity within a unity of aesthetic design. (Theoretically, of course, there is a sixth possibility: totality through multiplicity within a unity of the symbolic model; but the concepts of multiplicity and symbolic model seem to invalidate each other.)

There are few modern novels, German or other, that cannot be assigned at least generally to one of these categories or combinations. Joyce's *Ulysses*, for instance, represents the totality of multiplicity within the unity of mythic action. Gide's *The Counterfeiters* suggests the totality of multiplicity within the unity of aesthetic design. And Virginia Woolf's *The Waves* attains a selective totality within the unity of aesthetic design. Most novels, of course, tend to fall into the category of Thomas Mann's symbolic realism. And in Chapter Ten we shall have occasion to consider the consequences of a fiction that ignores either of these two basic requisites, totality and unity.

Our consideration of these landmarks in the development of the modern German novel, which has focused primarily on the author's response to the totality of the world and his attempts to render it as an aesthetic unity, has necessarily emphasized the differences between five important and representative works. To determine their similarities we must now stand back and take a broader view of the grand vistas of modern literature: of the features that assure its integrity as well as of its uniqueness when seen against the greater background of the past.

Part II

European Contexts

chapter six

The Discordant Clocks

(1)

WHEN Ingmar Bergman wished to express a premonition of death in *Wild Strawberries*, he was able to establish the mood instantly in the striking scene that opens the film. His aging hero dreams that he is taking his usual morning walk, which leads past the shop of a watchmaker-optometrist. He has always been amused by the slightly grotesque sign outside the shop: a large clock, beneath which is suspended the picture of a pair of giant eyeglasses with staring eyes. But this time, the scenario continues:

> To my amazement, the hands of the clock had disappeared. The dial was blank, and below it someone had smashed both of the eyes so that they looked like watery, infected sores. Instinctively I pulled out my own watch to check the time, but I found that my old reliable gold timepiece had also lost its hands. I held it to my ear to find out if it was still ticking. Then I heard my heart beat. It was pounding fast and irregularly. I was overwhelmed by an inexplicable feeling of frenzy.[1]

This brief, wordless scene makes it instantly clear to the viewer that Professor Isak Borg has been cut off from public time and hurled back upon his own inner time by the approach of death. But the effect narrowly escapes triviality, for in 1957 Bergman was well aware that he could count on an immediate, conditioned response from his audience. Fifty years of literature had seen to that.

[1] *Four Screenplays of Bergman*, trans. Lars Malmstrom and David Kushner (New York: Simon and Schuster, 1961), p. 161.

183

The Discordant Clocks

The modern novel is a riot of clocks. Think of James Joyce. In the story "Counterparts" (in *Dubliners*), Farrington pawns his watch in sullen defiance of the exacting schedule demanded by his employer in the office. In *Stephen Hero,* it is the clock of the Ballast Office, one of the focal points of Joyce's Dublin, that prompts the often-quoted remarks on the epiphany—the epiphany, which pierces through all deceptive temporal appearances to the timeless core of things. In the last chapter of *A Portrait of The Artist as a Young Man,* all the clocks tell a different time as Stephen Dedalus makes his tardy way, out of touch with the world about him, to a lecture. Leopold Bloom's watch stops at 4:32 P.M.: precisely at the moment, he later calculates, when his wife Molly consummated her infidelity.

Kafka's clocks are either fast or slow, but never, as he noted in his diary, "in unison." His people are usually late, and the disjuncture of their personal time and public time intensifies the anguish in which they live. When Gregor Samsa, in "The Metamorphosis," awakens to discover that he has changed into a great insect, his discomfiture at this fact is no greater than his distress at the realization that he is going to miss his train. "He looked over at the alarm clock that was ticking on the night table. 'Good God!' he thought. It was six thirty, and the hands moved calmly forwards. It was even past the half-hour mark, it was already approaching a quarter to." Similarly, *The Trial* begins with time out of joint: "The cook of Frau Grubach, his landlady, who brought him his breakfast every day around eight o'clock, did not come this time. That had never happened." From this moment on, Josef K. is on a different psychic schedule. Like Karl Rossmann, the hero of Kafka's *Amerika*, he resembles "a poorly functioning clock."

For Kafka and Joyce, human time is often out of step with

public time, but the clocks are still intact. Very soon, however, the image changes and becomes more radical: as human time alienates itself ever more from public time, the clocks themselves fall apart. Hans Castorp's watch falls from the night table and is smashed; since it has become useless, in any case, in the timeless "hermetic" world of *The Magic Mountain*, he does not bother to have it repaired. After his first setback in *Berlin Alexanderplatz*, Franz Biberkopf withdraws for days to his room, where he can find nothing better to do than to tinker perplexedly with his broken clock. In Faulkner's *The Sound and the Fury*, Dilsey's clock has only one hand, and even that is slow. But the breakdown of mechanical time does not distress Dilsey, who, alone of the main characters of the novel, is so wholly attuned to the natural world that her inner time is instinctively right.

> On the wall above a cupboard, invisible save at night, by lamp light and even then evincing an enigmatic profundity because it had but one hand, a cabinet clock ticked, then with a preliminary sound as if it had cleared its throat, struck five times.
>
> "Eight o'clock," Dilsey said.[2]

Quentin's monologue in the same novel is punctuated by intrusions of the timepieces that pursue him inexorably with the demands of a temporality that he detests. It is a watch, in the first sentence, that establishes contact between his waking consciousness and the world. "When the shadow of the sash appeared on the curtains it was between seven and eight o'clock and then I was in time again, hearing the watch." Before he commits suicide Quentin tries to destroy time by shattering the crystal of his watch and twisting off its hands, but

---

[2] Quoted here and below from the Modern Library edition (New York, 1946), pp. 290, 95, and 104.

everywhere he goes he is tormented by the sight and sound of the watches, clocks, chimes, and bells of Harvard and Boston. At one point he steps into a jeweler's shop to find out whether any of the watches in the window show the correct time, but they have not yet been regulated for the day:

> I went out, shutting the door upon the ticking. I looked back into the window. He was watching me across the barrier. There were about a dozen watches in the window, a dozen different hours and each with the same assertive and contradictory assurance that mine had, without any hands at all. Contradicting one another. I could hear mine, ticking away inside my pocket, even though nobody could see it, even though it could tell nothing if anyone could.

Mrs. Dalloway's day is shattered by the stately tolling of Big Ben, but none of Virginia Woolf's figures is more deeply offended by the intrusion of public time upon personal time than is the heroine of *Orlando*:

> Now as she stood with her hand on the door of her motor-car, the present again struck her on the head. Eleven times she was violently assaulted.
>
> "Confound it all!" she cried, for it is a great shock to the nervous system, hearing a clock strike. . . .[3]

> Like thunder, the stable clock struck four. Never did any earthquake so demolish a whole town. . . . Her own body

---

[3] Quoted here and below from the Penguin edition (New York, 1946), pp. 198-99, 208, and 209. There are countless other examples in the works of Virginia Woolf. In *The Waves* (published in one volume with *Jacob's Room* in the Harvest Books edition [New York, 1966]), p. 366, she writes: "Yes, but suddenly one hears a clock tick. We who had been immersed in this [timeless and poetic] world became aware of another. It is painful."

quivered and tingled as if suddenly stood naked in a hard frost. Yet, she kept, as she had not done when the clock struck ten in London, complete composure (for she was now one and entire, and presented, it may be, a larger surface to the shock of time).

She was standing with her eye fixed on his hand when the quarter struck. It hurtled through her like a meteor, so hot that no fingers can hold it.

This obsession with timepieces is not limited to literature. Who is not familiar with the languishing watches often draped across the surreal landscapes of Salvador Dali or the grandfather clocks drifting through the painted fantasies of Marc Chagall? In the German film *Waxworks* (1929), Ivan the Terrible frantically reverses a huge hourglass, for he has identified its trickling sand with the passing of his own life.[4] Nor must the symbol always be a tragic one. In his *Galgenlieder* (1906), describing a clock incorporating the features of the two clocks on the Jewish Council Hall in Prague, Christian Morgenstern paired a serious concern with the problem of time and satiric wit:

Die Korfsche Uhr

Korf erfindet eine Uhr,
die mit zwei Paar Zeigern kreist
und damit nach vorn nicht nur,
sondern auch nach rückwärts weist.

Zeigt sie zwei,—somit auch zehn;
zeigt sie drei,—somit auch neun;
und man braucht nur hinzusehn,
um die Zeit nicht mehr zu scheun.

[4] Cited by J. B. Priestley, *Man and Time* (New York: Doubleday, 1964), pp. 106-7.

The Discordant Clocks

Denn auf dieser Uhr von Korfen
mit dem janushaften Lauf
(dazu ward sie so entworfen):
hebt die Zeit sich selber auf.[5]

Yet in all these cases the symbolic meaning of the time-piece is remarkably consistent. It represents the temporal order of the public world, the world of business, science, and everyday affairs (Joyce, Kafka, Woolf)—an order, moreover, that is often sanctified by tradition (Faulkner, Mann, Chagall). It is an order, finally, that is inextricably linked to the physical life of the individual. At the same time, it is an order against which some part of the individual rebels. In virtually every case, that is, the clock is summoned forth as a negative symbol by the subjective consciousness of an individual who wishes to assert his own private time against the claims of public time. Clocks in modern literature seem to exist only to be ignored, dropped, shattered, deformed, or improved upon. To this extent they reflect admirably the attitude of modern man toward the objective time in which he is destined to live.

Critics have often noted the centrality of the theme of time in modern literature—and not only in the novel, of course. T. S. Eliot's *Four Quartets* are as much concerned with time as are Rilke's *Duino Elegies*.[6] Surveying the literary situation

---

[5] Korf's Clock

Korf invents himself a clock / that circles with two pairs of hands / and thus points not only forward / but also back.

If it shows two—then also ten; / if it shows three—then also nine; / and you only need to look at it / to lose your fear of time.

For on this clock of Korf's / with its Janus-like path / (that's why it was designed that way): / time is canceled out by time.

[6] See Christine Bourbek, *Die Struktur der Zeit in heutiger Dichtung* (Berlin: Herbert Renner, 1956). Though tendentiously Christian in its approach, the study contains a generous selection of modern German poetry dealing with the theme of time.

in 1941, Stephen Spender concluded that "modern literature is obsessed with problems of time. Writers who differ in everything else share this pre-occupation. The least political, the least philosophical, even those who disclaim any interest in ideas are yet strangely concerned with time."[7] Yet it is not this general preoccupation with time in itself that distinguishes our age—time has long been a problem for writers—but rather the particular form that this obsession assumes in the twentieth century.

(2)

In 1927 there appeared two highly symptomatic books that exemplify the form taken by the problem of time in the twentieth century. Wyndham Lewis, the violently antiromantic painter-writer-critic, was so grievously alarmed at the "mystical time-cult" threatening to engulf modern society that he devoted a substantial and sometimes almost hysterical volume to the problem of *Time and Western Man*.[8] Lewis felt that "Time-worship" and "time-jingoism" were undermining civilization, because they emphasized an inner flux of being at the expense of the concrete reality of space. Among the "time-snobs" he singled out as his particular whipping boys were such thinkers as "Whitehead, Alexander, and the other space-timeists" as well as such "time-children" of literature as Gertrude Stein, Ezra Pound, and James Joyce. But as the most heinous villains in his intellectual rogues' gallery he indicted Henri Bergson, who "put the hyphen between Space and Time," and Albert Einstein, the "finicky, fastidious and at the same time bizarre architect" who engineered the "mathematical Boro-Budur" of Relativity. "Both Einstein and Bergson are river officials of the great River Flux, of its conserv-

---

[7] "Books and the War, II," *New Writing* (1941).

[8] Quoted here from the Beacon Press edition (Boston, 1957), pp. 218, 221, 15, 55, 419, 271, 400.

ancy staff," sneered Lewis; "they both, in different ways, administer it."

Little did Lewis suspect that the worst was yet to come. At the very time that he was collecting evidence for his diatribe, a thirty-seven-year-old professor from the University of Marburg was sitting in a ski hut on the highest elevation in the Black Forest, quietly composing the dense treatise that was to bestow absolute philosophical priority upon subjective time. Martin Heidegger's *Sein und Zeit* (1927) was the first major attempt to systematize the very time-consciousness that Lewis so deplored. "The concrete elaboration of the question regarding the meaning of *Being* is the purpose of the following treatise," Heidegger stated in his preface. "The interpretation of *Time* as the possible horizon of any understanding of Being at all is its preliminary goal." Bergson had argued that the physical concept of time is insufficient to explain the experience of duration in human psychology. Einstein had taught that classical notions of time are not adequate to embrace all the phenomena of modern physics. Now Heidegger and the other existential philosophers of the twentieth century insisted that the study of all being had to be oriented around the concept of *experienced* time (*erlebte Zeit, temps vécu*).[9]

This is not to suggest that Lewis and Heidegger had any immediate influence upon modern fiction. Many of the novels that we now regard as major had already appeared by 1927. In any case, the positions and language of their respective works are so radical that they are more easily parodied than imitated. There is surely more than a touch of Lewis in some of the rabid opponents of relativity who are caricatured in modern fiction (e.g., Illidge in Aldous Huxley's *Point Counter Point* or Zacharias in Broch's *The Innocents*).

[9] In this connection see Otto Friedrich Bollnow, *Existenzphilosophie* (4th edn.; Stuttgart: Kohlhammer, 1955), esp. pp. 104ff.

And Günter Grass devotes a substantial section of his novel *Dog Years* to a parody of Heidegger's language and thought. Yet the radicality of the positions taken by the two books symbolizes the extent to which the conflict between public and private time had intensified by 1927. Each represents a strong claim on the conscience and consciousness of twentieth-century man. Society cannot survive without the classical notion of objective time defended by Lewis; yet the individual feels increasingly that his being must indeed, as Heidegger argued, ultimately be comprehended within his own subjective time.

The awareness of subjective time is nothing new, of course; it has existed as long as man himself. But only in the recent past has the dichotomy between public and private time been aggravated into a central conflict in man's consciousness. For it was not until the twentieth century that man sought the very meaning of his existence in the fact of his temporal duration. Earlier ages had been able to look elsewhere for meaning and value. We can make out three stages of development through which man has passed since the Middle Ages.[10]

Until the seventeenth century, the meaning of human existence was vouchsafed by the eternal order of God, within which man took his place. Time was seen as a hierarchy of durations ranging upward from the temporality of man to the timelessness of God, but there was no conflict between human time and eternal time, for God's time was the ultimate value toward which all men aspired, and no premium was

[10] In the following paragraphs I follow Georges Poulet's brilliant introduction to his *Etudes sur le temps humain* (Paris, 1950) and the chapter on "Time and the Modern World" in Hans Meyerhoff, *Time in Literature* (Berkeley and Los Angeles: University of California Press, 1955), pp. 85-119. I should like to express my general admiration for Meyerhoff's book, the most profound and imaginative study of the problem of time in literature. Both Poulet and Meyerhoff deal extensively with pre-twentieth-century conceptions of time.

placed on subjective time. In the seventeenth century man discovered that his own consciousness was somehow isolated from all other creation and from the duration of all other things. This feeling, first apparent in Montaigne's essays, found its most apt formulation in the *cogito ergo sum* of Descartes, which denies any transcendental temporal continuity and reduces human duration to "a chaplet of instants" linked only by the creative consciousness.[11] As the belief in an eternal order was displaced, "historical time became the only medium in which human life unfolded and fulfilled itself."[12] From its beginnings in the seventeenth century until it reached its climax with Hegel, Marx, Darwin, and other thinkers in every field of nineteenth-century scholarship, historicism became the accepted way of looking at life. Historical laws, which again gave meaning and order to human life, assumed the proportions of a secular surrogate for the eternal order of God. Just as, up until the seventeenth century, the order of God had guaranteed man's meaning and duration, now history provided the necessary order and values. The discontinuity of existence, which was noted by Descartes, Hume, and other thinkers of the age, posed no problem as long as life's meaning could be found in a history that transcended the individual.

But when the world of history, toward the end of the nineteenth century, became so vast and complex that no unified order could possibly be read into or out of it, history was fragmented into a set of pluralistic systems of value which defied survey. In the face of this virtually meaningless pluralism, the individual was hurled back upon himself in his

[11] Poulet, quoted here and below in the translation by Elliott Coleman, *Studies in Human Time* (Baltimore: The Johns Hopkins Press, 1956); here, p. 14.

[12] Meyerhoff, *Time in Literature*, p. 95.

search for meaning, value, and duration. The eternal order of God had failed; the secular order of history had failed. It was the hour for Bergson and for the modern philosophies that sought man's meaning in his own existence and in the fact of his duration.

Many areas of Bergson's thought had been anticipated. The romantic generation knew of the discovery of the self through memory. The nineteenth century was aware of the continuous becoming of things. And the notion that duration is the only reality goes back at least as far as the seventeenth century. But Bergson prepared the way for the twentieth century through his insistence that man's *becoming* is not necessarily predetermined, that duration is not the fact of being changed or shaped by external forces, but the act of shaping one's own existence. "It is, without doubt, in this that the originality of Bergson consists, and his share in establishing the thought of his century. Not in his conception of memory, nor in his philosophy of the continuous, but in his affirmation that duration is something other than history or a system of laws; that it is a free creation."[13] It is at this juncture, of course, that the conflict between public and private time, between time and duration, can emerge as a central conflict of the modern consciousness. Whereas up to this point human value had lain elsewhere—outside the individual, in the order of God or of history—now, for the first time, meaning was sought in the very fact of man's duration. Human duration thus becomes more meaningful and more valuable than anything that obtains in the realm of public time. This philosophical dilemma reflected, and in part intensified, the situation that was gradually developing in other areas. For during the past hundred years, public or scientific time has become an increasingly dominant factor in human life and activity.

[13] Poulet, *Studies in Human Time*, p. 35.

The Discordant Clocks

(3)

IN HIS intellectual autobiography *The World of Yesterday*,[14] Stefan Zweig stresses the great abyss that separates his own generation from the generations of the past. Looking back, Zweig is overcome with amazement at the fullness and variety of experience compressed into a life that began in the nineteenth century and spanned the technological progress of the first half of our own century. "My father, my grandfather, what did they see? Each lived his life in a state of uniformity. A single life from beginning to end, without rises, without falls, without shocks and danger—a life with small tensions, imperceptible transitions; in the same rhythm, steady and quiet, the wave of time bore them from the cradle to the grave." A man living such a life was only indirectly aware of the passage of public time. But modern man, by foreshortening the past and rendering the entire sweep of the present simultaneous, has deprived himself of the privilege of escaping the present. "Earlier generations could flee, in times of catastrophe, into seclusion and the isolation of existence off the beaten path. It was reserved for us to be compelled to know and experience, in the same hour and second, everything bad that happens on our planet."

Even discounting a certain degree of idyllicism in Zweig's account, we must concede that his analysis of the time-experience of his forefathers is acute. Today we are so accustomed to the tyranny of time that we may well tend to forget the attitude of generations that did not live by the clock. It was not until 1879 that Sir Sandford Fleming, engineer in chief of surveys for the Canadian Pacific Railways, came up with the idea of standardized time zones, which was first accepted by railway personnel in North America and gradually

[14] *Die Welt von Gestern; Erinnerungen eines Europäers* (Stockholm: Bermann-Fischer, 1946), p. 11 and (below), p. 453.

spread all over the world. In fact, it was specifically the rapid expansion of train traffic in the nineteenth century that abruptly synchronized the world, forcing man into conformity with a public time that increasingly conflicted with his private world. Hitherto every town and country had lived more or less according to its own schedule. There were no airline schedules to be kept, no radio or television programs to be strictly synchronized.[15] The frustrations of the traveling salesman Gregor Samsa would be unimaginable in a century that lived less by the clock than our own.

The problem of time in the twentieth century is actually the result of a twofold process. On the one hand, there has been an unparalleled development in the scientific precision with which time can be measured, and this continues from year to year. In October 1964, the International Bureau of Weights and Measures adopted a new standard for measuring the second (9,192,631,770 cycles of vibrations of a cesium atom), abandoning the relatively inexact astronomical standard (which can vary "as much as" 3/10 of a second in the course of a quarter century). This phenomenon, upon which modern science and technology wholly depend, is so remote from human experience that it would be irrelevant were it not accompanied by a new emphasis on time in our daily lives, from the precise timing necessary in wars and the launching of man-made satellites to the staggering of lunch hours and vacations. In many sports, athletes now compete against the stopwatch rather than against one another. In the name of science the timepiece has invaded the bedroom, where it records the temporal stages of love. Even the dignity of death has often been assaulted by our ghoulish obsession with the exact time, down to the fraction of a second,

---

[15] Isaac Asimov, *The Clock We Live On* (rev. edn.; New York: Collier Books, 1963), provides a readable account of the history of scientific time.

at which a public figure dies or is killed. The dominance of public time, in other words, has contributed immeasurably to the dehumanization taking place in every phase of modern life. It goes without saying that this modern temporal regimentation would be totally incomprehensible to the inhabitants of eighteenth-century Königsberg, who were content to set their clocks by Professor Kant's daily walk, or to the townsman of only a hundred years ago, who regulated his day by the tolling of the church bell in his own village or in his own part of town.

Now, the increasing importance, even tyranny, of what Hans Meyerhoff has called "the social meaning of time" comes into direct conflict with the modern sense of subjective duration that was popularized by Bergson, given scientific canonization (at least in the popular imagination) by Einstein's theory of relativity, and thrust into the center of being by the various forms of existential philosophy. "And all our intuitions mock / The formal logic of the clock," wrote W. H. Auden in his *New Years Letter* (1941). In opposition to an increasingly precise, increasingly insistent public time, modern man clings more and more to this intuition, to his private sense of duration. J. B. Priestley is undoubtedly correct when he attributes the astonishing popularity of "time-traveling" in science fiction, from H. G. Wells's *The Time Machine* (1895) right down to the current paperbacks in every drugstore, to our unconscious desire to "escape from relentless chronology."[16] Time travel is essentially a reified metaphor for our resistance to public time: our retreat into

[16] Priestley, *Man and Time*, p. 110. It might be noted in this connection that science fiction generally tends to reflect the preoccupations of the times. In earlier works of "science fiction"—e.g., Mary Shelley's *Frankenstein* (1818) or the romantic tales of E.T.A. Hoffmann—the main concern is travel in space (as a symptom of resistance to geographical restrictions) or physical transformation (as a reflection of the romantic belief in organic unity of all being).

the inner world of private duration is spatialized as a physical flight into the past or future. Ray Bradbury becomes the Proust of the 1960's. But the popularity of science fiction also proves that the sense of private time is intuitive and unconscious. It is a universal phenomenon, in other words, of which Bergson, Einstein, and Heidegger are more the symptom than the cause.

The conflict between public and private time that underlies so much of modern fiction does not necessarily, then, imply any understanding of, or influence by, the modern theories of duration, relativity, or being.[17] Very often, of course, the writers are fully aware of the philosophical and scientific debate, at least in general. Proust, who was best man when Bergson married a first cousin of his, was acquainted at first hand with the time debate stirred up by his in-law. By the same token, it is inconceivable that Rilke, who lived in Paris for many years between 1902 and 1910, could have helped but know of Bergson, whose lectures were as much a social as an intellectual event and whose ideas spread rapidly from salon to salon. There is good reason to believe that Kafka heard a lecture on Einstein's theory of relativity shortly after the Special Theory was published in 1905. And the witty references in *Finnegans Wake* to the "dime-cash problem," the "sophology of Bitchson," and the "whoo-whoo and where's hairs theorics of Winestain" are as eloquent a testimony to Joyce's general familiarity with these figures as is his amusing tale of The Mookse and The Gripes ("Eins within a space and a wearywide space it wast ere wohned a Mookse"). Yet critics still argue about the precise degree to

[17] This is a general principle of intellectual history and literary criticism, but one that is often not regarded. For instance, the popular *mis*understanding of Rousseau and Nietzsche had a far greater impact on their times than a correct comprehension could ever have had. Similarly, if Heinrich von Kleist had not misread Kant, the world might well be poorer by several great stories and dramas.

197

which Bergson might have influenced Proust's theory of memory. Thomas Mann wrote what is probably the greatest "time novel" of the century, *The Magic Mountain*, before he had read either Bergson or Proust. And it has, legitimately enough, occurred to no one to search for the influence of Bergson or Einstein in the works of Rilke and Kafka. Certainly it is the exception rather than the rule when a writer explicitly and systematically bases a theory of fiction on the theory of relativity, as in the case of Hermann Broch.[18] And, it should be conceded, this rarely improves the fiction *qua* fiction.

Hans Reichenbach, in an incisive study of *The Direction of Time*, criticizes what he calls the "emotional" attitude toward time represented by Bergson and his followers, maintaining that "it is a hopeless enterprise to search for the nature of time without studying physics."[19] As far as public and scientific time is concerned, Reichenbach is undoubtedly correct. But otherwise, Reichenbach is preempting the word "time" for only one of its legitimate meanings: he excludes the sense of private time altogether. Moreover, writers are generally not interested in anything so abstract as "the nature of time." As J. B. Priestley has noted, "Time is a concept, a certain condition of experience, a mode of perception, and so forth; and a novel or a play, to be worth calling one, cannot really be about Time but only about the people and

[18] In this connection see my article on "Hermann Broch and Relativity in Fiction," *Wisconsin Studies in Contemporary Literature*, 8 (Summer 1967), 365-76. In his chapter on "Time in Fiction and Drama," *Man and Time*, pp. 106-35, J. B. Priestley discusses his own attempts to incorporate various theories of time into his plays. See also Irwin Morgenstern, *The Dimensional Structure of Time, together with The Drama and Its Timing* (New York: Philosophical Library, 1960).

[19] *The Direction of Time,* ed. Maria Reichenbach (Berkeley and Los Angeles: University of California Press, 1956), p. 17.

things that appear to be *in* Time"—in other words, about the dramatic confrontation between subjective time and objective time. Thomas Mann confirmed this when he wrote, in *The Magic Mountain*, "Is it possible to narrate Time, Time itself, as such, in and for itself? Truly, no. That would be a foolish undertaking. A story that went: 'Time passed, it flowed, Time streamed along' and so forth—no one in his right mind could call that a story."[20] Even without Bergson and Einstein, without Wyndham Lewis and Heidegger, modern novelists would undoubtedly still have the conflict between individual time and public time as their central concern: it is a conflict, as we have seen, that is given by the age itself.

The foregoing remarks should explain, at least in part, both the abundance of clocks in modern art and literature and the general theme of time as it is precipitated in the novels under discussion. The conflict between public time and private time in the twentieth century has been generated by a clearly definable set of social and historical circumstances. This is not to say that special studies dealing with the impact of Bergson, Einstein, or Heidegger on certain writers are not interesting and revealing.[21] But the universal nature of the problem of public and private time suggests a more general approach to the treatment of time in literature, one that transcends these specific issues.[22] In particular, many structural and technical

[20] In the chapter "Strandspaziergang" ("Walk on the Beach"; in the Lowe-Porter translation, "By the Ocean of Time").

[21] In this connection I should like to mention especially Margaret Church, *Time and Reality; Studies in Contemporary Fiction* (Chapel Hill: University of North Carolina Press, 1963). Miss Church, whose study is focused "more toward values and meaning than toward structure and technique" (p. 19), tends to rate authors more or less according to their understanding of Bergson and Proust. Her book contains a multitude of useful observations, as well as an excellent bibliography of works on time in English, German, and French.

[22] This approach differs, it should be stressed, from the extremely valuable method of Günther Müller, *Die Bedeutung der Zeit in der*

features of the modern novel can be understood as a response to the confrontation of two kinds of time. Each writer, to be sure, has responded to the dilemma in a different way. But the basic question to which the novel addresses itself seems to be remarkably similar in each case.

(4)

IF WE look back at the novels that we have considered, we note that in every case the author has taken great care to construct a fairly rigid framework of public time. The flux of private duration is meaningful only when placed in dialectical opposition to clock or calendar time. For this reason Leopold Bloom's voyage through Dublin and Mrs. Dalloway's day are systematically punctuated by public time. Without the shaping influence of chronological time, private time would dissolve into a shapeless mass inaccessible of fictional rendition. This accounts for the predominance of clocks and watches that we mentioned in the opening pages of this chapter: they constitute part of the tools that the writer requires in order to create the outer form of his work.

At this point two general statements can be made. First, clocks are particularly conspicuous in works of limited temporal duration (*Ulysses, Mrs. Dalloway, The Sound and the Fury*, the first day of *The Magic Mountain*, the individual

---

Erzählkunst (Bonn: Universitätsverlag, 1947), which is concerned above all with the discrepancy between "narrated time" (*erzählte Zeit*) and "duration of narrative" (*Erzählzeit*) and with its implications for the structure and values of the fiction. My own approach is closer to, though not identical with, that of Hans Robert Jauss, *Zeit und Erinnerung in Marcel Prousts 'A la recherche du temps perdu'; Ein Beitrag zur Theorie des Romans* (Heidelberg: Carl Winter Universitätsverlag, 1955). Jauss, p. 37, distinguishes between "duration of the phenomenon" (*Dauer der Erscheinung*) and "appearance of duration" (*Erscheinung der Dauer*).

day-units of *The Trial*). In works with a longer temporal rhythm, the clock gives way to the calendar and to such indications as seasonal change (*Malte, The Sleepwalkers, Berlin Alexanderplatz*, the major portion of *The Magic Mountain*). But in every case the framework of public time is not only given, but stressed. *The Trial* lasts exactly one year. Hans Castorp's seven years on *The Magic Mountain* end with the outbreak of war in 1914. *Berlin Alexanderplatz* lasts from the autumn of 1927 to the winter of 1928-1929. Each section of *The Sleepwalkers* lasts precisely six months, from spring to fall of the years 1888, 1903, and 1918. Even in the most elusive work, *The Notebooks of Malte Laurids Brigge*, we have a clear succession of seasons, beginning with Malte's arrival in Paris in late August and his first entry on September 11.

Secondly, the more the fiction is interiorized, the more regularly it is likely to be punctuated by chronological time. In works in which a narrator has control of the disposition of events—*The Trial, The Sleepwalkers, Berlin Alexanderplatz* —he usually manages to suggest the sequence of external time in such a way that it can be calculated without specific reference to clocks or calendars. The very disposition of the episodes suggests the orderly passage of time, even when time is progressively telescoped, as in *The Magic Mountain*, or broken up into cycles of repetition, as in *The Trial*.

But when the narrative is turned over immediately to the consciousness of one or more of the figures in the novel, the passage of objective time obtrudes rather forcefully upon their senses to compensate for the lack of external shape. A striking example of this can be seen in Heinrich Böll's *Billiards at Half-past Nine* (1959), which is composed of roughly consecutive interior monologues delivered from various points of view over a period of some twelve hours. The compositional focal point in the work is a cathedral tower that all the characters can either see or hear in the course of their monologues, and that thus ties the various strands of the narrative together. Similarly, although the five episodes in *The Sound and The Fury* take place at different points of time, each is punctuated conspicuously by external time (e.g., Dilsey's clock and Quentin's watch). Malte's notebooks, as we have seen, are aestheticized to the extent that they are often wholly removed from reality, but the flux of the individual incidents is frequently controlled by a reference to chronological time. Thus, at the end of the three-page scene in which Malte experiences the epiphany of a wall, he writes: "You will probably say that I stood before the wall for a long time; but I am willing to take an oath that I began to run as soon as I recognized the wall." Even in Hermann Broch's wholly interiorized *The Death of Vergil*, which extends over some of five hundred pages, the poet's last hours are clearly punctuated by natural phenomena that obtrude upon his consciousness: birds, stars, varying stages of light and dark.

Objective time is stressed, then, in order to give shape to the narrative. We would be unable to understand a work that failed (at least by subtle hints) to refer to standards of time exterior to the subjective consciousness.[23] But more importantly, it is

[23] Thus E. M. Forster, in his chapter on "The Story" in *Aspects of the Novel* (New York: Harvest Books, 1927), p. 29, writes that "it is never possible for a novelist to deny time inside the fabric of his novel: he must cling however lightly to the thread of his story; he must touch the interminable tapeworm, otherwise he becomes unintelligible, which, in his case, is a blunder." The notion that temporality provides the form for human perception is, of course, one of the central principles of Edmund Husserl's *Phenomenology of Internal Time-Consciousness*. But since this work, based on a series of lectures delivered in Göttingen in 1904 and 1910, was not edited and published until 1928 (and then by Martin Heidegger!), Husserl's ideas can concern us merely as a reflection of, not as an influence upon, contemporary literary theory and practice.

The Discordant Clocks

the regular movement of public time that makes possible and emphasizes the suspension of time characteristic of private duration. In each of the novels, while the author keeps a firm grip on the chronology of public time, the hero is rapidly led into a state in which he experiences a kind of timeless suspension. Thus Malte, five floors up in his lonely room, barely experiences the seasonal changes of which he allows us to become aware. Only his first diary entry contains a date, and after "learning to see" he retreats more and more into the world of his own imagination, in which time is suspended: his days, as he puts it, are like "a clock without hands." Similarly, a calendar year passes from the time of Josef K.'s arrest until his death, but for him the passing of this public time—which we perceive as clearly as the fragmentary nature of the novel allows—is reduced to a series of repetitions in which time becomes meaningless. Seven years elapse while Hans Castorp experiences the "eternal sameness" of the Magic Mountain, but only during the first few months does he make any pretense of conforming to public time; later, as we have noted, his watch is broken, and he fails even to keep a calendar. After each of his three setbacks Franz Biberkopf retreats to a realm of private time: to his room, where he tinkers with his broken clock; to the hospital and then to Eva's room, where he recovers from the loss of his arm; and finally to the sanatorium at Buch, where he holds his silent dialogue with Death. Finally, the six months between Huguenau's desertion and his return to the world of reality are expressly spent in a timeless "vacation" state. In each novel, despite differences in technique, there is a pronounced disjuncture between private time, experienced as timeless suspension, and the orderly sequence of public time that gives the work its form.[24]

[24] Because both aspects—rendition of public and private time—are conspicuously present in all these works I am unable to accept the

The Discordant Clocks

For most authors this state of timeless suspension manifests itself as the experience of simultaneity. In his introduction to *The Magic Mountain* Thomas Mann argues that his work is a "time novel" in two (actually three) senses. It deals with a specific historical time; it treats time as one of its themes; and it attempts to *be* what it is *about.* "For while it portrays the hermetic enchantment of its young hero in a timeless realm, it endeavors itself through its artistic means to do away with time: to bestow upon the entire musical-conceptual world that it embraces total *presence* in every moment and to produce a magical *nunc stans.*"[25] This notion of the simultaneous presence of the work of art is one that Mann often repeated, for instance in his report on the composition of *Doctor Faustus*: "A work of art is always conceived as a whole; and even though the philosophy of aesthetics may claim that the work of words and of music, in contrast to that of the visual arts, is dependent upon time and its succession, nevertheless it too strives to be wholly present at every moment."[26]

Hermann Broch was similarly obsessed with the idea of simultaneity. In his essay on Joyce he contended that "the demand for simultaneity remains the true goal of all epic, indeed, of all poetry."[27] And in making some observations on his own *The Death of Vergil* he called the problem of

---

rigid differentiation suggested by Paul West, *The Modern Novel* (London: Hutchinson, 1963). In his introduction (pp. 3-55), West speaks of novels of metaphysical defiance and social analysis. Most of the works we have considered, however, combine both elements; indeed, their tensions stem from the confrontation of these aspects. This is certainly the case with Broch, Döblin, and Thomas Mann. Otherwise, West's study is often provocative and valuable.

[25] "Einführung in den *Zauberberg* für Studenten der Universität Princeton" (1939), *GW* (1960), xi, 611-12.

[26] *Die Entstehung des Doktor Faustus* (1949); in *GW*, xi, 292.

[27] "James Joyce und die Gegenwart" (1936); in *Essays I*, p. 192.

simultaneity "one of the most difficult problems of epic writing." "All epic representation must come to grips with the question of simultaneity, that is, must represent situations of a single moment in temporal succession and nevertheless maintain the impression of instantaneity."[28]

Broch and Thomas Mann are probably the two most eloquent theoreticians of simultaneity, but no matter where we turn, we find the major writers of the twentieth century obsessed with the problem. Thus Döblin, in an essay on "The Spirit of the Naturalistic Age," wrote: "A time is always a *mêlée* of various ages, . . . a symbiosis of many souls."[29] In Huxley's *Point Counter Point*, Philip Quarles says that "the essence of the new way of looking is multiplicity. Multiplicity of eyes and multiplicity of aspects seen. . . . What I want to do is to look with all those eyes at once."[30] In *Jacob's Room* Virginia Woolf talks about this same multiplicity of aspects: "But if you look at them steadily . . . multiplicity becomes unity, which is somehow the secret of life."[31] The rationale behind this desire for multiplicity and simultaneity is articulated by Walter Jens in his "Dialogue about a Novel":

> You see, my friend, we live at a time which, day after day, brings us as close to the Malayan farmer as to the waiter in Mexico City. We know the forests of Chad and the sky above New York; but we also know the vessels that Hannibal's soldiers used to dip water; we know, very precisely,

[28] "Bemerkungen zum *Tod des Vergil*"; in *Essays I*, p. 267.

[29] "Der Geist des naturalistischen Zeitalters" (1924); in *Aufsätze zur Literatur*, p. 80.

[30] *Point Counter Point* (New York: Modern Library [ca. 1928]), p. 228.

[31] *Jacob's Room*, p. 131. In *The Waves*, p. 264, Mrs. Woolf says the same thing more metaphorically: "in efforts to make a steel ring of clear poetry that shall connect the gulls and the women with bad teeth. . . ." This poetic world, moreover, is "a world immune from change" (p. 249).

the face of the moon and the motion in cells. We know the largest and the smallest; we peer into the shaft of time and survey all space as though it were a dish of modest proportions. We have laid out roads into the cosmos, given speech to the dead and redeemed the microbes from the curse of never being seen.[32]

All of this experience, however, requires an entirely new sort of literary figure, one reminiscent of the heroine of Virginia Woolf's *Orlando*. "Invent a figure, a thousand-mask figure, which leaps across continents in the space of a second and, between two breaths, plunges from one century into another . . . that homo fictus which, like us, is at home nowhere and everywhere," Jens's fictional critic suggests. Most authors would be unwilling to go to these lengths. Yet Jens has pinpointed precisely the difficulty that bedevils modern authors. In the foreshortened world of today, reality thrusts itself upon us as one instantaneous simultaneity. And it is precisely this simultaneity that ambitious novelists, as we have seen, are anxious to capture in their works.

Simultaneity, then, is the novelists' answer to the problem of *experienced* time. In other words, in contrast to the measured flow of chronological time, private time is experienced as simultaneously present. Succession is reunified into simultaneous experience. If life is explained as a series of discontinuous "existential moments," if past and future are meaningful only in their relation to the present moment, then that moment must be experienced in such a way as to embrace not only past and future, but also all multiple aspects of the present.

---

[32] *Herr Meister* (Munich: Piper, 1963), pp. 100-101. At this point I should like also to mention Jens's essay "Uhren ohne Zeiger: Die Struktur des modernen Romans," in *Statt einer Literaturgeschichte* (Pfullingen: Neske, 1957), pp. 23-58. This is one of the most imaginative and stimulating studies of time in the modern novel from Proust to Faulkner yet written.

The Discordant Clocks

The attempt to do this has produced a variety of fictional techniques that, for the sake of convenience, can be divided into two groups: those that achieve the effect of vertical simultaneity in time, and others that aspire to horizontal simultaneity in space. Among the techniques of the first group, Thomas Mann has particularly singled out the leitmotif, "that magical formula which points forward and backwards and which is the means of bestowing present validity upon its inner totality at every moment."[33] But each author provides his own examples. In *The Magic Mountain* Hans Castorp's dreams of the past and his visions of the future are used to this effect. Malte's associative visions, his epiphanies, and the typological prefigurations of the historical figures also establish the effect of temporal simultaneity, as do the repetitions in *The Trial*, which foreshadow the repetitions that link the three parts of *The Sleepwalkers*. In his novella *The Journey to the East* Hermann Hesse portrays a timeless realm in which figures from wholly different historical periods exist side by side.[34] And Döblin suggests through the montages of *Berlin Alexanderplatz* that Job and Orestes are present in the figure of Franz Biberkopf.

Along with these techniques that render the experience of vertical simultaneity,[35] there are others that lend themselves to the representation of horizontal simultaneity. Döblin exploits the device of the montage in order to reproduce

[33] "Einführung in den *Zauberberg*," *GW*, XI, 603.

[34] In this connection see my study of *The Novels of Hermann Hesse*: (Princeton: Princeton University Press, 1965), esp. Chap. 3: "Timelessness: The Chiliastic Vision."

[35] Roger Shattuck, *Proust's Binoculars: A Study of Memory, Time and Recognition* (New York: Random House, 1963), analyzes three methods that Proust employs to organize his *instantanés*: the cinematographic principle, the montage principle, and the stereoscopic principle. Robert Humphrey, *Stream of Consciousness in the Modern Novel* (Berkeley and Los Angeles: University of California Press, 1959), provides an intelligent discussion of various techniques used to convey the effect of stream of consciousness.

Franz Biberkopf's experience of the multiplicity of the city as instantly and totally present. The narrator of *The Sleep-walkers* contrives the parallel strands of his story in such a way as to reflect the simultaneity of their occurrence. Hans Castorp's encyclopedic studies, as well as the essayism of Broch and Robert Musil, tend to allow the reader to experience present multiplicity simultaneously. Virginia Woolf, Huxley, Gide, and Hesse all experimented with fictional variations of the musical fugue expressly as a means of reducing multiplicity to simultaneity. There is no need to rehearse once again the variety of techniques that we have observed in the course of the individual analyses. By now it should be clear that most of these techniques, in addition to those employed by Proust, Joyce, and others, represent an attempt to render the simultaneity that is felt to be the essence of the experienced moment.[36]

(5)

SIMULTANEITY, however, is a mode of perception, not of action. Action can take place only in time, not out of it. For this reason the various novels also represent different possi-

---

[36] In this connection see A. A. Mendilow, *Time and the Novel* (London and New York: Peter Nevill, 1952), p. 63: "In the final analysis, virtually all the techniques and devices of fiction reduce themselves to the treatment accorded to the different time-values and time-series, and to the way one is played off against the other." The usefulness of this study, which contains a number of brilliant comments on fictional technique, is vitiated by three big weaknesses: an insufficient understanding of the philosophical problems underlying the modern problem of time (e.g., p. 8, where Heidegger is confused with Heisenberg); a lack of awareness of foreign novels and critical works on time; and a tendency to resolve modern experiments "into little more than the development of devices foreshadowed in the eighteenth century" (p. 160). The last remark, of course, runs counter to the central theme of Poulet and Meyerhoff, and of my own chapter.

bilities of rhythmical variation in the relationship between perception and action, between timelessness and time. Hans Castorp's only real act is his decision to return to the plain when war breaks out; otherwise, as we have seen, the novel consists exclusively of talk and of Castorp's suspension between the various ideological positions presented by the other figures of the work. Hence *The Magic Mountain* reveals itself to us as a seven-year stretch of timelessness bounded by the temporality from which Hans Castorp emerges at the beginning and to which he ultimately returns. *The Trial* displays precisely the same pattern: Josef K.'s "awakening" jolts him out of the temporality to which he is returned only in the moment of his execution. Between these two events life presents itself to him as a series of timeless repetitions.

In *Berlin Alexanderplatz* the pattern is different. Franz Biberkopf emerges from the timelessness of Tegel Prison into the temporality of Berlin: three times he is beaten back into the timeless suspension of reflection before, ultimately, he becomes capable of surviving in the world of temporal action. The situation in *The Sleepwalkers* is far more complex. Bertrand Müller, the narrator of the entire trilogy, never emerges from his state of timelessness: totally alienated from the temporal world, he writes his essays and stories as an exercise in cognition. His three heroes, on the other hand, return after their six-month periods of suspension to the world of action and time; Huguenau's "holiday" ends when he murders Esch, rapes Mother Hentjen, and then settles down to his new life as a prosperous and respectable businessman.

But this tension between perception and action, produced by the rhythmical alternation of timeless suspension and temporal movement, produces a deeper ethical tension between freedom and responsibility. Past, present, and future, according to the existential view, "are for our inner temporality no longer parts of one and the same temporal continuum, but the three directions in which the temporal behavior of man extends and of which the present moment is constituted."[37] Any view of this sort, which liberates the present from any causal connection with the past, necessarily implies that the future is also a matter of the free choice of the individual. As Hans Meyerhoff puts it: "If such a temporal perspective is introduced, departing so radically from any objective metric and order, it is not difficult to take another step and say that the ordinary modalities of time—past, present, and future—are, strictly speaking, indistinguishable in experience; that they are contained (even those not actually experienced) as infinite possibilities within *any* moment of the life span of an individual."[38] The experience of subjective time as simultaneous duration, in other words, is an experience of freedom and potentiality. In these moments the individual perceives, as he is unable to do when he is pulled along by the relentless movement of public time, that he is free to determine his own future.

Now we have seen that, historically, the conflict between private time and public time emerged as one aspect of the struggle between determinism and freedom. In fact, Bergson's first major work, *Essai sur les données immédiates de la conscience* (1889), was devoted largely, as the title of the English translation indicates, to the question of *Time and Free Will*. Mechanism and determinism, he writes, "cannot hold good against the witness of an attentive consciousness, which shows us inner dynamism as a fact."[39] We are free, he continues, "when our acts spring from our whole personality"— at those moments, in short, when our acts are shaped by our perception of reality as a simultaneous duration. "In a word,

[37] Bollnow, *Existenzphilosophie*, p. 106.

[38] *Time in Literature*, p. 26.

[39] Quoted here and below in the translation by F. L. Pogson (New York: Harper Torchbooks, 1960), pp. 172-73.

if it is agreed to call every act free which springs from the self and from the self alone, the act which bears the mark of our personality is truly free, for our self alone will lay claim to its paternity."

In the light of these observations, the experience of timeless duration, the representation of the world as simultaneously apprehended, can be understood as an extended metaphor for the moment of freedom in which the individual contemplates the world from the standpoint of his new perception and reaches his decision to act accordingly. This interpretation seems to bear out our understanding of the various texts. For in each of them the period of perception and reflection is followed by a return to temporality—even, if we can believe his version of the legend of the Prodigal Son, in the case of Malte Laurids Brigge. The experience of duration and simultaneity acts as an impulse to ethical action.

At the same time, this very freedom is coupled with a sense of guilt and is largely responsible, as we shall see in Chapter Nine, for the prevalence of the metaphor of the criminal in modern fiction. For the freedom of simultaneous perception removes the hero from the ethical responsibility that exists only in the realm of temporal action. As long as he is lifted out of time—like contents of the vacuum jars of which Hans Castorp speaks or like Huguenau in his "vacation state"—man is not functioning in his capacity as an ethical being. Thus Malte is keenly aware that he belongs to the "outcasts." Hans Castorp regards his experiments in perception as an "aventure dans le mal." Josef K. clings deperately to his state of timeless repetition in order to avoid for as long as possible the responsibility and punishment that await him in temporality. Franz Biberkopf remains involved with crime until he finally comes to terms with the temporal world and stops fleeing at every instigation into a timelesss retreat. And Huguenau perpetrates the most reprehensible crimes—theft, rape, murder—before he resumes his life in the world of everyday time.

We see, then, that man's attempt to escape the clocks leads on the one hand to a state of heightened perception, and on the other to a loss of ethical responsibility. The paradoxical dilemma of modern writers is revealed most poignantly by the fact that they ultimately send their heroes, armed with intensified awareness, back to the responsibility of the temporal world, while they themselves by necessity remain in the timeless state of aesthetic detachment. Huguenau returns to the world, but Bertrand Müller remains in his lonely room, wiser but sadder. Yet despite the uneasy conscience that plagues so many writers (Broch spoke of "the immorality of the ivory tower") they cling to their vision of simultaneity. To understand why, we must go a step further.

(6)

THE GREAT moments of modern literature are instants of a sudden, intense, almost blindingly vivid perception: what Virginia Woolf in *The Waves* called "rings of light."[40] Wherever we look, we are confronted with these moments of revelation. Joyce called them epiphanies, and his works are in one sense a catalogue of these moments of Thomist *claritas*. But the moments can come in different forms: Proust's *madeleine* and Hans Castorp's vision in the snowstorm; Malte's instants of "seeing" and Franz Biberkopf's dialogue with Death; even Josef K.'s agonizing realization, at the end of his life, that he

[40] *The Waves*, p. 264. This is merely one of many vivid images in that novel through which Virginia Woolf stresses the characteristic luminosity of these moments wrested out of "the loop of time" (p. 189). This same radiance is mentioned explicitly by many other writers: Joyce, Rilke, Hofmannsthal, Musil. See, in this connection, my article on "James Joyces Epiphanie und die Überwindung der empirischen Welt in der modernen deutschen Prosa," *Deutsche Vierteljahresschrift*, 35 (1961), 595-616.

is dying "like a dog." The insight gained in such moments ultimately justifies the state of timeless suspension in which the hero lives. "The moments during which we thus grasp ourselves are rare," writes Bergson, "and that is just why we are rarely free. The greater part of the time we live outside ourselves"[41]—in the world of public time.

This leads us to a final remark. The moments of light receive their meaning only in counterpoint to the knowledge that time is moving inexorably toward death. "And do you not understand," Gide wrote in *The Fruits of the Earth* (1897), "that no instant would ever assume that admirable luster unless set off, so to speak, against the very dark background of death?"[42] The entire discussion of time must be seen, in the last analysis, in connection with the theme of death. The search for the duration of private time reveals itself as a reaction against the realization that time leads toward death. As Hans Meyerhoff notes, "The significance of a timeless dimension in experience, the self, the work of art, or beyond experience can be fully appreciated only when it is placed within the context of the melancholy, gloomy reflections ensuing from the direction of time toward death and nothingness."[43]

It is the awareness of death that makes the individual cling to the experienced moment, in which he seeks meaning and duration.[44] "Death is woven in with the violets"—this is the

[41] *Time and Free Will*, p. 231.

[42] *Nourritures terrestres*, in André Gide, *Romans* (Paris: Gallimard, 1958; Bibliothèque de la Pléiade), p. 172.

[43] *Time in Literature*, p. 74.

[44] See Frederick J. Hoffman, *The Mortal No: Death and the Modern Imagination* (Princeton: Princeton University Press, 1964), p. 4: "Death turns us toward life and forces us to admire or cherish it (even though we may despair of it as well), to begrudge the passing of time (which is signified by changes occurring in objects) and eventually to despair of conclusions." I mention Hoffman's book here

image through which Virginia Woolf asserts the inextricable bond between the intensified poetic experience and death.[45] It is the threat of death that causes men to rip the hands off their watches and to throw away their clocks. It is the fear of death that causes the conflict between private time and public time. Yet inevitably man must return, at the end of his life or at the end of his novel, from the realm of duration to the realm of public time, from the irresponsibility of simultaneous perception to the ethical arena of time. For it is only in reality that the clocks function. It is only here that a man finally discovers, in the words of two other writers oriented toward time and death, for whom the bell tolls.[46]

---

rather than in the following chapter because, despite its title, it is not so much about death as about the intensified turn to life and temporal experience found in modern literature.

[45] *The Waves*, p. 273.

[46] From among the many studies of time in literature, I should like to single out for mention two more works that are of general interest, though not applicable in our specific context: Emil Staiger's *Die Zeit als Einbildungskraft des Dichters* (Zurich and Leipzig: Niehans, 1939), which deals with the poetry of Brentano, Goethe, and Keller; and Jean Pouillon's *Temps et roman* (Paris: Gallimard, 1946), which is less concerned with time than with point of view and psychology.

chapter seven

The Metaphysics of Death

(1)

To THE uninitiate, a catalogue of the important works of modern German literature reads like a necrophile's delight, a literary feast for the morbid sensibility—just the sort of thing one might expect from such poets as Rilke, that self-styled "pupil of death" who knew few pastimes more beguiling than that of deciphering the inscriptions on Italian Renaissance gravestones in order to let himself "be educated by their limitless knowledge."[1]

In Vienna the modern age opened with the lyrical dramas in which Hofmannsthal celebrated Titian's death (*Der Tod des Titian*, 1892) and depicted the confrontation between a foolish aesthete and Death (*Der Tor und der Tod*, 1893). The stories of Arthur Schnitzler, written mainly between 1895 and 1910 and typologically characteristic of the literature of the times, usually revolve around death ("Sterben," "Die Toten schweigen," "Der Tod des Junggesellen"). Schnitzler was fond of casting his tales in the form of farewell letters of dying men ("Andreas Thamayers letzter Brief," "Der letzte Brief eines Literaten"), and one of his experiments with interior monologue ("Fräulein Else," 1924) renders the last hours of a woman who has taken her own life by poison. Like Hofmannsthal's aesthete, the protagonist of Richard Beer-Hofmann's novella *Der Tod Georgs* (*The Death of George*, 1900) is a recluse who learns to appreciate life only through the experience of three great scenes of death, both real and imagined.

[1] Rilke, *Briefwechsel mit Benvenuta* (Esslingen: Bechtle, 1954), p. 93: "ein Schüler des Todes."

The Metaphysics of Death

The centrality of death in the works of Viennese neoromanticism has often been noted,[2] but it was by no means these writers alone who succumbed to the lure of thanatopsis. Gottfried Benn gave his first collection of poems the symptomatic title of *Morgue* (1912). Many of the stories recounted by Malte Laurids Brigge in his notebooks deal with death, and in the tenth of his *Duino Elegies* (1922) Rilke painted an apocalyptic landscape of death that rivals Grünewald's Isenheim Altar. With the title *Death in Venice* (1911) Thomas Mann epitomized one of his most characteristic themes; indeed, *The Magic Mountain*, which was originally begun as a comic counterpart to that famous novella, might well have been known as "Death in Davos." In *Berlin Alexanderplatz* Death appears as the most powerful of the voices that speak to Franz Biberkopf and bring about his spiritual rehabilitation. And death was a central theme for Hermann Broch long before he devoted over five hundred pages to a detailed poetic rendition of *The Death of Vergil* (1945).

This obsession with death is not, of course, unique to modern German literature. Around the turn of the century writers all over Europe were gravitating toward this compelling theme. The somber preoccupations of the aging Tolstoy in such late masterpieces as *The Death of Ivan Ilych* (1886) were matched by the mysterious presentiments of Maeterlinck's *Pelléas et Mélisande* (1892). Joyce's *Dubliners* (1904) opens with the death of a priest and closes with "The Dead." Proust, in search of time past, repeatedly came face

[2] Martin Buber, "Geleitwort," in Richard Beer-Hofmann, *Gesammelte Werke* (Frankfurt am Main: S. Fischer, 1963), p. 5; also Erich Kahler's introduction to Hermann Broch's *Gedichte* (Zurich: Rhein, 1953), pp. 12-14. What still remains to be studied is the extent to which this obsession is related to contemporary psychological theories, especially to those of Ernst Mach.

to face with death, and these encounters prompted some of his most memorable scenes and reflections. It is not only true, as one critic noted, that "twentieth-century literature began on the note of death."[3] The last years of the nineteenth century also resounded with its knell.

Every age, of course, has been philosophically aware of death. In the *Phaedo* Plato pointed out that the sage's life is lived in constant observation of death. The medieval antiphony of death—*media vita in morte sumus*—found its visual equivalent in the dance of death of the late Middle Ages. Indeed, the attitude toward this most universal of experiences is in every case so characteristic of the age in which it occurs that R.W.B. Lewis has been led to suggest that "the best way to distinguish the two or three literary generations of our century is in their manner of responding to the fact of death."[4] This is precisely what Walther Rehm set out to do for earlier generations in his profound study of death in German literature: "From a man's attitude toward death it is possible fully to grasp all his other relations to the whole of the phenomenal world as well as to the other great moments of existence."[5]

Generally speaking, Rehm detects and outlines two principal trends in literature from medieval times up to the age of romanticism. The great humanist movements with their orientation toward man in this world—Renaissance, Reformation, Enlightenment, and classicism—regard death as existing only in order to make life possible. This attitude, culminating in the humanism of Goethe, can be traced right down to its presence, in rather trivialized form, in the bland expostula-

[3] R.W.B. Lewis, *The Picaresque Saint; Representative Figures in Contemporary Fiction* (Philadelphia and New York: Keystone Books, 1961), p. 17.

[4] *The Picaresque Saint*, p. 19.

[5] *Der Todesgedanke in der deutschen Dichtung vom Mittelalter bis zur Romantik* (Halle an der Saale: Max Niemeyer, 1928), p. 1.

tions of Settembrini in *The Magic Mountain.* Opposed to this view are such heaven-directed movements as late medieval mysticism, baroque, eighteenth-century sentimentalism, and romanticism, which hold that life exists primarily in order to enrich eternal death. This view, which found its sublime expression in Novalis' *Hymns to Night,* is still present, at least in caricature, in the rabid nihilism of Naphta. It is this "romantic" attitude toward death, finally, that underlies both Hegel's theory of history and Freud's conception of repression and sublimation.[6] Hegel's dialectics of constant change can be traced back to the thought in his *Science of Logic,* that "the nature of finite things as such is to have the seed of passing away as their essential being: the hour of their birth is the hour of their death." And the subtle gymnastics of the human psyche are understood by Freud as a response to the principle stated in his essay *Beyond the Pleasure Principle*: "The goal of all life is death."

From the psychoanalytical point of view, there is a great deal of truth in the implication that the generation of Joyce, Mann, and Proust was enacting in its works a rite of aesthetic sublimation of death. "Art was the answer given back by the first generation to the universal pressure of death."[7] In a more radical formulation, R. M. Albérès has even gone so far as to suggest that "the novel is a substitute for death."[8] According to this view, the very act of artistic shaping somehow re-

[6] See Norman O. Brown, *Life against Death; The Psychoanalytical Meaning of History* (Middletown: Wesleyan University Press, 1959), esp. Chap. 8: "Time, Death, and Eternity." Brown offers a persuasive analysis of Hegel and Freud, but he fails to note: a) their dependence upon earlier romantic sources, and b) differences between their attitude and that of many other modern thinkers.

[7] Lewis, *The Picaresque Saint,* pp. 20-21.

[8] *Histoire du roman moderne* (Paris: Albin Michel, 1962), p. 9: "*Le roman est un substitut de la mort.* . . . le roman a remplacé l'idée de l'éternité, dont il est un *ersatz* sans cesse renouvelé."

moves the threat of death by transposing death into another realm altogether. But if Rehm's analysis is correct, the situation is more complex. When we look closely at specific works we quickly see that the view of death represented there is not the characteristic romantic view, in which life is nothing but a stage along the road to death, nor is it a humanistic view in which death must be overcome at all costs. The typically modern attitude turns out to be neither "for" life nor "for" death. Recognizing, rather, that death is immanent in life, it attempts to achieve a harmonious synthesis of the two forces in the awareness that true knowledge of life must involve a cognition of death.

The speculative basis for this attitude is best exemplified, perhaps, by the thoughts on death articulated by the philosopher and sociologist Georg Simmel (1858-1918). Simmel's "Metaphysics of Death" first appeared as an essay in 1910, but his ideas reached their widest audience as a chapter in his famous book on *Rembrandt* (1916) and as a section in the summation of his *Lebensanschauung* (1918).[9] Although Simmel's direct impact on the public consciousness of his time was slight, his ideas were widely transmitted through his influence on Rilke and other writers with whom he was in personal contact. His thoughts made their way into academic philosophy indirectly, through their decisive effect on Heidegger's philosophy of death.[10] And essentially the same ideas are implicit in Oswald Spengler's *Decline of Western Civili-*

[9] "Zur Metaphysik des Todes," *Logos*, 1 (1910), 57-70; *Rembrandt: Ein kunstphilosophischer Versuch* (Leipzig, 1916); *Lebensanschauung* (Munich and Leipzig, 1918), esp. "Tod und Unsterblichkeit."

[10] In this connection see the introduction to Georg Simmel, *Brücke und Tür; Essays des Philosophen zur Geschichte, Religion, Kunst und Gesellschaft*, ed. Margarete Susman and Michael Landmann (Stuttgart: K. F. Koehler, 1957), p. vi. I refer to the text of Simmel's essay as it is reprinted in this edition on pp. 29-36.

zation (1918), which so accurately reflected the spirit of the times (though perhaps not the spirit of history).[11]

Simmel explains the immanence of death in the following way: "In every single moment of life we *are* such as shall die, and our life would be different if this inherent destiny did not somehow affect it. Just as we are not fully present in the moment of our birth (since some part of us is being constantly born), similarly we do not die only in our last moment. This fact alone makes clear the form-giving significance of death. It delimits, that is to say: it shapes our life not merely in the hour of death. Rather, it is a formal element of our life that colors all its contents: the limiting of the life-whole through death has an anticipatory effect on each of its contents and moments." Death, then, is so pervasively immanent that it decisively shapes life—a thought that we shall encounter again in Rilke and other writers. Life, in turn, can be understood only by reference to death.

But the meaning of death is even greater, for Simmel holds that all human values are based on the fact of death. Death is a limiting factor par excellence. Now limitations are the necessary prerequisite to values of any kind; without limitations there are no differences, but merely an eternal flux within which good and evil, right and wrong merge and blend indistinguishably. It is only within the limitations imposed by death that we become aware of the ethical dimensions of our choices. A life, once lived, cannot be redeemed by the living out of another role. The fact of death not only makes values possible; by separating a life from the values it has ob-

[11] E.g., *Der Untergang des Abendlandes* (one-volume special edn.; Munich: C. H. Beck, 1963), p. 160: "Death is given in birth. . . . Along with the knowledge of life, which remained alien to animals, the knowledge of death grew to be the power that dominates the entire human consciousness."

served, death makes the values ideal and eternal rather than contingent.[12]

Finally, Simmel sees life and death as thesis and antithesis, each necessary to the other. But rising out of this opposition as a synthesis is a higher unity that Simmel calls "reality," and that embraces both life and death. It is man's highest goal to achieve cognition of this unity. "This actual unity can only be lived and, as such, cannot be achieved intellectually." The notion of an immanent reality transcending life and death appealed to the writers of Simmel's generation. But more than that: Simmel's conviction that this unity or reality can only be experienced and not attained by rational means turned out to be a rather accurate prediction of developments to come. For systematic philosophy had for many years tended to ignore the problem of death; this problem was appropriated almost by default by the writers, who had, or sought, means to render the experience of this reality.

It would be irresponsible to deny the differences, both substantial and subtle, between the ideas of the various figures to be discussed in this chapter. But overriding all distinctions, a common modern attitude seems to emerge from their views. In contrast to the earlier polarity of life and death outlined by Rehm, these writers regard death as immanent in life, constituting a higher reality or unity; and they are convinced that a knowledge of death is essential to any true understanding of life itself. In other words, this modern attitude, which is common to many great writers between 1890

[12] Simmel's idea seems to reflect Gide's meaning in *Nourritures terrestres* (Gide's *Romans*, p. 172): "I would no longer try to do anything if I were told, if it were proved to me, that I have all the time in the world to do it. I would be satisfied, from the very start, with having wished to undertake something, knowing that I have time to do all other things *as well*. Whatever I might do would never matter if I did not know that this form of life must come to an end. . . ."

221

and 1930, cannot be regarded simply as an attempt somehow to get around the fact of death by aestheticizing it. The preoccupation with death is but one aspect of a deeper and more serious commitment to life itself.

It is not our function to analyze here in any detail the philosophical beliefs of the era. We want, instead, to ask three related and central questions. First, why did this striking new obsession with death emerge at this particular time in literature? Second, in what way does this new sense of death affect theme and structure in the works themselves? Third, through what devices did the writers attempt to render the experience of the immanence of death if, as Simmel claims, it cannot be grasped and expressed intellectually?

(2)

SEVERAL factors help to account for the new prominence that death assumes toward the end of the nineteenth century. The first and most obvious one would be the new sense of time that we observed in the preceding chapter. The consciousness of an irreversible time proceeding ineluctably toward an inevitable death—the two concepts go hand in hand. "This," says Hans Meyerhoff, "is, without doubt, the most significant aspect of time in human experience, because the prospect of death thus enters, as an integral and ineradicable part, into the life of man."[13] This concept differs quite radically from older notions of death. Christianity proclaimed the overcoming of death because it saw life as extending beyond death into eternity. Likewise, the conception of the Parcae and the thread of life, the fatalistic view that death comes at random, ignored the connection between time and death. But the modern awareness of time is linked closely to the organic conception of an immanent death that is born with life and,

---

[13] *Time in Literature*, p. 66.

at the same time, gives life its form by delimiting it at the end. It is the awareness of death, in turn, that intensifies man's desire to experience the world simultaneously, as we noted in the preceding chapter.

A second factor is necessary as a complement to the new awareness of time. In ages with a strong faith in transhuman meaning—either in God or in history—the obsession with death and time has no cause or occasion to thrive. It has been noted by various thinkers—notably Johan Huizinga in *The Waning of the Middle Ages* and the Catholic existentialist philosopher Louis-Paul Landsberg in his *Essay on the Experience of Death*[14]—that the consciousness of death is most acute in periods of social disintegration. In such times as late antiquity, the late medieval period, and the early twentieth century, when all traditional values seem to be giving way to chaos, the individual is hurled back upon himself and must come to grips with death privately. This is precisely the situation at the end of the nineteenth century. There is no need to rehearse again the phenomenon that has been so frequently noted and analyzed. The stages of disintegration of traditional beliefs, proclaimed loudly by Nietzsche and recorded by many recent cultural historians, are well known.[15] For our purposes it should suffice to note that the modern sense of death is linked to the emergence of subjectivity as the central standard of judgment in the course of the nineteenth century. This individual relativism, in turn, is possible only in a

[14] *Essai sur l'expérience de la mort* (Paris: Editions du Seuil, 1951).

[15] Erich Kahler, *The Tower and the Abyss; An Inquiry into the Transformation of Man* (New York: Compass Books, 1967); Gerhard Mazur, *Prophets of Yesterday; Studies in European Culture, 1890-1914* (New York: Macmillan, 1961); H. Stuart Hughes, *Consciousness and Society; The Reconstruction of European Social Thought* (New York: Vintage, 1961); Fritz Stern, *The Politics of Cultural Despair* (New York: Anchor Books, 1965).

period of pluralism, when strong central values have given way to conflicting sets of values. In the face of this conflict of beliefs, death once again looms large in the mind of the individual man.

The factors of time and cultural disintegration are intensified, in turn, by a third factor. For the keen new sensitivity to death found in the writers and thinkers of the age was not paralleled at all in the public consciousness. Indeed, the age of positivism, as Broch noted,[16] seemed to be involved in a naïve conspiracy to ignore death, to overcome it not by faith in eternity or in the meaning of history but by science and technology. And this blithe positivistic attitude is in no way limited to the nineteenth century. The more insistently death thrusts itself upon us, the more ingeniously man contrives to dismiss it. In a letter of 1949 Broch complained that the United States is "not a proper place to die. The notion of being displayed in cosmetic make-up in a funeral parlor is ghoulish; in this country death is denied."[17] This trivialization of death is a phenomenon that has been well publicized in the United States by Jessica Mitford's best-selling indictment of *The American Way of Death* (1963). On another level altogether, it is perfectly apparent to any observer that our public consciousness attempts to deny death. Ready examples can be seen in the news coverage of any great public death, such as the assassination of President Kennedy or the burning of the three American cosmonauts. On all such occasions it is more than apparent that the public, rather than succumbing to the dignity and grief of the simple fact of death, attempts to escape its impact by taking refuge in a

[16] In the essay "Das Böse im Wertsystem der Kunst" (1933); in *Essays I*, p. 316. This observation is not unique with Broch, of course. See Jacques Choron, *Death and Western Thought* (New York: Collier Books, 1963). In his useful survey Choron is concerned with philosophy rather than literature.

[17] Letter of February 15, 1949; *Briefe*, p. 327.

study of the contingent circumstances: the precise second at which the conflagration broke out, the number of seconds between the shots, and so forth. In the face of this barrage of endless facts, the simple and unequivocal meaning of death virtually disappears.

This trivialization of death is anything but a contemporary American phenomenon, as Broch tended to assume. In *The Notebooks of Malte Laurids Brigge*, Rilke poured out his indignation at the lack of respect and appreciation for the simple dignity of death in Paris at the turn of the century:

> This distinguished Hôtel is very old; even in King Clodwig's time people died here in a number of beds. Now the dying goes on in 559 beds. Factory-like, of course. Where production is so enormous the individual death is not so well made. But that doesn't really matter. It is quantity that counts. Who cares anything nowadays for a finely tailored death? No one. Even the rich, who could after all afford the luxury of dying elaborately, are beginning to be careless and indifferent; the wish to have a death of one's own is growing ever rarer.[18]

The images of tailoring seem to be permanently associated in Rilke's poetic indignation with tawdriness, for twelve years later, in the fifth of the *Duino Elegies*, he lampooned the sterile deaths of the modern world in the figure of the modiste "Madame Lamort," who shapes life into falsely colored ribbons, frills, artificial fruits, and flowers for "the cheap winter-hats of Destiny."

The tendency to trivialize death, to ignore it, to aestheticize it, constitutes an important factor in almost all the works we have mentioned. Hofmannsthal's Claudio has attempted to escape death by retreating into art, Franz Biberkopf tries blindly to ignore its call, Broch's Vergil begins by despising

---

[18] *Malte*, pp. 713-14.

death and Rilke's Malte by fearing it. In short, the literary obsession with death reflects, at least in part, the public tendency assiduously to overlook the immanence of death in life and to deny its cognitive value. (Only Hans Castorp begins with an intuitive sense of the dignity of death, and in his case this sense is aroused by the general disregard of death that he encounters in the sanatorium.)

A fourth factor, finally, must be taken into account. Schopenhauer was the first modern philosopher to deal extensively with death in an attempt to make it a part of his system. In *The World as Will and Idea* he asserted that death is the "Musagete" or inspiring genius of all philosophy.[19] Nevertheless, Schopenhauer's exhortation remained largely ignored by the positivistic philosophers of the nineteenth century, who had no room in their systems for such a metaphysical notion as death. To be sure, there were isolated thinkers who stressed the importance of death. In his epoch-making work on ancient grave symbolism, Johann Jakob Bachofen had uncovered the importance of death in classical cults.[20] Similarly, it was a central principle of Wilhelm Dilthey's seminal studies of experience and poetry that the relation of life to death is the one that most deeply determines the feeling of our existence, for "the delimitation of our existence through death is always decisive for our understanding and our estimation of life."[21] Wagner's Tristan and Isolde (1859) were intoning exultant arias to death long before Nietzsche's

[19] *Die Welt als Wille und Vorstellung*, Part II, Chap. 41. It was this long section on "Death and its Relation to the Indestructibility of our Being in Itself" that had such a profound impact on Thomas Buddenbrook in Thomas Mann's earlier novel (Part X, Chap. 5).

[20] *Versuch über die Gräbersymbolik der Alten* (Basel, 1859).

[21] *Das Erlebnis und die Dichtung* (6th edn.; Berlin and Leipzig: Teubner, 1919), p. 230. Dilthey's essays, published as a book in 1905, had appeared separately from 1865 on. This quotation occurs in the section on Goethe (1877).

The Metaphysics of Death

Zarathustra (1883) proclaimed the value of "The Free Death."

But generally speaking, the impact of these thinkers was not felt until the twentieth century, while the hardnosed philosophers of the nineteenth century dealt with more pragmatic matters. Even Simmel's ideas had a greater influence on artists and writers than on the professional philosophers of his generation, partly because he tended to express himself in essayistic fashion rather than systematically and because he obtained a chair of philosophy only a short time before his death in 1918. In any case, the logical positivism that dominated Viennese and Anglo-American philosophy in the twenties and thirties had little patience with such metaphysical concerns. Even today, most Anglo-American philosophers of the analytical school hold that the study of death belongs properly to the fields of psychology and social science, not to philosophy.[22] Of all the directions philosophy has taken since Schopenhauer, only existentialism has conspicuously concerned itself with the phenomenon of death. And this development is so recent that it delimits and reflects the tendencies of "modern" literature rather than contributing in any essential way to it.

The feeling, then, that philosophy had reneged on its responsibility to deal with death led the writers to take the problem, which was growing ever more acute, into their own hands. As the result of the congruence of various complex factors, death had emerged as one of the central concerns of modern times. And the philosophy of the age was unwilling to come to grips with it or even to take cognizance of the problem. It was this state of affairs that led Broch to grumble that since philosophy and science had completely appropriat-

[22] See Robert J. Olson's article on "Death" in *The Encyclopedia of Philosophy*, ed. Paul Edwards (New York: Macmillan and The Free Press, 1967), ii, 307-9.

ed the realm of life, the only proper subject remaining for literature was death! This observation went hand in hand, moreover, with Simmel's feeling that the synthetic "reality" of life and death was a unity that could never be comprehended rationally, but only experienced intuitively.

(3)

THE BELIEF in the immanence of death in life and the conviction that a true knowledge of life can be attained only through cognition of death—these are the two attitudes that characterize much modern thought and, specifically, most literature of the modern period. Both emerge clearly and paradigmatically in Hofmannsthal's poetic dialogue between Death and the Fool, for in the short verse drama the theme of death is not complicated by other main or secondary themes. Claudio, whose very name is etymologically symbolic, represents the aesthete who has attempted consistently to "close himself off" from life, and hence from the threat of death. But he is compelled to realize that Death has been his constant companion throughout his life, touching him in the depths of his soul with a sacred and mysterious power in every truly great hour that he has experienced:

> In jeder wahrhaft grossen Stunde,
> Die schauern deine Erdenform gemacht,
> Hab ich dich angerührt im Seelengrunde
> Mit heiliger, geheimnisvoller Macht.[23]

[23] *Der Tor und der Tod* (1893), in Hugo von Hofmannsthal, *Gedichte und lyrische Dramen* (S. Fischer, 1952), p. 209. Regarding the theme of death, see esp. Richard Alewyn's essay on "Der Tod des Ästheten," in his book *Über Hugo von Hofmannsthal* (Göttingen: Vandenhoeck and Ruprecht, 1958), esp. p. 74: "This is the initiation that Claudio now receives: Everywhere life borders on death, not only as a continuing possibility (in the sense of Christian death), but also as an ever-present reality."

The Metaphysics of Death

This recognition of the immanence of death in life is paired, moreover, with Claudio's ultimate acknowledgment of the cognitive power of the very experience that he has so assiduously sought to avoid. As Death directs the parade of figures from Claudio's past through the aesthete's chamber, Claudio for the first time perceives the facts of his life and his human relationships in their true perspective. He dies with a murmured query on his lips: "Why, O Death, must you be the first to teach me to see Life?"

Despite certain variations, this theme links all the novels we have considered and even, as we shall see, determines certain of their stylistic characteristics. The story that Malte Laurids Brigge confides to his notebooks is in one important respect the record of his attempts to come to terms with death. Rilke was obsessed as few men have been with death, throughout his life and in all of his works.[24] But his characteristic attitude began to crystallize in the "Book of Poverty and Death" (written in 1903) that constituted the third part of his *Stunden-Buch* (*Book of Hours,* 1905). Here, for the first time, Rilke speaks of "der eigene Tod," a conception that was to play a great role in Malte's reflections. For our purposes, the debate regarding the source of this conception of a unique, personal, private, individual death is irrelevant. Scholars most frequently point to the Danish writer Jens Peter Jacobsen, whom Rilke admired and in whose novels (especially *Marie Grubbe* and *Niels Lyhne*) a similar notion is developed.[25] However, Walter Rehm is undoubtedly correct when he attributes equal importance to Simmel's meta-

[24] For the most exhaustive study of Rilke's conception of death, see Walther Rehm, *Orpheus; Der Dichter und die Toten* (Düsseldorf: L. Schwann, 1950), pp. 377-669. Rehm, unfortunately, has little to say about *Malte* specifically (pp. 586-89).

[25] Lydia Baer, "Rilke and Jens Peter Jacobsen," *PMLA*, 54 (1939), 900-932 and 1133-80.

physics of death.[26] Moreover, Rilke was soon to find a new confirmation of his thoughts on death in Kierkegaard. Most recently, attention has been drawn to the influence of the Danish novelist Herman Bang, particularly of his novel *The Gray House*.[27] The obvious conclusion to be drawn from this variety of possible sources is simply this: the theme of an immanent death—another way of saying "one's own death" —was so widespread at the time that its origin can hardly be pinpointed.

In his *Stunden-Buch* Rilke includes a brief prayer in which he implores God for the kind of individual death that emerges from every life that has known love, meaning, and despair. For men, he continues, are merely the leafage or shell preceding or containing the true fruit, Death, that each man bears within himself:

> O Herr, gieb jedem seinen eignen Tod.
> Das Sterben, das aus jenem Leben geht,
> darin er Liebe hatte, Sinn und Not.
>
> Denn wir sind nur die Schale und das Blatt.
> Der grosse Tod, den jeder in sich hat,
> das ist die Frucht, um die sich alles dreht.

This inchoate sense of the immanence of death was intensified to an almost unbearable pitch by the experience of Paris, where for the first time Rilke was confronted both with death as intensified by the modern metropolis and with the phenomenon of the trivialization of death. His poems from 1903 until 1909—especially the *New Poems* and the two great "Requiems" that he wrote in 1908—revolve around the experience of death. In the face of all the death to which he

---

[26] *Orpheus*, p. 586.

[27] Hans Aarsleff, "Rilke, Herman Bang, and *Malte*," Proceedings of the IVth Congress of the International Comparative Literature Association (The Hague and Paris: Mouton, 1966), pp. 628-36.

was witness, Rilke felt that the only possible escape was to embrace death in the hope of learning from it. The poem "Todes-Erfahrung" ("Experience of Death," 1907) employs the metaphor of the stage, which stands in the same relation to reality as does human life to the greater reality of life beyond death. We can know nothing of the actual demise, "which doesn't share with us." But at the moment when a beloved person dies, a "patch of reality" breaks into the stage of life by way of the opening through which the deceased has departed:

> Doch als du gingst, da brach in diese Bühne
> ein Streifen Wirklichkeit durch jenen Spalt
> durch den du hingingst. . . .

Those left behind continue to act out the drama of life. But from time to time the existence of the departed can come over us, "sinking down like a knowledge of that reality," so that we can continue to play at life:

> . . . aber dein von uns entferntes,
> aus unserm Stück entrücktes Dasein kann
>
> uns manchmal überkommen, wie ein Wissen
> von jener Wirklichkeit sich niedersenkend,
> so dass wir eine Weile hingerissen
> das Leben spielen, nicht an Beifall denkend.

It would be a mistake to conceive of this "experience of death" in the traditional romantic sense. Indeed, Rilke specifically denied any such intent, most articulately in a letter of consolation written in 1923, which virtually expands into an essay on death.[28] "Believe me, Death is a *friend*, our closest, perhaps our only one who is never, never disconcerted by

[28] Letter of January 6, 1923, to the Countess Margot Sizzo-Noris-Crouy; Rilke, *Briefe* (Wiesbaden: Insel, 1950), II, esp. 378-82.

our behavior and vacillation . . . and I do *not* mean this, of course, in that sentimental-romantic sense of denial of life, the opposite of life. But our friend expressly when we are most passionately committed to existence in this world, to action, to nature, to love." In the same letter, after reproaching all modern religions for preaching the consolation of death in euphemistic terms instead of teaching their believers how to get along with death, Rilke continues with expressions of the greatest praise: "Death is not *beyond* our power; it is the measuring line at the edge of the vessel; we are *full* whenever we reach it." Rilke avers that he does not want to insist that we should love death. But we should love life so generously that death is automatically included in this love. "It would be conceivable that Death is infinitely closer to us than life itself . . . What do we know of it?!" One truth, he goes on, has become ever clearer to him through the years: "The sole goal of our effort can be to predicate the *unity* of life and death, so that this unity may eventually reveal itself to us. As prejudiced as we are *against* death, we never manage to liberate it from our own misrepresentations." Here, only three years before his own death, Rilke has formulated his thoughts quite lucidly. But when we look back, we recognize essentially the same attitude in Malte Laurids Brigge, who spends so many hours drawing up the catalogue of deaths that fills his notebooks.

Malte's journal begins with death. "So, this is where people come in order to live; I should sooner think that this is a place for dying." In this first sentence life and death are radically juxtaposed, and many months pass before Malte reaches, tentatively, that understanding that Rilke expressed in so many of his poems and letters. For the act of "learning to see" reveals death to Malte in many unexpected forms. He not only encounters death as it goes on "factory-like" in the hospitals of Paris; he also realizes that the misery he perceives at every turn is nothing but what might be called a secularization, a premonition of death. The trivialization of death in modern society leads Rilke, in accordance with his "sacred law of contrasts," to recall other deaths that he has experienced: the death of his grandfather Brigge, a "genuine" death that went on for weeks and was so powerful and immense that it cast its spell not only over the household but over the surrounding countryside as well. Malte forces himself to recall in graphic detail the death of his own father, who had specified in his last wishes that a needle be inserted into his heart to make certain he was dead. As he sits in his chamber Malte intones a veritable litany of deaths: women, children, dogs, neighbors, even flies. And their deaths all had one thing in common. "When I think of the others that I have seen or of whom I have heard: it is always the same. They all had their own death."[29] When he runs out of deaths that he has personally witnessed or been involved in, history provides him with a limitless supply of examples. These he relates, often at great length: Christian IV of Denmark; the French poet Felix Arvers; the Portuguese saint Jean de Dieu; the False Dmitri (Grishka Otrepioff); Duke Charles the Bold of Burgundy; Charles VI of France; Pope John XXII.

Structurally, the theme of death determines in large measure the choice of subject matter and its disposition. Malte attempts to get at the nature of people in reverse—not from their births and what follows, but from the light cast back upon their lives by the manner of their deaths. After he has discovered in his dead father's pocket a slip of paper with the anecdote regarding the death of Christian IV, Malte notes: "I now understand quite well, by the way, why a person car-

[29] *Malte*, p. 720.

ries the description of an hour of death deep in his wallet through so many years. It wouldn't even have to be a particularly special one; they all have something rare about them."[30] And it is this rare, unique quality that reveals, almost as in an epiphany, the meaning of the whole preceding life. Death thus serves as a means of cognition of life.

At the same time, Malte's obsession with death, which began in the opening pages as a defensive reaction to his fear and anxiety in Paris, ends by leading to Malte's own overcoming of the fear of death. "Since then [the death of his father] I have thought a great deal about the fear of death, not without taking into account certain of my own experiences. I believe I can say that I have felt it. It attacked me in the city, right in the midst of all the people, often with no apparent reason."[31] But his reflections lead him to conclude that men fear death only because they do not know it. Nothing can lead us toward ourselves more surely than a preoccupation with the death that is immanent in our lives. "Sometimes I imagine how heaven came to be, and Death: through the fact that we distanced our most precious possession because there was still so much to do beforehand and because it was not secure with such busy people as we. Now times have passed, and we have become accustomed to lesser things. We no longer recognize our possession and are terrified by its extreme greatness. Couldn't that be the case?"[32] Our fear of death, then, stems from the fact that we have alienated from our being something that inherently belongs to it. This anxiety can be overcome only by a renewed reflection on death and by a conscious attempt to unify again what was originally one and the same: death and life. For this reason Rilke praised "the great lovers." In one of his most extensive utterances on death Rilke explained, with specific reference to Malte Laurids Brigge, that "the lovers do

[30] *Malte*, p. 862.   [31] *Malte*, p. 859.   [32] *Malte*, p. 862.

not live out of this world that has been cut off from the whole. . . . *for they are full of death while they are full of life.*"[33]

The meaning and significance of death, which Rilke stressed so often—but always poetically and obliquely— emerge more coherently in the works of Thomas Mann. In his essay "On the German Republic" (1922), Mann suggests: "And isn't sympathy with Death a symptom of depraved romanticism only if death is opposed to life as an autonomous spiritual power rather than being absorbed, in a sanctifying and sanctified capacity, into life? Interest in death and disease, in the pathological, in decay is merely a sort of expression of interest in life and mankind."[34] Like Rilke, Thomas Mann rejects the imputation that this conception of death is in any sense romantic. He too sees disease, poverty, and suffering as a prolongation of death, its foreshadowing in life. Mann concludes his remarks with a cryptic reference to *The Magic Mountain*, which was at that time nearing completion: "It could be the purpose of a *Bildungsroman* to show that the experience of death is ultimately an experience of life, that it leads to *mankind!*" Many years later Mann unequivocally stated the theme of the same novel: "What he [Hans Castorp] learns to comprehend is, that all higher health must have gone through the profound experience of sickness and death, just as the knowledge of sin is a prerequisite for salvation." With such sentences as these, which can be documented repeatedly in his works, Thomas Mann affirms his

[33] Letter of November 8, 1915, to Lotte Hepner; *Briefe* (1950), II, 56.

[34] "Von deutscher Republik"; *GW*, XI, 851. Lydia Baer, *Concept and Function of Death in the Works of Thomas Mann* (Dissertation: University of Pennsylvania, 1932), traces the emergence of this theme in Mann's works without distinguishing his attitude from the typically romantic view. Joseph G. Brennan, *Thomas Mann's World* (New York: Russell and Russell, 1962), p. 67, explains Mann's whole preoccupation with disease psychoanalytically, seeing it as a substitute for his curiosity about death, which cannot be directly experienced.

belief in the immanence of death and in its cognitive power.

In no novel did he more clearly attempt to put these thoughts into practice than in *The Magic Mountain*. Death, to be sure, was as pervasive a theme for Thomas Mann as for Rilke, from the early story "Death" ("Der Tod," 1897) to the disease, insanity, and death of Adrian Leverkühn in *Doctor Faustus* (1947). But in none of his works—with the exception of *Death in Venice*, which *The Magic Mountain* was originally to complement—are the theme and structure so dominated by death as here. For Davos is a place of death. Within his first hour on the mountain, Hans Castorp is jolted out of his conventional assumptions when he learns that one of the sanatoriums uses bobsleds to transport its corpses down to the village in the winter. In his first conversation with Settembrini, the latter jestingly refers to the two doctors of Sanatorium Berghof as Minos and Rhadamanthes, two lesser divinities of the underworld. From the beginning, the tone set for talk of death is intentionally jocular, but this does not vitiate the deeper meaning of the theme. Indeed, the effect of alienation produced by the humor draws attention to the theme. Within six months Hans Castorp's pursuits have led him through the encyclopedic stage, during which he investigates the physiological processes of life and death, to the "Dance of Death"—the chapter devoted to his missions of mercy to the moribund patients of the sanatorium. His motives are rather complex. "His protest against the dominant egotism was only one of them. Another factor that played a role was especially the need of his spirit to be permitted to take suffering and death seriously and to respect them."[35]

Speaking quite generally, it is this understanding of death that distinguishes Hans Castorp from the other figures in the novel, all of whom misunderstand and misinterpret his motives in their own ways. For Hans Castorp has had a priv-

[35] *Zauberberg*, p. 412.

ileged relationship with death ever since his childhood;[36] but this is a fact that gradually becomes clear to him only after his arrival in this realm of death and after his dream about his grandfather's death. It is this deep-rooted desire to take death seriously that prevents Hans from falling into the routine of the other patients, who tend to ignore, to physiologize, to trivialize, or to ridicule the fact of death. His preoccupations with death and with the dying represent the preliminaries to his great vision in the snow, in which he suddenly perceives for the first time the immanence of death in life and man's position between the two powers, as Lord of the Antinomies.

It is this realization that leads to his final rejection of Settembrini and Naphta, who represent the blind positions of, on the one hand, a naïve humanism, contemptuous of death, and on the other a rabid terrorism that worships death. (But as we noted earlier, this amounts to a rejection of the two attitudes toward death that were conventional in German literature before the modern period.) Life cannot exist without death, he sees in his vision of unity. So Hans Castorp resolves to remain true to death in his heart, but always to remember that this fidelity to death and the past becomes pernicious if it is allowed to dominate our thoughts and actions. *"Man shall, for the sake of goodness and love, concede to death no power over his thoughts."*[37] This insight, italicized in the text to indicate its significance as the high point of Hans Castorp's development, shows the extent to which both the theme and the structure of the novel are dependent upon death. All of Hans's arcane researches, even his subtle questioning of Counselor Behrens regarding the art of painting

---

[36] So much so that Hermann J. Weigand, *Thomas Mann's Novel Der Zauberberg* (New York and London: Appleton-Century, 1933), p. 28, numbers death among Hans Castorp's four *Urerlebnisse* or basic psychic experiences.

[37] *Zauberberg*, p. 686.

skin and his curious manner of wooing Madame Chauchat, are related ultimately to his quest for a greater knowledge of life by way of sickness and death.

The fact that the novel ends with a question mark—both regarding Hans Castorp's fate in the war and regarding the possibility of love emerging from the death of battle—in no way disqualifies the vision of unity that underlies the total conception. Like Malte before him and Franz Biberkopf later, Hans Castorp is confronted at the start with the apparent discrepancy between two great powers, life and death. His development is determined in large measure by his exposure to the presence of death, and culminates in the acknowledgment of the immanence of death in life and of its cognitive value.

Although differing sharply in structure and style, *Berlin Alexanderplatz* reveals the same theme. Here, in contrast to Malte's notebooks and *The Magic Mountain*, death is not so conspicuous at the beginning. It is not until Book 5 that the theme is gently announced through the first verses from the old folksong about Death the Reaper ("Es ist ein Schnitter, der heisst Tod"), which then recur several times as an element of the montage. But at the end death emerges as a far more vigorous force than in the other two works, for in Franz's hallucination Death is personified with all the power of a medieval mystery play. This vision, moreover, casts a retroactive light over the entire preceding action, so that we recognize the presence of death even in scenes where we had not seen it earlier. (It is for this reason, of course, that Döblin reduced the variety of voices that speak in the novel to a single one in the radio version: the voice of Death.) Structurally, despite the vast differences between the delicate neoromantic playlet and the powerfully surging novel, the scene displays a remarkable similarity to Hofmannsthal's *Der Tor und der Tod*—a bit of literary parody, by the way, of which Döblin would have been fully capable (e.g., the Hebbel parody discussed above).[38]

As Franz lies in a coma in the sanatorium, he is still unwilling to see the truth and to acknowledge his guilt and stupidity, his *hamartia*. To convince him, Death unrolls once again the whole panorama of action, demonstrating how often he had appeared to Franz and how consistently Franz had rejected his admonitions. "When Lüders deceived you, I spoke with you for the first time, you got drunk and—held back! Your arm was crushed, your life was in danger, Franz, confess, you didn't think of Death for a single instant, I sent everything to you, but you didn't recognize me, and whenever you divined my presence, you ran away from me, ever wilder and more terrified."[39] The message that Death now hammers into Franz is the immanence of death: "I'm going to put it on record, Franz Biberkopf, you're lying here and you want to come to me. Yes, you were right, Franz, to come to me. How can a man get along if he doesn't seek out Death. The true Death, the real Death."[40] Death has been present at every crucial moment of his life, but Franz has always turned away in his blind attempt "to be respectable." The insight that he now is vouchsafed through the experience with Death amounts to the same vision of unity that both Malte and Hans Castorp attained. At this point the voice of Death crescendos from the calm, reflective cadences of his first speeches to the screeching, sarcastic dialect of the streets of Berlin: "Shut up! You got no head, got no ears. You aren't even born, man, never came into the world. You lousy abortion with crazy ideas! With smart-alecky ideas, Pope Biber-

[38] In the postscript to his edition of *Berlin Alexanderplatz*, Walter Muschg refers (p. 521) in this connection to Ernst Barlach's drama *Der tote Tag* and to expressionist literature generally; but these parallels are not as close as Hofmannsthal's play.

[39] *BA*, p. 475.   [40] *BA*, p. 474.

kopf, he had to be born so that we would find out how things are. Well, let me tell you, buddy, the world needs other guys than you, brighter ones who aren't such wise guys and who see how things are, not made out of sugar, not made out of filth, but sugar and filth together, all mixed up."[41]

In this case it is almost fitting to say that Death *is* cognition. To acknowledge the immanence of death in life is equivalent to realizing that the world is composed of good and evil alike. It is this realization, however, that permits man to overcome evil; for once man is aware, then he faces life, like the new Franz Biberkopf, "with open eyes." For this reason Döblin is able to portray Franz's recovery symbolically, in his final apocalyptic vision. "The Whore of Babylon has lost, Death is the victor and drums her away."[42] After his recovery the city no longer presents itself to Franz as the chaotic Whore of Babylon, the roofs no longer threaten to slide from the houses. He has found himself through the prescience of death, and his new awareness steadies the world in his eyes.

The final pages of *Berlin Alexanderplatz*, following this mighty conjuration of Death, have often been criticized for their triviality—not unlike the vision of peace and love that Thomas Mann puts forward in the last lines of *The Magic Mountain*. However, the meaning of Death with which we are left is no less valid for that reason. "Sacrifice, sacrifice, that is Death!" is Franz's final insight.[43] In this context death means the act of self-sacrifice involved in giving up one's pretensions to naïve respectability in a world that demands shrewd judgment, decision, and commitment. It is only when Döblin, in the last two pages, seeks to render the vision in a dream of a glorified brotherhood of man that the work sinks into triviality, like a movie from the 1930's. To this extent the novel is dated, like the novels of Steinbeck or the

[41] *BA*, p. 479.   [42] *BA*, p. 488.   [43] *BA*, p. 489.

plays of Clifford Odets. This is a dream in which we no longer easily believe. Yet up to this point the theme of death as immanent and as the means of cognition is anything but trivial: it is consistent, moreover, with the conception of death that is central to many of the writers of Döblin's era. And his rendering of Death has a ghastly grandeur rarely matched since the dance of death of the late Middle Ages.

(4)

HERMANN BROCH is by all odds the greatest metaphysician of death in the twentieth century. He devoted many years of his life to an elaborate theory of values based upon the premise that death is the absolute non-value. Reasoning that in an age in which transcendental absolutes no longer exist, Earthly Absolutes can be determined only by a relative process, he maintained that "all value is determined with respect to the absolute non-value, which is death."[44] And in a long essay on "Evil in the Value System of Art" (1933), value is defined simply as "the conquest of death."[45] Yet despite this attitude, which seems quite remote from the views discussed above, the same basic theme found there can be established in Broch's writings as well. For like Rilke, Thomas Mann, Döblin, and other writers, Broch was obsessed with totality and simultaneity. And this totality must embrace all poles of being: both rationality and irrationality, both life and death. Death, however, as the barrier between this life and the unknown, is "the only gate through which the

---

[44] In *Erkennen und Handeln; Essays II*, ed. Hannah Arendt (Zurich: Rhein, 1955), p. 232. Death is such a fundamental conception in Broch's thought that it is discussed in virtually every work on Broch. Two helpful analyses are the essay by Erich Kahler cited in note 2 and Hannah Arendt's introduction to *Essays I*. Both deal with the general role of death in Broch's philosophy.

[45] *Essays I*, p. 316.

Absolute in all its magical significance streams into real life"
and "constantly fills the soul of man with its psychical
being and its metaphysical existence."[46] Thus death is immanent, and cognition of death is necessary if we are to have
any grasp of totality. It is for this reason that Broch, in his
splendid study of "Hofmannsthal and His Age" (published
in 1952), had high praise for Hofmannsthal, Schnitzler, and
Beer-Hofmann, who alone among their Viennese contemporaries sought to come to grips with the problem of death.
"For where there is no genuine relation to death and where
its claim for absoluteness in this world is not acknowledged,
there can be no true ethos."[47]

Everything of human value is referred to the fact of death.
"All religiosity is a coming to grips with death," Broch noted
in the essay "Life without a Platonic Idea" (1932).[48] And a
few pages later, the same thought is generalized: "For the
essence of humanism is, again, nothing but a coming to grips
with death in the sphere of the real." Twelve years later he
wrote to a correspondent that "Myth is always the winning
of a new insight into the phenomenon of death: the meaning
of life is determined from the standpoint of death, hence also
the meaning of history."[49]

Reflection on death becomes a particularly acute need for
men in an age of disintegrating values. It is imperative "to
become privately acquainted with the experience of death:
this is needed by everyone to whom the religious tradition
cannot grant the traditional consolation."[50] *The Death of*

---

[46] *Essays I*, p. 316. This is quite close in imagery and attitude to
Rilke's poem "Todes-Erfahrung."

[47] "Hofmannsthal und seine Zeit"; in *Essays I*, p. 123.

[48] "Leben ohne platonische Idee"; in *Die Unbekannte Grösse
und frühe Schriften*, ed. Ernst Schönwiese (Zurich: Rhein, 1961),
p. 276.

[49] *Briefe*, p. 201.

[50] *Briefe*, p. 271.

The Metaphysics of Death

Vergil was Broch's response to imprisonment by the Nazis and the possibility of an imminent death. "The *Vergil* was not written as a 'book,' but (under Hitler's threat) as my private discussion with death," he later explained.[51] "I was concerned with naked cognition of death, and because it was in the form of literature I chose for this purpose a dying poet, and one who lived under similar circumstances of life as we ourselves. In this connection it was my task to grasp the total being that is turned toward death—hence the physical as well as the emotional and the cognitive."[52]

So poetry, in addition to religion, humanism, and myth, is turned into a vehicle for the cognition of death. How is this to be accomplished? Broch justified his means in a letter to Aldous Huxley, who had criticized the excessive irrationality of the work in a review. "My task was to transmit to the reader perception as it came to me. I had to let the reader re-experience how a person draws near to the knowledge of death (draws near, but never reaches it while still alive) through *Zerknirschung* and self-extinction."[53] Broch would surely not be flattered by the comparison, and certainly *The Death of Vergil* has little else in common with *Berlin Alexanderplatz*. But it should be remarked that *Zerknirschung* is an astonishingly precise word for the process of being racked and crushed that Franz Biberkopf undergoes during his vision of Death; and "self-extinction" is very much implicit in the notion of self-sacrifice that emerges, toward the end of Döblin's novel, as the meaning of Death.

The Death of Vergil is Broch's greatest hymn to the immanence of death and the cognition to which it leads. It is also unquestionably the most spectacular rendition of death in the twentieth century. Since here the theme of death has become the totality of Broch's lyrical novel, only a few points

[51] *Briefe*, p. 376. [52] *Briefe*, pp. 192-93.
[53] *Briefe*, p. 214.

243

can be singled out for mention. The most important in our context is this. Like the other works we have considered, the book begins with images of polarity and disharmony, as, in the first section, the dying Vergil is borne through the streets of Brundisium to the palace of Augustus. It is the actual experience of death, some eighteen hours later, that resolves these apparent conflicts and brings about the great *coincidentia oppositorum* in a vision.[54]

The first three parts of the novel present the preliminaries. But in the short fourth part Broch attempts to render the actual experience of death—an attempt that is unique and remarkable in its poetic power even if the mortal reader is in no position to judge its truth. For as Vergil gradually loses touch with life, he actually experiences the stages of creation —in reverse! He moves progressively back through earlier stages of being: through Paradise; through the stages of animal, plant, and mineral life; back through the original division of light and dark, to the source of all being. And at that point, when he is finally reunited with God, he turns back and, in one grand vision, surveys all of life and reality. The polarities have disappeared. From his sublime position of reunification with the all he now perceives the pattern of wholeness in life, as life and death become one and the same. Broch's sublime vision of unity and simultaneity is more sustained and more intensely lyrical than any other such rendition in modern literature. At the same time, it displays a pronounced structural similarity to Hans Castorp's vision in the

[54] See the brilliant analysis by Hermann J. Weigand, "Hermann Broch's *Death of Vergil*: Program Notes," *PMLA*, 62 (1947), 525-54. Also useful are D. Meinert, *Die Darstellung der Dimensionen menschlicher Existenz in Brochs "Tod des Vergil"* (Bern and Munich: Francke, 1962), and Götz Wienold, "Die Organisation eines Romans: Hermann Brochs *Der Tod des Vergil*," *Zeitschrift für deutsche Philologie*, 86 (1967), 571-93.

snow, which also is built upon the conjuration of mythic images in the mind of its hero.

The Death of Vergil was Broch's most consistent monument to death, but he was obsessed with death in all his works, from *The Unknown Quantity* (1933), whose title refers to death, among other things, down to *The Innocents* (1950). In *The Sleepwalkers* death is no less central to the theme of the novel, but here it is on the epistemological level that it must be sought. There are surprisingly few actual deaths in the book: Joachim's brother dies in Volume One; Bertrand commits suicide in the second volume; Huguenau murders Esch in the third. But these deaths cannot compete, in psychological impact, with the catalogue of deaths in Malte's notebooks or with the "Dance of Death" on *The Magic Mountain*. Furthermore, there are no grand visions of death, as in *The Death of Vergil* or *Berlin Alexanderplatz*. Yet death dominates the book, for much that the figures of the novel experience stems, though they are not aware of it, from a suppressed and unconscious fear of death.

The feelings that dominate and torment the characters of Broch's world are loneliness and anxiety; these are the sensations about which they think and talk. Yet Broch makes it clear that both these feelings are ultimately traceable to a metaphysical fear of death. Thus the narrator of "The Disintegration of Values" speaks of the problem "that alone legitimizes all philosophical thought: fear of nothingness, fear of time which leads to death."[55] The thought of death as the ultimate loneliness is invoked repeatedly: from the gentle words of Bertrand to Elisabeth ("You are alone, as alone as in your lonely dying")[56] to the crude vernacular of the third volume: "A guy is always by himself when he kicks the

[55] *Schlafwandler*, p. 426.
[56] *Schlafwandler*, p. 104.

The Metaphysics of Death

bucket."[57] For Broch's psychology the origin of loneliness and anxiety in death has vast implications. For when the metaphysical problem of death is secularized into psychological terms that the individual can understand, it precipitates itself as feelings of guilt and hostility. Failing to comprehend that his anxiety is a universal metaphysical state, the individual believes that he has brought it upon himself by some wrong, and hence feels guilty. At the same time, since men tend to project their guilt upon others (for Broch, as for Kafka), this guilt produces feelings of distrust and hostility.

Since the source of loneliness and anxiety is fear of death, they can be overcome only through a return to and acknowledgment of death. Hence the longing for redemption through death that all the characters instinctively feel. "Only he who casts himself into the fearful overintensification of loneliness and death, only he perceives unity," Esch says.[58] Bertrand Müller repeats the same thought to Marie: "You know that death alone, this last moment alone, will overcome the estrangement."[59] This paradoxical thought is explained in the last pages of the novel, for death produces a "lucid reality in which things fall apart and disperse to the poles and to the boundaries of the world, where all separate things become one again, where distance is invalidated. . . ."[60] This experience is called "the mystery of unity."[61] The states of alienation into which man is cast by the very fact of his birth can be overcome only by following this lonelines to its utter conclusion, to death. Man was separated from the all by birth; he will be returned to it again by death. Thus death is, once again, immanent in life, and the principal, even sole, means of cognition.

Now these speculations are related to the action of the

[57] *Schlafwandler*, p. 488.   [58] *Schlafwandler*, p. 533.
[59] *Schlafwandler*, p. 612.   [60] *Schlafwandler*, p. 683.
[61] *Schlafwandler*, pp. 105, 283.

novel through the theme announced in the title. For in the state of sleepwalking the individual escapes the bonds of ordinary reality long enough to experience what Broch calls "an anticipatory dream of death."[62] "When wishes and goals are concentrated, when dreams move ahead to the great turning points and crises of life, then the path narrows to darker ravines, and the anticipatory dream of death sinks down upon the man who has until now walked in his sleep: all that has been, wishes and goals, they glide past him once again as past the eyes of a dying man, and one can almost call it chance if it does not lead to death." The sleepwalking state in which the principal characters of the book move is structurally equivalent, then, to the grand visions in the earlier novels. It is a state of heightened awareness, of unity. "In this hovering reality the things stream in upon me, they streamed into me, and I did not have to make any effort to understand them."[63] But sleepwalking has this privileged nature solely through its relation to death. Only death brings true cognition of unity, and sleepwalking offers at best a temporary substitute, a state that the individual cannot sustain indefinitely and from which he must awake to plunge back once again into his human fears and loneliness. At the same time, it is largely because of the cognition of death represented in them that Broch, as we have seen, considers his novels a kind of "prophecy."

(5)

THIS view of death helps to put into proper perspective a characteristic of the modern German novel that distinguishes it in large measure from the European novel in general: its use of the phenomena of mysticism. Students learning German are often confronted with a famous story by Arthur

---

[62] *Schlafwandler*, p. 314: "Vortraum des Todes."
[63] *Schlafwandler*, p. 609.

The Metaphysics of Death

Schnitzler in which the narrator recounts a tale that he has heard from a man who, as it later turns out, must have already been dead at the time of the interview (*Das Tagebuch der Redegonda*, 1911). The tale itself, in turn, intensifies the mystification: a man and a woman who know each other only by sight have constructed in their separate imaginations the circumstances of a love affair between themselves; the two versions later turn out to be identical down to the smallest detail. Another frequently cited instance of such mysticism is the séance described near the end of *The Magic Mountain*, in which Hans Castorp sees the apparition of his dead cousin Joachim. It is not the simple fact of the apparition that has disconcerted readers: that alone could be explained by rational means. The eeriness of the scene arises from the fact that Joachim is clad in the field-gray uniform and combat helmet that were still unknown in the Germany Army before the First World War. The vision, in other words, is also precognitive.

Malte Laurids Brigge records in his notebooks an apparition of his dead aunt, Christine Brahe—a phenomenon taken very much for granted by the other members of the household, who had already witnessed a similar phenomenon shortly after the death of another aunt, Ingeborg. And in another passage we hear that as a child he once saw a disembodied hand emerge from the wall beneath a table and grope about on the floor for a crayon. The narrator of *Berlin Alexanderplatz*, an otherwise emphatically realistic work, does not hesitate to describe the angels who walk the streets of twentieth-century Berlin. One of the central scenes in *The Sleepwalkers* depicts a telekinetic vision: Esch encounters Bertrand in a dream, and, although Esch has never laid eyes on him, all the circumstances of Bertrand's appearance and behavior are absolutely consistent with reality. Other novelists employ similar effects. Harry Haller, the narrator of Hesse's

248

Steppenwolf, has conversations with Goethe and Mozart, while in *The Journey to the East* Hesse nonchalantly intermingles persons from his own circle of friends and figures from past history and literature.

These examples and numerous others might lead us to believe that we are dealing here with a company of convinced clairvoyants. As a matter of fact, several of the writers evinced a pronounced curiosity about spiritualism. Few men, for instance, have been more sensitive to the four-dimensional experience of places than Rilke.[64] He once told his friend Carl J. Burckhardt that in Paris, wherever one turns, "all the dead live on."[65] In Duino Castle, where he conceived his great elegies, he felt that the entire past history of the castle had "materialized," and he was constantly apprehensive lest he disturb the spirits of its past inhabitants. Despite the peace and quiet that he found there, he never felt that he was alone: the dead made a constant claim on his time and thoughts. Similarly, at Muzot, where he later died, Rilke was again preoccupied with the presence of past inhabitants, especially Isabelle de Chevron, whose shade was reported by popular legend to wander disconsolately through the castle. Yet despite all this, Rilke never claimed to have seen a revenant. The cycle of poems "From the Literary Remains of Count C. W." (1920) represents possibly the closest contact that Rilke ever had with the dead; namely, it was his conviction that in these poems he acted merely as a medium, transmitting the poetic impulses of the deceased count.

Along with his friend the Princess of Thurn and Taxis, who was a member of an international Society of Psychical

[64] In this connection see the references to Rilke in Gaston Bachelard, *Le poétique de l'espace* (Paris: Presses Universitaires de France, 1957); esp. Chap. 1, on "the house."

[65] The following examples, and others, are recounted by Walther Rehm in *Orpheus,* pp. 622-25.

249

The Metaphysics of Death

Research, Rilke took part in a number of séances and on occasion even heard the voice of "an Unknown Woman."[66] But generally speaking, Rilke regarded spiritualism with the same mixture of skepticism and unwilling fascination as did Thomas Mann. In his essay on "Experiences of the Occult" (1924),[67] which reports the actual séance that supplied the material for the scene in *The Magic Mountain*, Mann begins by conceding that he anticipates nothing but a contemptuous astonishment from many readers, who will no doubt be amazed to find him dealing with a subject so suspect. He records the various phenomena that he witnessed in the course of a séance conducted in Munich by Dr. Albert von Schrenck-Notzing: sounds, mysterious movements in the darkened room, automatic typing, and the materialization of a disembodied hand. After presenting the various scientific theories that have been advanced in order to explain telekinesis, exteriorizations, and ideoplastic manifestations, Mann concludes that spiritualism, for the most part, is the product of fraud and trickery. And yet, like Rilke, he cannot rid himself of a fascination with occultism, for he sees in it what he calls "empirical-experimental metaphysics."

This last phrase, I believe, points directly to the source of the interest. We have seen that many modern writers believe in a mystical unity of being embracing both life and death. In his "Metaphysics of Death" Simmel used the word "reality" to designate this state, and "reality" is the term that crops up repeatedly whenever the writers discuss these matters. It is used by Broch to describe the cognition achieved by the sleepwalker in his anticipatory dream of death. In "Todes-Erfahrung" Rilke speaks of the "patch of reality" that breaks

---

[66] Hans Egon Holthusen, *Rainer Maria Rilke in Selbstzeugnissen und Bilddokumenten* (Reinbek bei Hamburg: Rowohlts Monographien, 1958), pp. 138-39.

[67] "Okkulte Erlebnisse"; *GW*, x, 135-71.

through into our lives from the realm of unity in the beyond. Hermann Hesse regularly puts quotation marks around the word "reality" when he intends it to designate, ironically, the life of this world as opposed to what he considers the true reality of unity. Even Kafka, as we shall see, conceives of reality in this way.

But how—and this is the central problem—is this "reality" of life and death to be rendered in literary form, since it is in essence metaphysical? This is where occultism comes in, for its phenomena, according to Thomas Mann, represent "empirical-experimental" evidence of the metaphysical belief. The use of such images does not, of course, demonstrate a naïve faith in occultism, any more than "The Metamorphosis" proves that Kafka held incredibly archaic notions regarding the laws of genetics. But occultism supplies concrete metaphors for the abstractions of metaphysics. Rilke, despite his barometric sensitivity to psychic pressures, never saw a revenant in Duino Castle. How he must have envied Malte, who was privileged to see the spirit of Christine Brahe move through the dining hall at Urnekloster. But that is the difference between life and art.[68]

The spiritualistic phenomena, regardless of the authors' attitude toward occultism, constitute metaphors for the immanence of death in life, for the reality of a unity in which death and life coexist simultaneously. And as metaphors, they must be understood within the fictions in which they occur. They have their reality, in other words, only within the hermetic and timeless world of the novel. But there they serve to embody visually the otherwise abstract metaphysical

[68] In a letter of October 21, 1924 to Hermann Pongs, Rilke said that Malte was made a Dane partly in order to make plausible his occult experiences: "because only in the atmosphere of the Scandinavian countries does the ghost appear ranged among the possible experiences and admitted (which conforms with my own attitude)"; Rilke, *Gesammelte Briefe* (Leipzig: Insel, 1939), v, 320.

faith. It is not so much in an underlying mystical belief that
the German authors differ from many of their European contemporaries, as in their willingness, in their fictional worlds,
to transcend the reality of everyday life in order to render
the reality of metaphysical unity. This emerges quite clearly
in a letter written by Aldous Huxley to Hermann Broch in
1945.[69] Huxley, in a review of *The Death of Vergil*, had criticized what he regarded as the excessive irrationalism of the
novel. "When I said, in my review, that I thought some of
the passages devoted to the exploration of the experience of
metaphysical reality were too long and should, in order to
clarify them for the reader, have been alternated with passages of 'straight' narrative, I was not at all thinking of intellectual commentary—I was thinking of passages describing
and expressing the immediate experience of the given, material world, that world which is the product of the Divine,
that world whose every particle and event is the *locus*, so
to speak, of an intersection between creative emanation
through the Logos and a ray of the pure Godhead." Huxley's estimate of Broch's novel is not at issue here. What
emerges from his letter, rather, is Huxley's equally mystical
belief in a metaphysical reality. But the Anglo-Saxon novelist
seeks to express this reality through the experience of the
material world—like Joyce in his epiphanies, like Proust in
his memory.

Broch and many German novelists, in other words, employed a source of metaphor that, for various reasons, was
left untapped by the European novel in general. But these
metaphors, though perhaps disconcerting at first sight, turn
out in the finest novels to be perfectly consistent with the
character of the protagonist and the atmosphere of the fictional world. We are prepared to believe in the vision of the
child Malte, of young Hans Castorp, of the deranged Franz

[69] In Broch's *Briefe*, pp. 218-20.

The Metaphysics of Death

Biberkopf; we would not be prepared to accept these visions from Rilke, Thomas Mann, and Alfred Döblin.

(6)

IF WE have postponed the discussion of Kafka to this point, it is not because he does not share the conception of death that was common to his generation. "I have said Yes to everything," Kafka remarked to Gustav Janouch when his tuberculosis forced him to leave for the sanatorium. "Thus suffering becomes enchantment, and death—it is nothing but an element of sweet life itself."[70] Just as he affirms the immanence of death, so also he believes in its cognitive power, as he implied on another occasion: "In the moment of death man probably surveys his whole life. For the first time—and for the last time."[71] In his "Observations on Sin, Suffering, Hope, and the True Way" (written mainly in 1917 and 1918), Kafka said that "a first sign of beginning cognition is the wish to die."[72] And he remarked on another occasion that "life is for the healthy man nothing but an unconscious and unacknowledged flight from the awareness that one will have to die someday." But this flight, he continues, brings no cognition. On the contrary: it merely interposes the egoistical self between the soul seeking truth and "the knowledge of death."[73] And along with the writers discussed above, Kafka believed that "death is just as real as life."[74]

Thus Kafka shares the belief in the cognitive power of death. But at this point his view begins to differ somewhat. In an undated aphorism Kafka speculates that "anyone who

[70] Gustav Janouch, *Gespräche mit Kafka*, p. 108.
[71] Janouch, p. 95.
[72] In Franz Kafka, *Hochzeitsvorbereitungen auf dem Lande und andere Prosa aus dem Nachlass* (Frankfurt am Main: S. Fischer, 1966), p. 40.
[73] Janouch, *Gespräche mit Kafka*, p. 59.
[74] *Ibid.*, p. 61.

has been in a state of pseudo-death can tell frightful things about the experience, but he cannot tell us how it is after death. Actually he has not even been closer to death than anyone else; he has only experienced something special, and everyday life, which is not 'special,' has become more precious to him for that reason."[75] Hence we can learn a great deal from such people, "but one cannot find out from them the decisive thing, for they themselves have not discovered it. And if they had discovered it, they would not have come back." The cognitive power of death, then, is qualified far more rigorously by Kafka than is the case with the other writers we have considered. Kafka does not, for example, have the assurance of Broch, who felt that he had actually approached the experience of death in *The Death of Vergil.* Kafka would answer that what Broch underwent in portraying death there was indeed a privileged experience, but no more than that. We can learn from it, but it is still not the experience of death itself, from which no man returns. Kafka indicates only one possible loophole. "A man who cannot come to terms with life," he noted in his diary in 1921, "needs one hand in order to ward off his despair at his destiny, . . . but with his other hand he can record what he sees among the ruins, for he sees different things and more than other people. After all, he is dead during his lifetime and the only real survivor."[76] With this metaphor Kafka does not claim such grandiose insights by far as Thomas Mann, Rilke, Broch, or Döblin. Yet it is interesting that he chooses precisely this image of "dead during his lifetime" to characterize the writer with a heightened perception of the misery and glory of life.

Kafka once told Max Brod that he expected to be quite content on his deathbed, provided the pains should not be

[75] "Vom Scheintod"; in *Hochzeitsvorbereitungen*, p. 433.
[76] *Tagebücher*, p. 545.

too great.[77] This unquestionably must refer to his hope that with death would come insight. But he specifically neglected to tell his friend, as the diary note continues, that this feeling had produced the best of his writing: those passages in which someone is dying a hard death because he feels that an injustice is being done to him, a feeling that the reader is expected to share. "For me, however, since I expect to be content on my deathbed, these portrayals are secretly a game; I get my pleasure from dying in the dying man and calculatedly exploit the reader's attention, which is focused on death." No passage indicates more clearly the sort of trickery or fraud that Kafka is capable of perpetrating on the reader by design; almost as though to conceal his true feelings, he purposely leads the reader's emotions in a completely false direction.

At the same time, it helps us to understand the meaning of death in his works. Many of Kafka's most famous works end with the death of the protagonist: "The Judgment," "The Metamorphosis," "The Hunger Artist," *The Trial*. Walter Sokel has suggested very persuasively that "the fragmentary form of most works not ending with the protagonist's death attests to the inability of arriving at certainty."[78] For the only certainties in Kafka's world are those that we attain at the moment of death: that is, cognition through death. At the same time, it is a kind of cognition that no one is privileged to receive along with the dead man. Hence it cannot be communicated. Moreover, a work such as "The Penal Colony" seems to refute even that tentative meaning. For in that story, which sets out to demonstrate the notion of illumination and insight at the moment of death through one of Kafka's most grisly metaphors—the machine that inscribes the prisoner's

[77] *Tagebücher*, p. 448 (December 13, 1914).

[78] *Franz Kafka*, in the series Columbia Essays on Modern Writers (New York: Columbia University Press, 1966), p. 11.

guilt on his very skin—the reverse turns out to be the case. For the officer who preaches this doctrine of illumination experiences no blissful insight when he places himself on the rack; he merely dies in meaningless agony. Kafka cunningly strives to withhold his most private insights from the reader, and his views on death belong to this category.

In the light of his various observations, nevertheless, it might be said with extreme caution that he believes both in the immanence of death and in its cognitive power. And any insights that he himself as a writer is privileged to record, he regards as stemming from his position as "dead during his lifetime." But because, on the other hand, this illumination belongs to death and to death alone, and because death is an experience that is absolutely incommunicable, Kafka never indulges himself, as do the other writers of his generation, in attempts to render these insights by means of metaphor or mystical phenomena. In most of the other cases we have observed, the protagonist is privileged to gain the insight vouchsafed by death in a vision that obtrudes into life itself, and hence to live his life with the heightened awareness that death provides. These novels, therefore, need not end with the physical death of the hero; the possible death or downfall of Hans Castorp or Malte is at most suggested by the author. Since Kafka denies the possibility of such foreknowledge, the only possible ending, if any insight is to be portrayed, is death. And even then the reader is not privy to the insight that Josef K. receives as the knife is plunged into his heart. We can only surmise. Kafka's attitude is perfectly illustrated by the parable of the Man from the Country. Nowhere in the parable are the existence and reality of the Law denied; it is there, but out of reach for the man during his lifetime. And since the parable only extends to the time of his death, the reader has no way of knowing whether or not the man attains the Law after his death.

The Metaphysics of Death

Thus Kafka occupies an intermediate position between the writers of his own generation and those of the next, who regard death as "a wall and not a doorway."[79] They turn away from the experience of mystical unity through cognition of death and toward that concentration upon experience in this world alone that R.W.B. Lewis defines as the "agonizing dedication to life"[80] characteristic of the next literary generation. Although Kafka shares the convictions of Rilke, Thomas Mann, Döblin, and Broch, he is unwilling to use his fiction as a vehicle for the rendition of this experience, since it is one that we cannot know. Yet this awakening to a new "reality" in a state of timeless suspension has surprising implications for the structure of the works in which it occurs.

[79] Hoffman, *The Mortal No,* p. 4.

[80] *The Picaresque Saint,* p. 27. It is perhaps worth noting at this point that death is the key issue on which Sartre, as a representative philosopher of the succeeding generation, differed with Heidegger and others who believed in an immanent death. For Sartre, death is a "contingent" fact that is undiscoverable: that is, neither immanent nor accessible of cognition.

chapter eight

The Novel of the Thirty-Year-Old

(1)

KAFKA'S *The Trial* begins with the awakening of its hero on the morning of his thirtieth birthday and ends, a year later, with his murder on the eve of his thirty-first birthday. At first glance this fact might seem to be no more than one of those singular but otherwise quite useless bits of literary trivia that are simultaneously the delight of pedantic professors and the despair of candidates for a degree in literature. For apart from the structural balance that it lends to the novel, the precise information regarding the hero's age does not seem to be particularly noteworthy. Critics generally point to the author's own crisis in his thirtieth year, thus obviating further discussion of the matter. Certainly Kafka's biography plays a role in the characterization of his hero which should not be overlooked: it is surely no accident that Josef K. is the same age as Kafka was when he wrote *The Trial*.

But if we look further in the fiction of the times, we begin to feel a nagging suspicion that the age of the hero perhaps warrants more attention in some broader connection. For the major novels of our century are positively teeming with thirty-year-old heroes. When Franz Biberkopf is released from Tegel Prison in *Berlin Alexanderplatz*, he is explicitly "a man at the beginning of his thirties." The three protagonists of *The Sleepwalkers*—Pasenow, Esch, and Huguenau—are all thirty years old in the volumes devoted respectively to each. Antoine Roquentin, who suffers from intolerable attacks of *nausée* in Sartre's novel (1938), is a thirty-year-old, as are Meursault, the "stranger" of Albert Camus' novel (1942), and the little curate of Ambricourt in Georges

The Thirty-Year-Old Hero

Bernanos' *The Diary of a Country Priest* (1936). Malte
Laurids Brigge is only twenty-eight at the beginning of Rilke's
"prose book," but he too approaches his thirtieth year during
his Parisian sojourn. And—to give a contemporary example
—Oskar Matzerath expressly concludes the memoirs of his
Tin Drum days (1959) on his thirtieth birthday.

Now it is striking that the age of the hero is even mentioned, let alone, as in most of these cases, explicitly emphasized. For often the precise age of the hero plays no role
in a novel and can only be calculated roughly, from various
hints in the text. So the simple verification of the repeated use
of this age suggests certain questions. For instance, is the age
thirty in itself remarkable in the tradition of the novel? Going
beyond literature, does the thirtieth year have any generally
recognized typological significance that is relevant in this connection? Above all: Can we perceive among these novels,
despite all undeniable variety, any similarities that permit us
to assume a common underlying attitude and structure? Is it
possible, in other words, to speak of a Novel of the Thirty-
Year-Old that bridges, say, the philosophical abyss between
the Catholicism of Bernanos and the atheism of Camus or
Sartre? That affords a literary link between the speculative
flights of Broch, the lyrical raptures of Rilke, and the
black humor of Günter Grass? Or are we dealing merely with
a curious, but otherwise insignificant, coincidence?

The first question can be answered easily. If we consider
some of the best-known fictional heroes of the eighteenth and
nineteenth centuries, we soon realize that most of them share
the sentiments of Schiller's Don Carlos, who cried out in
frustration: "Dreiundzwanzig Jahre, / Und nichts für die
Unsterblichkeit getan!"[1]—which, by the way, is probably an
echo of the words attributed to Alexander the Great, who

---

[1] *Don Carlos*, II, 2: "Twenty-three years old, and I've done nothing
for immortality."

according to a well-known legend was disconsolate because at twenty-three he had not yet conquered the world. Indeed, in the representative novels of the period from 1730 to 1830, very few heroes seem to reach the relatively ripe old age of thirty. Novalis' Heinrich von Ofterdingen is twenty years old. Tieck introduces William Lovell as "a lively cheerful youth," and although his lively cheerfulness is of no great duration, he still doesn't age much in the course of his three-year escapade. The standing epithet for Franz Sternbald is "young," and Count Friedrich, who has just left the university, is scarcely older than Eichendorff himself was when he wrote *Presentiment and Present*: namely, twenty-two. The Chevalier des Grieux has romped through the whole gamut of passions with Manon Lescaut—before his twenty-second year! Tom Jones's comic and tumultuous misadventures land him in the lap of wedded bliss before he becomes twenty-one. Stendhal's Julien Sorel, Voltaire's Candide, and Chateaubriand's René are all in their early twenties.[2]

In comparison with the blush of such tender youthfulness, the protagonists of Jean Paul's *Years of Indiscretion* (*Flegeljahre*, 1804-1805), Goethe's *Wilhelm Meister's Apprenticeship* (*Wilhelm Meisters Lehrjahre*, 1795-1796), Benjamin Constant's *Adolphe* (1816), or Gottfried Keller's *Green Henry* (*Der grüne Heinrich*, 1854-1855; final version 1879-1880) strike us as creaking old-timers. Walt and Vult are twenty-four; both Wilhelm Meister and Adolphe, at the end of their fictional careers, reach their twenty-sixth year, as

[2] *Candide* appeared in 1759 and *René* in 1802 (*René* was published separately in 1805). All the other novels fall within the same period: Novalis (Friedrich von Hardenberg), *Heinrich von Ofterdingen* (1802); Ludwig Tieck, *Die Geschichte des Herrn William Lovell* (1795-96) and *Franz Sternbalds Wanderungen* (1798); Joseph von Eichendorff, *Ahnung und Gegenwart* (1815); L'Abbé Prévost, *Manon Lescaut* (1731); Henry Fielding, *Tom Jones* (1749); and Stendhal, *Le rouge et le noir* (1831).

does Heinrich Lee soon after his return to his home in Switzerland. In these novels, all of which conclude with the integration of the hero into the existing social structure, we find an exemplary confirmation of Hilaire Belloc's "Cautionary Tale" of Lord Lundy:

> It happened to Lord Lundy then,
> As happens to so many men:
> Towards the age of twenty-six
> They shoved him into politics.[3]

It is hardly necessary to cite further examples, because they would merely confirm the tendency we have already noted: in comparison with the typical hero of most older novels, the modern hero displays a pronounced shift in age.[4] Now, if we take into consideration the fact that the tradition of youthful heroes is still vigorous in our own times (some critics have spoken of the "primacy of adolescence" in the twentieth century,[5] and one needs only to think of Proust, Mauriac, Salinger, Golding, Böll, or Hesse to see how true this is) then the thirty-year-old hero distinguishes himself from a dominant trend even within modern literature.

(2)

WE CAN approach this anomaly most easily, perhaps, if we first glance for a moment at some representative views regarding age. For centuries the thirtieth year has traditionally been regarded as the high point of a process of development

---

[3] Hilaire Belloc, *Cautionary Verses* (New York: Alfred A. Knopf, 1959), p. 64.

[4] This generalization applies, of course, only to those novels with a single hero, and not, for instance, to the novel of manners with several leading protagonists (e.g., Goethe's *Die Wahlverwandtschaften* or *Les Liaisons dangereuses* of Choderlos de Laclos).

[5] See Justin O'Brien, *The Novel of Adolescence in France* (New York: Columbia University Press, 1937).

culminating in the integration of the individual into the particular order of the world accepted at a given time.[6] Aristotle, for instance, designates the years from thirty on as the intellectual and physical zenith of life, while Isidore of Seville characterizes the period from twenty-eight to forty-nine as *firmissima aetatum omnium*. For medieval Christianity the thirtieth year marked the beginning of the *aetas canonica,* because Christ went forth at that age to proclaim his teaching. And according to a rabbinical legend, Adam was thirty years old when he was created. Similarly, the numerological calculations of the Romans and of the Germanic tribes yield this as the age at which man's preparation is fulfilled. According to the seven-year stages of the Romans it was the twenty-eighth year, and according to the system of the Germanic tribes the thirtieth, in which a youth fully assumed the responsibilites of adulthood—what the Romans called *aetas legitima.* Everywhere we look, we find the same phenomenon: the years around thirty symbolize a turning point in human development, the integration into society, the goal of all previous education and training. Thirty is the age at which a man reaches certain conclusions about life and wants to write them down. Thus in 1461 François Villon began his "testament":

[6] I have gotten much of the following material from Ulrich Helfenstein, *Beiträge zur Problematik der Lebensalter in der mittleren Geschichte* (Zurich: Europa, 1952). See also Philippe Ariès, *L'Enfant et la vie familiale sous l'ancien régime* (Paris: Plon, 1960), trans. by Robert Baldick as *Centuries of Childhood; A Social History of Family Life* (New York: Vintage Books, 1962). The shift in age from twenty to thirty is doubtless connected with the absence, established by Ariès, of the concept of "adolescence" before the nineteenth century. It is worth noting, finally, that Dante's age at the beginning of *The Divine Comedy* (thirty-five) belongs to another tradition and group of associations: it marks the midway point—"nel mezzo del cammin di nostra vita"—in the biblical threescore and ten.

262

The Thirty-Year-Old Hero

En l'an de mon trentiesme aage,
Que toutes mes hontes j'eus beues,
Ne du tout fol, ne du tout sage,
Non obstant maintes peines eues. . . .⁷

Such a conception of the thirtieth year is possible, however, only within the framework of a stable world-order. As
long as the world and its order remain intact, the thirtieth
year constitutes the threshold to a golden age, to what Balzac
in *La Femme de trente ans* called "ce bel âge de trente ans,"
defining it further as the "sommité poétique de la vie des
femmes." But the reaching of this "poetic peak" implies at
the same time the end of the tumultuous life that characterizes the years of youth. As soon as a man submits to the
existing order of things, life offers little more that is really
worth the telling. His further destiny is virtually predetermined by the function that he voluntarily assumes within the
social structure. As long as the faith of the author in the order
of his world remains unshaken, nothing can happen that
might jeopardize the harmony attained by the thirty-year-old.
Even if the hero perishes in his youth, at the end he ultimately
acknowledges—like William Lovell or the Chevalier des
Grieux—that he has destroyed himself through his own deviations, his own *Zerrissenheit*, his own *désordres*. The
sacred order is maintained and affirmed. Within the framework of such a stable reality, then, it is primarily the period
of youth that offers material for the novelist, whose attention
focuses above all on the critical struggles of his hero's years
of apprenticeship. Thus, in the works of dozens of novelists,
from Grimmelshausen to Fontane, from Fielding to Henry

---

⁷ Quoted from *The Works of François Villon*, ed. Geoffroy Atkin-
son (London: Scholartis Press, 1930), p. 72. "In the thirtieth year of
my age / When I've drunk all my shame, / Not fully mad nor wholly
sage, / For all my suffered blame.

James, we encounter in endless variation the formula of trials and tribulations, of *Irrungen, Wirrungen*. The crisis of the hero may shift in nature according to the religious, philosophical, or social modes of the times; but the typical structure inevitably ends with the awareness of the mature hero that the existent order of the world is good.

It is within this framework that we should also assess the many negative utterances, according to which the thirtieth year is not so much a turning point as a dead end. Thus Montaigne observed: "Among all the fine human deeds that have come to my attention, by far the most of them—today as well as centuries ago—were achieved before the age of thirty."[8] François Mauriac intoned in his *Journal of a Man of Thirty*: "It's too late now—since the war is over—to hope for anything else but the satisfactions of work in peace and quiet with the few people who don't annoy you. Not that you don't regret those whom you have missed forever. But it's too late. At thirty one no longer switches his course in life."[9] (To anyone who recalls the splendid tributes celebrating Mauriac's eightieth birthday, this lament doesn't sound quite so pathetic.) Or listen to Reginald, the hero of Saki's stories, who "in his wildest lapses into veracity never admits to being more than twenty-two": "To have reached thirty," Reginald remarks with the characteristic heartlessness of the *fin de siècle*, "is to have failed in life."[10] We could go on and on: from Thoreau's grumblings in *Walden* ("I have lived some thirty years on this planet, and I have yet to hear the first syllable of valuable or even earnest advice from my seniors")

[8] From the essay "De l'Aage" (I, lvii), cited here from *Oeuvres Complètes*, ed. A. Armaingaud (Paris: L. Conard, 1924), II, 510.

[9] *Journal d'un homme de trente ans* (Paris: Egloff, 1948), p. 24 (entry for July 1915).

[10] "Reginald" and "Reginald on the Academy" in the volume *Reginald* (1904), cited here from *The Short Stories of Saki* (New York: Viking, 1937), pp. 4 and 10.

to Lord Byron's eloquent lament at the end of the first canto of *Don Juan*. But this negative attitude is summed up most cogently by a slogan current on the Berkeley campus during the recent excitement there: "Never trust anybody over thirty!"[11]—a piece of advice somewhat more charitable than that of the Baccalaureus in Goethe's *Faust*, who opines (verses 6787-89) that since anyone over thirty is already as good as dead, it would be best to put an end to such a person immediately.

What is expressed in all these partly melancholy, partly contemptuous observations is simply the other side of the same coin. For they share with the more positive utterances the basic belief that the thirtieth year constitutes a threshold, an axis of life; the sole difference lies in the fact that the negative conception expects nothing from life beyond thirty but peace and quiet, indifference, or—at worst—even dishonesty and betrayal. Yet the role of the thirty-year-old is still viewed from a point *within* a stable world-order, even if that order is regarded by youthful rebels as not particularly desirable. Their very rebellion demonstrates their rather touching belief in its existence. (Note, for instance, the hippies' premise of a "straight" establishment, from which they think they are "dropping out.")

But if the system of belief that has given meaning to the symbolic threshold threatens to collapse, then the thirtieth year takes on a wholly new significance. This sense of disintegration is implicit, for instance, in the words of the twenty-four-year-old Ivan Karamazov:

[11] This saying, of course, has become a national slogan since the disturbances in California. See the amusing column by John Fischer in *Harper's* (March 1966), pp. 16-28; and C.D.B. Bryan, "Why the Generation Gap Begins at 30," *The New York Times Magazine* (July 2, 1967), pp. 10-11 and 34-39. Most recently there has even been a volume of essays entitled *Never Trust a God Over 30*, ed. Albert H. Friedlander (New York: McGraw-Hill, 1967).

The Thirty-Year-Old Hero

I've been sitting here thinking to myself: that if I didn't believe in life, if I lost faith in the woman I love, lost faith in the order of things, were convinced in fact that everything is a disorderly, damnable, and perhaps devil-ridden chaos, if I were struck by every horror of man's disillusionment—still I should want to live and, having once tasted of the cup, I would not turn away from it till I had drained it! At thirty, though, I shall be sure to leave the cup, even if I've not emptied it, and turn away—where I don't know. But till I am thirty, I know that my youth will triumph over everything—every disillusionment, every disgust with life.[12]

As the precursors of an essentially modern and problematic view of life, Dostoevsky's heroes—Ivan Karamazov, the twenty-five-year-old "idiot" Prince Myshkin, or the twenty-four-year-old "underground man" (that is, during the narrative portion of the book)—sense an impending hour of collapse and disintegration. But as the heirs of a romantic narrative tradition they are normally at an age where their immense sense of life still supports them in the face of despair —where, in other words, narrative action is still possible. It is only in the twentieth century that we encounter certain documents that circle with an almost masochistic fascination around the dilemma of the man who has reached the symbolic year and sees stretching before him, not the anticipated consolation of total affirmation but the gaping horror of emptiness.

(3)

TODAY it is a commonplace of intellectual history to say that the disappearance of a stable reality has become the central

[12] *The Brothers Karamazov*, Book v, Chap. 3. In the translation by Constance Garnett (Modern Library College Edn.; New York, 1950), p. 273.

experience of our century. But who is capable of experiencing this disintegration tragically, or even in a manner accessible of narrative representation? Surely not the rootless contemporary, to whom the patterns of relativism and pluralism are evident almost before he emerges from childhood. No, the tragedy of disintegration manifests itself above all in the man who was scrupulously educated during his youth to acknowledge an integral world-order, who, so to speak, already has a *Bildungsroman* behind him. Then, when the symbolic moment of affirmation arrives, the meaninglessness of the world is suddenly unmasked and he finds himself compelled to doubt and question all the beliefs that he has inherited, experienced, or learned. The thirtieth year has become, for better or for worse, a typological turning point, a symbolic peripeteia that one inevitably reaches. But instead of the bliss of fulfillment, only nothingness leers at the thirty-year-old from beyond the threshold. Instead of affirming a given world-order, he finds that he must now examine anew the entire meaning of life that he has so painfully constructed for himself in the course of thirty years of experience and learning. It is surely no accident that Nietzsche's Zarathustra is thirty years old when he departs for ten years of reflection in the mountains.[13]

Let us consider, as a first literary expression of this crisis, a little poem by Ogden Nash. Like all first-rate humorous

[13] In *Thus Spake Zarathustra* Nietzsche consciously parodies many biblical elements, both in style and structure; Book IV is an outrageous travesty of Christ's last day. It is probably safe to assume, in view of this tendency, that Nietzsche had in mind Jesus, who also went into the wilderness when he was thirty. In "The Wanderer and His Shadow" (the second volume of *Menschliches, Allzumenschliches*, 1880) Nietzsche outlines his own theory of age in §269 ("Die Lebensalter"). Neither the first nor the last twenty years should count, he argues, but only the three decades from twenty to fifty—the spring, summer, and autumn of life. The thirties, according to this system, are the years of work and achievement.

poems, it reveals in comic distortion the most important elements of the experience of a generation:

> Unwillingly Miranda wakes,
> Feels the sun with terror.
> One unwilling step she takes,
> Shuddering to the mirror.
>
> Miranda in Miranda's sight
> Is old and gray and dirty;
> Twenty-nine she was last night;
> This morning she is thirty.[14]

The chief elements in the experience of the thirty-year-old stand out clearly here: first, the sudden and unpleasant awakening; second, the disintegration of a familiar world in the face of a new reality (beautiful yesterday; today, old and gray and dirty); and third, the urgent compulsion toward self-scrutiny, however painful it may be.

If we make a leap in time from the dejected Miranda of Nash's poem to another lady who has experienced a similar awakening, we find precisely the same typological elements intensified into a state of despair that has nothing more in common with the "sommité poétique" that Balzac attributed to the woman of thirty. I refer to the first paragraph of Ingeborg Bachmann's story "The Thirtieth Year":

> When a person enters his thirtieth year people will not stop calling him young. But he himself, although he can discover no changes in himself, becomes unsure; he feels as though he were no longer entitled to claim to be young. And one morning he wakes up, on a day which he will forget, and suddenly lies there unable to get up, struck by

[14] "A Lady Thinks She Is Thirty," from the volume *Many Long Years Ago* (Copyright 1936, by Ogden Nash); quoted here from *Verses from 1929 On* (New York: Modern Library, 1959), p. 42.

harsh rays of light and denuded of every weapon and all courage with which to face the new day. If he shuts his eyes in self-defense, he sinks back and drifts away into a swoon, along with every moment he has lived. He sinks and sinks . . . and he crashes down into a fathomless abyss, until his senses fade away, until everything which he thought he was has been dissolved, extinguished and destroyed. . . . He casts the net of memory, casts it over himself and draws himself, catcher and caught in one person, over the threshold of time, over the threshold of place —to see who he was and who he has become.[15]

Here the typological experience is defined more precisely. The motif of self-scrutiny is transposed from the physical to the psychological realm: it is now a question of contemplating one's own past and of determining a new meaning for one's life. And this self-reflection is further characterized as a state that is lifted, as it were, out of time. The person who (as the quotation continues) no longer simply exists from one day to the next, experiences in the symbolic moment of reflection a certain paralysis of time, until, with a jolt of decision, he injects himself once again into the stream of temporality.

Precisely the same experience is mirrored in the words of another thirty-year-old of our day:

It happens that the stage sets collapse. Rising, streetcar, four hours in the office or the factory, meal, streetcar, four hours of work, meal, sleep and Monday Tuesday Wednesday Thursday Friday and Saturday according to the same rhythm—this path is easily followed most of the time. But one day the "why" arises and everything begins in that weariness tinged with amazement. "Begins"—this is impor-

[15] Ingeborg Bachmann, "Das dreissigste Jahr," in her *Gedichte, Erzählungen, Hörspiele, Essays* (Munich: Piper, 1964), p. 67.

tant. Weariness comes at the end of the acts of a mechanical life, but at the same time it inaugurates the impulse of consciousness. It awakens consciousness and provokes what follows. What follows is the gradual return into the chain or it is the definite awakening. At the end of the awakening comes, in time, the consequence: suicide or recovery.[16]

We recognize the voice of the thirty-year-old Albert Camus. But here in *The Myth of Sisyphus* the dilemma is formulated even more radically than it was in Ingeborg Bachmann's story. The awakening to the absurdity of life—that is, the awakening to the disintegration of a familiar reality—leads either back to a false existence or forward to death or recovery. And the symbolic age for this awakening, in the essay as well as in the novel *The Stranger*, is again the thirtieth year, when, for the duration of the decision, time is suspended.[17] So there emerges from these documents (to which one

[16] Albert Camus, *The Myth of Sisyphus and Other Essays*, trans. Justin O'Brien (New York: Vintage Books, 1959), p. 10.

[17] Curiously, the age of the narrator is not clearly stated either in the novel or the essay—in contrast to all the other works under consideration here. But in both cases it is clearly implied. The next paragraph of the essay notes that men usually pay little attention to these events of everyday life: "Yet a day comes when a man notices or says that he is thirty. Thus he asserts his youth. But simultaneously he situates himself in relation to time. He takes his place in it." This striking association of the crisis with the age thirty can be no more accidental than Meursault's observation shortly before the end of the novel: "In reality I was not unaware that it makes little difference whether one dies at thirty or at seventy. . . ." It is reasonable to assume that the young narrator, who chooses the age seventy as a contrast, is himself about thirty. It is of further interest that Camus himself had not yet reached thirty when these two works appeared, in 1942. This might mean that instead of using an autobiographical age or one chosen at random, he wanted to exploit the symbolic implications of the age thirty. That would explain the curious phrase "a man notices or says that he is thirty" ("l'homme constate ou dit qu'il a trente ans"). It

could easily add others)[18] a clear-cut profile that permits us to speak of a modern typological significance of the thirtieth year that differs sharply from the traditional view, in which the chief element was affirmation.

The typological experience of the thirty-year-old begins with a shock of recognition and ends with a conscious decision. Between this absolute beginning and absolute end, the thirty-year-old lives in a state of timeless suspension during which all action is paralyzed; the analysis of his own past and of his own present existence moves into the foreground. It is the attempt to shape this experience fictionally that has produced what might be called the Novel of the Thirty-Year-Old. For it can be demonstrated that the same typological experience underlies each of the novels mentioned at the beginning of this chapter. We can see this most clearly if we first consider five novels in which the form of the narrative coincides absolutely with the structure of the experience. In fact, the correspondence is so precise that each novel might be defined virtually as the metaphorical elongation of the basic experience.

---

might be mentioned at this point that the age thirty does not necessarily have any bearing at all on the age of the author, who is sometimes about thirty himself, but often much older at the time of writing (Broch, Döblin, Bernanos).

[18] For instance, Alfred Andersch, *The Cherries of Freedom* (*Die Kirschen der Freiheit*, 1952). This autobiography, one of the most compelling documents of postwar German literature, provides a perfect example of the crisis of the thirty-year-old in real life. Andersch, to be sure, does not choose the age thirty for symbolic reasons; he is recounting certain events of his life as they occurred. But the critical instant upon which the entire report focuses is, in the last analysis, that of his decision to desert from the German Army—a flight into freedom that he made at age thirty. And this main episode ("Die Wildnis") reveals all the elements of the typological experience as we have outlined it above. My colleague Michael Curschmann has also called my attention to the equally characteristic entry that Paul Klee made in his diary on his thirtieth birthday.

The Thirty-Year-Old Hero

(4)

The Trial, Nausea, The Diary of a Country Priest, The Note-books of Malte Laurids Brigge, and the three parts of *The Sleepwalkers* all begin with the sudden realization on the part of their heroes that the world as they have previously known it has fallen apart. In place of the leisurely opening of the traditional *Bildungsroman* or of the novel of manners, the introductory passage marks a radical break between past and future. Josef K. learns one morning upon awakening that he is under arrest, and this fact, which jolts him out of the normal patterns of his existence, forces him for the first time in his life to give serious consideration to the question of his guilt or innocence. Roquentin's notes begin just as abruptly: "Something has happened to me. I can no longer doubt it." He has noticed, and his nausea is the external symptom of the fact, that the reality he previously accepted now disgusts him. In the middle of a country lane, Bernanos' little priest is suddenly paralyzed by the realization that his parish is being inwardly consumed by the "rot of despair," by ennui. A trip to Paris catalyzes a similar sensation in the case of Malte Laurids Brigge. "Is it possible," he asks in his introductory ruminations, "that nothing real and important has yet been seen, perceived, and said?"[19] The separate parts of Broch's trilogy begin just as abruptly: August Esch, dismissed from his job because of a colleague's embezzlement, is compelled by this glaring injustice to question his whole conception of cosmic order; Wilhelm Huguenau's complete break with the old systems of values is symbolized on the first page by his desertion from the army.

These beginnings, moreover, are anything but dramatic. As Camus emphasizes, it is precisely the triviality of the instigation that unmasks the absurdity of the world and shatters

[19] *Malte*, p. 726.

"the chain of daily gestures."[20] But this abrupt beginning marks the arrival at a radically new vantage point—what Kafka once called the Archimedean point from which conventional reality takes on a wholly new appearance.[21]

The abrupt beginning is followed, for the duration of the novel, by a suspension of time. In the third part of *The Sleepwalkers* Broch characterizes the time explicitly as a *Ferienzeit* ("vacation time"), the action as a *Ferialhandlung* ("holiday action"). Huguenau drifts along during these six months "as though under a glass bell," which is to say that his life is no longer subject to the normal categories of the world surrounding him. The same holds true for Josef K.'s period of arrest, in which the "paralysis of time" has often been noted. His alienation from the world is indicated by, among other things, the fact that his private sense of time is completely out of touch with the mechanical time of the outside world: he always arrives too early or too late; he lets others wait or he waits for others who, like Beckett's Godot, never come; he slams the door on an unpleasant scene, yet when he returns, weeks later, the same scene is still being enacted, ri-

---

[20] *The Myth of Sisyphus*, p. 10: "All great deeds and all great thoughts have a ridiculous beginning. . . . The absurd world more than others derives its nobility from that abject birth. In certain situations, replying 'nothing' when asked what one is thinking about may be pretense in a man. Those who are loved are well aware of this. But if that reply is sincere, if it symbolizes that odd state of soul in which the void becomes eloquent, in which the chain of daily gestures is broken, . . . then it is as it were the first sign of absurdity."

[21] It is perhaps worth noting that this inner awakening to a sense of disintegration is often reflected, at the end of the novel, by the public event of the First World War, which enacts in reality the spiritual breakdown. There have been studies of the war as subject matter. But we still need a good book on the symbolic meaning of the war in *The Sleepwalkers, The Magic Mountain*, Hesse's *Demian*, Musil's *The Man without Qualities*, Joseph Roth's *Radetzky March*, and other works. In literature, the meaning of the First World War differs wholly from that of the Second World War.

gidified in what Northrop Frye has called a state of "refrigerated deathlessness."[22] The critical month during which Roquentin searches for a valid and authentic attitude toward life is similarly lifted out of time. "Time had stopped," he notes during the access of nausea in the famous scene under the chestnut tree. Likewise, Malte Laurids Brigge passes his Parisian months in a suspended state in which past, present, and future blend indistinguishably into one another. He has as little sense of the exigencies of everyday life as does Bernanos' country priest.

This state of suspension, as we saw in Chapter Six, is essential to the meaning of these works. For it is only when he is lifted out of time that the hero is able to be truly free. Up to this point he has characteristically accepted the world in a conventional manner: Josef K. was happy in his work at the bank, Esch with his job as accountant. Swept along by the stream of events, they had no opportunity to view life with minds liberated of everyday restrictions. But within the state of freedom made possible by the suspension of time, the heroes concern themselves with the characteristic questions imposed on them by the problems which concern their respective authors. Josef K. wrestles with the problem of his guilt and Bernanos' country priest with his crisis of faith. Roquentin wins his existential freedom from *mauvaise foi,* while Broch's heroes grope desperately for an ethical prop in the general disintegration of values. And Malte Laurids Brigge sets out in pursuit of the "vocables of his anguish."

But in each case, the crisis of the thirty-year-old ends with a conscious decision that determines his future attitude toward the world. Roquentin discovers that he can overcome

[22] *Anatomy of Criticism* (New York: Atheneum, 1966), p. 186. Frye coins this phrase with reference to comic strips, whose central characters persist unchanged for years. But it is equally applicable to many scenes in Kafka.

his nausea only by devoting himself completely to the existential encounter with the world and with himself. He discards his historical studies and decides to write a novel. "A moment would probably come when the book would be written, it would lie behind me; and I believe that something of its radiance would fall upon my own past."[23] Josef K., who is incapable of bearing the terrible freedom imposed by the acknowledgment of his own guilt, lets himself glide back into "bad faith" by denying that guilt; but this denial is nonetheless a conscious decision.[24] Bernanos' priest dies of his cancer, a disease which of course symbolizes the moral rot threatening him and his parish; but he dies with the affirmation of a renewed faith on his lips: "Tout est grâce." Broch's protagonists, as incapable as Josef K. of sustaining absolute freedom, decide unanimously to slip back into the false security of their partial systems of values. And Malte Laurids Brigge commits himself so wholly to the pure love of reality that he surrenders his own tormented personality and is subsumed in the myths of his own notebooks.

Without reconsidering in detail the complex problems of interpretation posed by the individual works, we can still see from these sketchy outlines how the essential structure of the novel is maintained in every case. Each novel begins, on the first page, almost in the first sentence, with a shock of awareness; each ends with a clear decision that leads the hero back out of the timelessness of reflection into engagement with life, either authentic or false. And in each case we are dealing with a thirty-year-old hero who, after years of quiet-

[23] *La nausée* (Paris: Gallimard, 1951; Livre de Poche), p. 250.

[24] The question of Josef K.'s guilt is a matter on which critics differ, of course. I regard him as guilty and unwilling to accept his guilt. (See Chap. Two.) But *both* schools of thought acknowledge a conscious decision on K.'s part; so this view of the structure of the novel is upheld regardless of interpretation.

ly accepting life at face value, is jolted for the first time into questioning the meaning of this life.

In the other novels the typological experience is no less effectively present, even though it does not coincide so precisely with the external structure of the work. In the novels of Günter Grass and Albert Camus (however greatly the stylistic exuberance of the one may differ from the simple understatement of the other) we find a similar structural treatment of the basic experience. In both cases the narrator reflects retrospectively, during a period of imprisonment. As in *The Trial*, it is the arrest that constitutes the shock of awakening and thus initiates the period of timeless suspension.

Oskar Matzerath is in the mental ward of a prison from the first page of *The Tin Drum* to the last, but the circumstances of his arrest are not described until the last chapter of the book. Since the last chapter also contains his decision to act, both his arrest and his release, events lying two years apart, are narrated in the same chapter. The abrupt beginning and the abrupt ending of the typological experience thus coalesce in an unusually effective conclusion.

The two parts of *The Stranger* are, of course, written in entirely different styles. The first part records the events leading up to the killing on the beach as they occur. ("Today, mother died," is the style in which the book begins.) The second part, by contrast, represents Meursault's recollections of his experiences after eleven months in prison. The event of the arrest thus falls between the two parts.

But this is what matters: both reports stand under the impact of the typological experience from start to finish, because they are written as a response to what we recognize to be the typical crisis of the thirty-year-old. Without the jolt of arrest, without the suspension of time in prison, it would have occurred to neither Meursault nor Oskar Matzerath to reflect on his life and to seek to come to terms with it. In both cases, therefore, we find all the characteristic elements of the experience, although, for narrative purposes, the abrupt beginning has been shifted to the middle or the end and hence no longer coincides with the first sentence of the text.

Five months of prison seem to Meursault to be no more than a single enduring day; and in general, he spends much of his time thinking about the new static aspect under which time reveals itself to him during his confinement.[25] On the first page of his report Oskar Matzerath mentions the "stillness woven through white metal bars" of his cell, whose "equilibrium and serenity" is interrupted only once a week by the "violation" of visiting day.[26] Even in these superficially different novels, then, a suspension of time prevails from the moment of arrest, and in this timeless state the decision of each hero slowly matures. For Meursault, despite the meaninglessness that becomes apparent to him during his lonely mnemonic exercises in jail, it is a matter of affirming life on the last page: "I too, I felt ready to live through everything once again."[27] And Oskar Matzerath, who has learned through writing his autobiography that his tumultuous tin drum life was in the last analysis nothing but a flight from

[25] *L'Etranger* (Paris: Gallimard, 1957; Livre de Poche), p. 119: "When the guard told me one day that I had been there for five months, I believed him, but I didn't understand. For me, it had been without interruption the same day that was unfurling in my cell and the same task that I was pursuing."

[26] *Die Blechtrommel* (Frankfurt am Main: Fischer Bücherei, 1964), pp. 9-10: "Einmal in der Woche unterbricht ein Besuchstag meine zwischen weissen Metallstäben geflochtene Stille. . . . Solange sein Besuch währt—und Anwälte wissen viel zu erzählen—raubt er mir durch diesen Gewaltakt das Gleichgewicht und die Heiterkeit."

[27] *L'Etranger*, p. 179: "Et moi aussi, je me suis senti prêt à tout revivre. Comme si cette grande colère m'avait purgé du mal, vidé d'espoir, devant cette nuit chargée de signes et d'étoiles, je m'ouvrais pour la première fois à la tendre indifférence du monde."

responsibility, concludes in the last chapter: "Today I am celebrating my thirtieth birthday. At thirty, one is obliged to talk about the theme of flight like a man and not like a boy." In both novels, a clear decision announces a totally new attitude toward life.

Alfred Döblin demonstrates still another possible way of shaping the typological experience. Franz Biberkopf's crisis is related only in the last book of *Berlin Alexanderplatz*. But it is this crisis that shows all that has gone before in the proper light, for the meaning of the whole novel emerges only with Biberkopf's analysis of reality and his final decision. After the three hard blows that fate, as he thinks, has inflicted upon him, Biberkopf lands in the mental hospital at Buch. The insights leading to his nervous breakdown constitute the shock of recognition that reveals to him the naïveté of his previous conception of life. The stupor in which he passes his days is so remote from the temporality of the outside world that not even medical treatments penetrate his hermetic isolation. Only the ultimate concession that his stubborn attempts "to be respectable" had led him to a false assessment of reality frees him from the past, thus opening the way for his decision to return to the world "with his eyes open."

(5)

IN EVERY case, then, the abrupt awakening of the thirty-year-old leads first into a timeless state of reflection and analysis of existence, which is finally ended by a conscious decision to act. Now, whether or not the experience of the thirty-year-old coincides absolutely with the structure of the book, each novel is constructed in such a way that the decision constitutes the high point of the narrative, illuminating and explaining all preceding action. For this reason the event of physical death, whenever it occurs, is incidental and is

278

virtually forced onto the novel by external considerations.[28] Josef K., Meursault, and Bernanos' country priest all die. But Camus does not consider it worthwhile to describe the death scene; the entire meaning of the novel is contained in Meursault's prior decision, and his execution thereby becomes almost irrelevant. For the same reason, the little priest's death is mentioned almost in passing, in a laconic appendix. Josef K.'s death is merely the external correlative of the more significant philosophical suicide that he has already committed through his decision in favor of *mauvaise foi*.

In general, the life of the hero after his crisis is regarded as unimportant. We are supposed to be able to predict his future behavior and attitudes in the light of his decision. This point of view is expressed most clearly in the last paragraph of the first part of Broch's *The Sleepwalkers*, where the narrator takes leave of his hero with the following words: "Nevertheless after some eighteen months they had their first child. It actually happened. How this came about cannot be told here. Besides, after the material for character construction already provided, the reader can imagine it for himself." Such an ending contrasts sharply with the conclusion of the traditional *Bildungsroman* or the novel of manners, and not only because certain facts conventionally considered of interest—births, deaths, marriage, and so forth—are ignored. There is a more important consideration: endings of this sort imply a radically different attitude toward the hero and the world. In the conventional novel it is the world-order that consoles us with regard to the hero's future; whatever may come to pass, nothing more can happen to jeopardize the hero in a stable reality. Here, on the other hand, it is the hero in whom we have confidence; no matter what hap-

---

[28] This has no bearing on the greater theme of death that we discussed in Chap. Seven, however. A new awareness of the metaphysics of death often plays a major part in the hero's awakening.

pens in a meaningless world, we know our man and know how he will react to any given situation in the future. This is the fictional form absolutely consistent with a world view that has lost all faith in absolutes and a stable order.

The same principle of total omission or relative foreshortening applies to the treatment of the hero's earlier life. In none of these novels is the adventurous story of youth told simply for its own sake, as is the case in the traditional novel. If we experience the life of youthful action before the crisis at all, we do so only from the radically relativized viewpoint of the thirty-year-old, who has learned that his previous manner of comprehending and judging was completely false. Therefore his entire youth must be lived once again in his memory, as it were, if it is to have any value. This is implied in the country priest's uncertainty about whether or not he actually recognizes the memory of his own youth: "because I was seeing it for the first time, I had never seen it before."[29] It applies even to *The Tin Drum*, which is inconceivable without the ironic tension that obtains between the thirty-year-old narrator and the life story that he recounts. And multiple examples of a similar attitude toward the past can easily be found in the works of Rilke, Sartre, and Broch, where the hero's life prior to his awakening merely supplies raw material for the new analytical powers of the thirty-year-old. Again, this literary phenomenon reflects the conscious-

[29] *Journal d'un curé de campagne* (Paris: Plon, 1964; Livre de Poche Université), p. 201: "En un éclair, j'ai vu ma triste adolescence —non pas ainsi que les noyés repassent leur vie, dit-on, avant de couler à pic, car ce n'était sûrement pas une suite de tableaux presque instantanément déroulés—non. Cela était devant moi comme une personne, un être (vivant ou mort, Dieu le sait!). Mais je n'étais pas sûr de la reconnaître parce que . . oh! cela va paraître bien étrange —parce que je la voyais pour la première fois, je ne l'avais jamais vue."

ness of an age that has suddenly grown skeptical of its own past.

The suppression of the future, together with the relativization of the past, produces an almost explosive concentration of tensions in the narrative present, which is compressed between an absolute beginning and an absolute ending. Hovering timelessly between past and future, the symbolic moment of analysis and decision is so psychically overcharged that many writers, in order to make this tension psychologically plausible, exploit the metaphors of illness, madness, or imprisonment. On the one hand, illness and imprisonment provide a rational justification for the paralysis of time in the novel; the stay in the hospital or cell or in the isolation of one's own room releases the patient or prisoner from the normal bonds of everyday life. On the other hand, illness affords a rich language of metaphor for the disintegration and inner decay of the traditional world. Consider, for example, the pervasive cancer symbolism of Bernanos, the macabre dermatological metaphors of Rilke, the brilliant surgical images of Broch. (In the last two chapters we shall examine the symbolic use of criminality and madness more extensively.) The depiction of the states of sickness or imprisonment, with their overlapping layers of time, is intensified, finally, by the frequent use of the first-person narrative: five novels of the group are written in the form of notebooks or autobiographical records. In the other cases (Kafka, Broch, Döblin) the same effect of immediacy and internalization is achieved by other stylistic devices: interior monologue, visions, stream of consciousness, and so forth.

It is clear that the fictional shaping of the typological experience leads to certain structural characteristics that distinguish these novels, as a group, from other novels. And what is perhaps equally striking: this form, this unique complex

281

of structural elements, sets off these novels even from other works by the same author. Compare, for instance, the radical conclusion of *The Trial* with the infinite spiral of Kafka's *The Castle*, or the concentrated experience of *Nausea* or *The Stranger* with the broad panoramic vistas of Sartre's multi-volumed *The Roads of Liberty* or Camus' *The Plague*. The Novel of the Thirty-Year-Old is simply the most adequate form for the shaping of this life-crisis. As such, it occurs most frequently in the twentieth century, the century when an awareness of relativism and of the disintegration of values has come to dominate the foreground of literary consciousness.

(6)

SINCE the crisis of consciousness is by no means an exclusive prerogative of our time, but a typological experience that can crop up in any period, it seems to be a confirmation of the validity of our pattern when we encounter the same structure almost paradigmatically anticipated in the work of an older writer with an uncannily modern sense of being. "Up to his thirtieth year this extraordinary man could have passed for the model of a good citizen," reads the second sentence of Kleist's *Michael Kohlhaas* (1810). Like his younger brothers in the twentieth century, Kleist's hero is torn out of his habitual patterns of existence at the beginning of the novella by an abrupt awakening: the world, which he has previously known as orderly and good, suddenly unmasks itself as arbitrary, shifting, and hostile. The novella begins, then, with an abrupt jolt of awareness. The hero finds himself, during the course of the concentrated narrative, in a state of suspension, outside all conventional bonds: his wife has died, he sells his farm, sends his children away, and passes his year of vengeful action in a timeless world of his own creation. The plot rushes along toward the moment of decision, when Kohlhaas has the choice of renouncing his legal claims and living in peace, or of obtaining justice at the cost of his own head. A thirty-year-old hero; the closed form with an abrupt beginning; suspension of time and disintegration of the known world; and an absolute end in the critical decision—in Kleist's novella we find prefigured almost as in a model all the characteristic structural elements that we know in the modern Novel of the Thirty-Year-Old. But this striking parallel compels us, in conclusion, to consider the whole structure once again under a somewhat broader aspect.

Our investigation began with the observation that thirty-year-old heroes occur in a number of modern novels. While considering the possible reasons for the anomaly, we arrived at a basic typological pattern that all the novels of this group seem to share. Now—at the risk of diminishing the catchiness of the concept, but in the hope of increasing its usefulness— let us waive the age of thirty itself as a characteristic. Immediately several other modern novels come to mind, revealing precisely the same structure but possessed of slightly older or younger heroes.[30] A conspicuous example in recent American literature is Saul Bellow's *The Dangling Man* (1944). Although Joseph is only twenty-eight, his experiences during the months while he waits for induction correspond, point for point, to the typological experience outlined above. The period of timeless dangling is initiated by an induction notice, and during his months of waiting Joseph's view of reality is so radically altered that he is forced, like Roquentin and Malte Laurids Brigge, to keep a journal in order to come to grips with the new reality he senses. His heightened perceptions bring about such a change that he is no longer the

---

[30] I do not believe that the limits can be stretched too far. We have already seen that the twenty-year-old hero requires a different fictional form. And another chapter could be written on the hero in his forties, whose experience has yet other characteristics.

same man. "Very little about the Joseph of a year ago pleases me," he notes. "I cannot help laughing at him, at some of his traits and sayings."[31] Bellow's Joseph responds to his crisis very much like his namesake Josef K. "To be pushed upon oneself entirely put the very facts of simple existence in doubt," he observes in one of his last entries. Unable to bear pure freedom, he longs to fall back into the patterns of a regulated security. "Hurray for regular hours!" he concludes on his last day of civilian life. "And for the supervision of the spirit! Long live regimentation!" Bellow's comic spirit saves his hero from the suicide of despair that claims two other modern thirty-year-olds: J. D. Salinger's Seymour Glass and the gigolo hero of Pierre Drieu la Rochelle's *The Fire Within* (*Le feu follet*, 1931).

At first glance Thomas Mann's *The Magic Mountain* seems to have few elements in common with the structure we have outlined, but if we look more closely we recall that Hans Castorp's seven-year sojourn on the Magic Mountain begins with an abrupt awakening to the new reality represented by life in the sanatorium. It continues during a period of pronounced timeless suspension coupled with a critical analysis of existence, all of which takes place in terms of the heightened sensibility of sickness and to the accompaniment of an elaborate rhetoric of fever images and tuberculosis symbolism. And it ends with the decision of the now thirty-year-old hero to return to the flatlands below, where World War I is raging. In this connection, moreover, we recall that Hans Castorp's future after his decision—including the possibility of his death—falls outside the narrator's scope; and that the hero's childhood and youth appear only in two brief flashbacks. All the interest centers on the period of crisis and decision. The same parallels can be established, finally, in Robert Musil's *The Man without Qualities*, whose thirty-two-

---

[31] *The Dangling Man* (New York: Meridian, 1960), p. 26.

year-old hero takes what the author calls "a vacation from life" (*Urlaub vom Leben*) in order to come to terms with his own potentialities for existence.

What conclusions do these reflections permit us to reach? If we formulate our observations modestly, we can ascertain something like the following. For centuries the thirtieth year has possessed a certain symbolic value as a crucial turning point in a man's life. And in our own time, the loss of a stable reality has emerged as the central experience of modern man. The thinking of our age has combined these two basic ideas into a typological experience with a distinct profile: abrupt awakening to the disintegration of the familiar world, suspension of time during a period of analysis, and an abrupt ending when the hero decides how he intends to act in the face of this new reality. The specific nature of the crisis varies in accordance with the problems which concern the individual author, but the essential structure of the experience remains constant. It is this structure that certain writers have appropriated (whether consciously or unconsciously is irrelevant here) in order to give fictional form to this life-crisis. Within the given structure there remains a broad area of freedom for the inventive genius of the author: the form of the novel can coincide wholly with the structure of the experience, or the actual narration of the abrupt beginning can be shifted to the middle or end of the novel; the duration of the crisis can be several hours or several years; the phenomenon of timelessness can be rendered symbolically, through illness or imprisonment; even the age of the hero need not be precisely thirty in every case (although it was the very reoccurrence of this age that caught our attention initially). But as long as the structure of the typological experience determines the form of the novel *to a decisive extent*, we are justified, I think, in speaking of the Novel of the Thirty-Year-Old.[32]

[32] After I completed this chapter, friends and colleagues called my attention to still other works with thirty-year-old heroes who fit the

The Thirty-Year-Old Hero

The authors who have employed this structure—or more precisely, the authors whose fictional situations produced this structure—are explicitly interested in rendering a general experience, rather than a highly individualized one. Malte finds release from his anguish only when he realizes that his experience is typical, not unique. For this reason his notebooks end with a parable in which his suffering has been objectified and thus universalized. Kafka was not content to insert a parable into *The Trial*; he constructed the novel as a whole in such a way as to make a parable of it, applicable to all men. For the same reason Broch called Huguenau "the adequate child of his time"; and the individual volumes of the trilogy suggest the representative qualities of Pasenow "the romantic," Esch "the anarchist," and Huguenau "the objectivist." Döblin repeatedly reminds us that we should recognize ourselves in Franz Biberkopf, and his references to Job and Orestes put the hero in a variety of contexts that transcend the individual. And despite Thomas Mann's ironic description of Hans Castorp as a "simple young man" (he turns out to be anything but that) his hero is still a representative of man as the "Lord of the Antinomies."

It is this representative quality of the figures, incidentally, that accounts for the titles of many modern novels. Rilke's "prose-book" is virtually the only one that has a conventional

---

general pattern. Léon Roudiez mentioned the heroine of Françoise Sagan's *La Chamade*. And I continue to stumble across others on my own: e.g., the hero of Georg Büchner's *Woyzeck*. Two extremely typical cases can be found in such radically different works as Witold Gombrowicz's *Ferdydurke* (1937), which reveals many other parallels to Sartre's *La nausée*, and Ray Bradbury's *Fahrenheit 451* (1953). Several people have also cited *The Great Gatsby*; but since in this case it is the narrator who is thirty years old and not the hero, the effect in Fitzgerald's novel is less pronounced. While it is true that Nick Carraway has a crisis, it is ultimately Jay Gatsby who determines the action and hence the structure of the work.

title referring to a specific hero. The other titles, by contrast, tend to generalize the meaning from the outset by subordinating the specific individual to some greater whole: to a group (*The Sleepwalkers, The Counterfeiters*); to a symbol (*The Tin Drum, The Glass Bead Game*); to a type (*The Stranger, Ulysses*); to an area of action in which many persons are involved (*The Magic Mountain, Berlin Alexanderplatz*); or to the process that the hero undergoes (*The Trial, Nausea*). By such devices the authors stress the general validity of their novels. Wilhelm Meister's "Apprenticeship" is so highly individualized that it belongs only to Wilhelm Meister. But we are all, in a sense, "sleepwalkers," or involved in our own "trial," or afflicted by a sense of "nausea." The Novel of the Thirty-Year-Old shares this generalizing tendency with the modern novel as a whole. But taken along with the other characteristics we have noted, the titles underline the generational aspect of this particular experience.

We should not insist too categorically on our conclusions. There may be thirty-year-old heroes who have no such experience; there may be novels of crisis that make no use of this basic typological structure. And finally: even when we have established the fact that we are dealing with a Novel of the Thirty-Year-Old, we are still only at the beginning of any thorough analysis or interpretation of the work in question.[33]

But if we have detected in a given work this phenomeno-

---

[33] To avoid any possible misunderstanding, let me stress that the Novel of the Thirty-Year-Old is in no sense an exclusive structure: it can include far more, particularly further implications of the age of thirty itself. Most of the novels, apart from *The Diary of a Country Priest*, do not exploit the possible parallels to Jesus. (At least one scholar has insisted that *The Trial* is to be read as a parallel to the life of Christ, but this view is not widely shared.) But *The Tin Drum* conspicuously parodies a number of elements from the life of Christ, including his setting out at the age of thirty to gather disciples and to teach. This aspect does not conflict with the more general structure; it augments it and adds interesting details.

logical framework, we do know a few basic things. We know that we are dealing with the fictional shaping of a very specific kind of crisis and are thus in a better position to understand the nature of the crisis. We become alert, further, to important principles of structure: for instance, the distribution of the typical elements of the experience; the rendering of the suspension of time; the treatment of the past and future; the meaning of death; and the function of sickness or confinement. We are able to relate the work to others of its kind for the purpose of meaningful comparison. And as we proceed from theme and structure to imagery, we perceive the further implications of such obsessive figures as the criminal and the madman, which suggest themselves to the thirty-year-old as the adequate metaphors for his existence.

chapter nine

A Portrait of the Artist as
a Criminal

(1)

FRANZ Biberkopf is an ex-convict who has spent four years in prison for manslaughter. Wilhelm Huguenau is a deserter who gets by, unpunished, with six months of swindling, rape, and murder. Josef K. is arrested and executed for his "guilt" a year later. Hans Castorp regards his experiences on the Magic Mountain as an "aventure dans le mal." Gide's Lafcadio pushes a man out of a speeding train as an "acte gratuit." Jean Genêt has become the darling of the intellectuals, thanks in part to the efforts of his staunchest admirer, Sartre. And surely more than one reader felt a tickle of irony at the recent report (in *Die Zeit*, October 10, 1967) that Döblin's most conspicuous literary heir, Günter Grass, had visited Tegel Prison in Berlin in order to read selections from *The Tin Drum* to the inmates. This obsession with criminality (both in literature and in life) will undoubtedly give pause to future cultural historians, yet it is by no means exclusively a modern phenomenon.

A morbid fascination with crime seems to number among the basic human traits, and writers through the centuries have never been slow to gratify this taste in appropriate literary forms. Enterprising reporters of the fifteenth and sixteenth centuries traveled around Germany singing their *Zeitungslieder* ("newspaper songs"), which recounted the gory details of the latest crimes in seven-line strophes. As soon as they had captured the attention of an avid audience, they sold their songs in the form of broadsheets or *fliegende*

289

Blätter. Debased versions of these ballads survived into the seventeenth and eighteenth centuries; they were known as *Bänkelsang,* because the balladmongers stood on benches at local fairs to sing their *Moritaten* (a corruption of *Mordtat* or "act of murder"). In England, meanwhile, prison chaplains did a flourishing business in the sale of firsthand accounts of the confessions of notorious criminals. These chronicles, known loosely under the collective designation of "Newgate Calendars," provided in turn the inspiration for many of the Newgate novels of the nineteenth century, which traditionally incorporated a daring prison escape into their reports of criminal adventures.

By the middle of the eighteenth century this pastime had advanced from the marketplace to the salon. In 1734 Gayot de Pitaval began publishing the twenty volumes of his *Causes célèbres* from the tribunals of Paris, a work that was to exert its attraction for over two centuries and on such connoisseurs of crime as Schiller, E.T.A. Hoffmann, and Ernst Jünger. Thirty-five years later, Pitaval's successor introduced a new edition with a rationalizing appeal to the favorite catchwords of the Enlightenment: "In general, I shall endeavor to unite, in my selection of *Causes célèbres,* the clear, the precise, the curious, the instructive, the reliable, the useful and, finally, the pleasant."[1] But the rationalistic vocabulary scarcely conceals the underlying fascination with crime that made this collection one of the most popular works of the century. By 1782 it had been translated into German, and in 1792 Schiller prefaced a four-volume selection (Jena, 1792-1795) with praise for "the important gains for the study and treatment of humankind" that could be obtained from the perusal of criminal cases. In 1842 the lawyer-turned-

---

[1] M.J.C. de la Ville, *Continuation des Causes Célèbres et Intéressantes; avec les jugements qui les ont décidées* (2nd edn.; Paris, 1769), pp. vii-viii.

writer Willibald Alexis published the first volume of his *Neuer Pitaval*, with cases gleaned from the law courts of the entire continent. Before his retirement in 1860 Alexis edited twenty-eight volumes of the series, which by 1890 had grown to sixty volumes, providing an inexhaustible source of material for Hebbel, Fontane, and other contemporary writers.

The *Causes célèbres*, that Enlightenment police gazette, was merely one of the new forms devised for indulging a more refined public taste for crime. (On another literary level altogether, Rousseau's *Confessions* accustomed the public to the most shocking disclosures of the intimate details of guilt.) By the end of the eighteenth century the literary market in Germany was choked with a miasma of *Ritter- und Räuberromane* (novels of knights and robbers) boasting such titles as *Thaten und Feinheiten renomirter Kraft- und Kniff-genies* (*Deeds and Ruses of Famous Geniuses of Strength and Roguery*; published in two volumes, Berlin, 1790-1791). An entire generation of hack writers, capitalizing on the revolutionary fervor of the times and portraying their heroes as titanic figures, made a living by describing in these works the more colorful or terrible deeds of the notorious "Sonnenwirt," Schinderhannes, and other criminals of the century. All of these works, and the Newgate novels as well, had at least two things in common. They focused on the criminal and his deeds; and they viewed the criminal with sympathy, as a kind of people's hero who dared to defy an unpopular authority. The criminal in these works is often related by descent to the picaresque rogue of the sixteenth and seventeenth centuries as well as to the titanic hero of the German *Sturm und Drang*: Goethe's *Götz von Berlichingen*, Schiller's *Räuber*, and the like.[2] The hero of Heinrich

[2] The connection with the picaro is argued most persuasively by Frank W. Chandler, *The Literature of Roguery*, 2 vols. (New York:

The Artist as Criminal

Zschokke's *Abällino, der grosse Bandit* (*Aballino, the Great Bandit*, 1794), which in translation helped to popularize the figure of the "noble brigand" in France, is a lineal ancestor of the "good" outlaws who gallop across our television screens every night.

The year 1828 saw the appearance of the work that was to change these concepts radically: the four-volume *Mémoires* conventionally (though wrongly) attributed to Français Eugène Vidocq (1775-1857). Vidocq was a onetime crook who had shrewdly calculated that it would be more to his advantage to work for the law than against it. In 1806 he offered his services to the Paris police and rapidly rose from the status of stool pigeon to the rank of chief of the Sûreté. He and the associates he recruited among other ex-convicts astounded Paris both by the number of criminals they apprehended in the lawless days of the Restoration (over eight hundred in one year) and by the daredevil methods they employed. Suddenly the "deeds and ruses" of the pursuer began to match and surpass those of the pursued. Whether or not Vidocq wrote the *Mémoires*, his exploits inspired Eugène Sue,

---

Houghton and Mifflin, 1907). This entire category, of course, can be regarded as a secularization of the "generous outlaw" or "sublime criminal" that Mario Praz considers in his chapter on "The Metamorphoses of Satan" (in *The Romantic Agony*). By the same token, it is not to be confused with those seers of evil whom Praz sees "In the Shadow of the Divine Marquis." For the noble bandit, though outside of the law, still believes in justice and virtue, while the Marquis de Sade and his followers, through their inversion of values, denied the existence of good altogether. In this connection see also Martin Greiner, *Die Entstehung der modernen Unterhaltungsliteratur* (Hamburg, 1964; rowohlts deutsche enzyklopädie, No. 207), esp. pp. 116-26, "Die edlen Räuber." With specific reference to Broch's categories, Greiner correctly points out that the entire age confused the "criminal" with the "rebel." We shall later have occasion to note, moreover, that until the close of the eighteenth century this confusion extended to the "madman" as well.

The Artist as Criminal

Dumas, Hugo, Dickens, Poe, and Gaboriau, and marked a turning point in popular crime literature. For with Vidocq, interest began to shift from the criminal to the "detective"— a designation that did not gain currency in English until Dickens' *Bleak House* (1852).

It is unnecessary, for our purposes, to make subtle distinctions between the *roman policier* and the detective story, between *Kriminalroman* and *Detektivroman*. It does not matter whether the detective works by ratiocination, brute strength, or animal cunning. The important point is simply that popular sympathy was displaced, generally speaking, from the criminal and was now firmly on the side of his pursuer, whose methods in themselves were often scarcely preferable to those of the men they hunted.[3] (In this respect, Mickey Spillane's Mike Hammer and Ian Fleming's James Bond are direct descendants of Vidocq and his gang of "police.") For without this shift of emphasis, without the transformation of the criminal from a titanic hero into a guilty man, the criminal would be useless as a metaphor and symbol in much modern literature.

By the time Poe's *Murders in the Rue Morgue* appeared in 1841, the romance of crime, which had flourished for centuries, had been in effect relegated to the cheap counters. In the detective story, the crime and the criminal have been reduced to a constant, not to say irrelevant, factor. Here, virtually all interest is focused on the analytical powers or physical prowess of the detective; the crime is either merely a *fait accompli* that precipitates the narrative or the threat

[3] Here I agree with Richard Gerber in his article on "Verbrechensdichtung und Kriminalroman," *Neue Deutsche Hefte*, 13 (1966), 101-17. Gerber objects to the dichotomy of "Kriminalroman" and "Detektivroman" of which many German encyclopedias are fond. In both, he argues, the emphasis is on the sleuth. "Der Kriminalroman ist kastrierte Verbrechensdichtung."

that the hero seeks to avert. The author's originality exhausts itself in the creation of ever new heroes: from Poe's Dupin through Sherlock Holmes, Hercule Poirot, and Father Brown, down to the latest Negro and rabbi sleuths of John Ball and Harry Kemelman. No one can forget Inspector Maigret, but who remembers the criminals he pursues? The titanism that characterized the criminals of old has been drained off into the detectives, and with a few notorious exceptions, crime, like the rest of society, has become institutionalized and faceless. We remember famous crimes—the Great Train Robbery, or the Valentine's Day Massacre—but the individual criminals have faded into anonymity, like Jack the Ripper, who is known only through his deeds. The criminal, in other words, has become the gangster, with all the collectivity implied in the term. It is perhaps not going too far to suggest that the titanism of evil, continued in the *Volksbücher*, the shilling pamphlets, and the penny dreadfuls of the nineteenth century, was deflected into the genre of horror fiction, which manifested itself on a literary level in *Frankenstein, Dracula,* or *Dr. Jekyll and Mr. Hyde.* But the criminal of modern popular literature is almost invariably condemned to a pallid existence.

Truman Capote's *In Cold Blood* (1965) is symptomatic of the fate of the criminal. In this "true account of a multiple murder and its consequences," it is the monstrosity of the crime, its absurdity, and the details of the investigation that fascinate the reader. In comparison with Dick Turpin, Jonathan Wild, and other criminals of the past, the two slack-jawed perpetrators of the Kansas murders are anything but titanic figures. To be sure, Truman Capote was dealing with reality; he did not invent a fictional situation. But the very fact that he chose to record this particular crime is characteristic of the turn that the literature of crime has taken. We no longer expect criminals to be titantic; they are merely sordid.

The entire development just outlined here is based, of course, on popular literature of crime—on folk ballads, chronicles, trivial romances, detective stories, works written for the gratification of public taste. Yet its history, which has often been recorded,[4] is linked in a very direct way to literature of another order altogether. And a grasp of this history is essential, I believe, to certain distinctions that must be made if one is to understand properly the role of the criminal in modern literature. Before the shift in public sympathy around 1830, a clearly defined genre featuring the criminal as a titanic man had emerged. This genre, with its distinct characteristics, has survived on a literary level right down to the twentieth century, even though popular crime works underwent the transformation we have noted. Around 1900, before the criminal had become the wretched creature of the present but after he had become an outlaw and an outsider who no longer engaged public sympathy, he emerged in a different literary role: as a metaphor for the artist himself. During the last forty years, finally, he has made his appearance in a third guise, stripped of all titanism and grandeur, but representative by his very sordidness of elements that many writers sense in our society. These three types exist side by side in the novel of the twentieth century: the criminal as Titan, as Narcissus, as Everyman. We can understand this phenomenon if we begin by considering a constellation of writers that may at first glance seem incongruous: Diderot, Schiller, Hoffmann, Dostoevsky, Nietzsche, and Genêt.

---

[4] The most exhaustive study still appears to be Régis Messac, *Le "Detective Novel" et l'Influence de la Pensée Scientifique* (Paris: Champion, 1929).

The Artist as Criminal

(2)

DIDEROT'S *Neveu de Rameau* seems to be one of the earliest examples of a literary preoccupation with the criminal.[5] "If I knew history, I would show you that evil has always come into the world through some man of genius." This fashionably titanic association of genius and evil, which anticipates a favorite theme among the romantics of succeeding generations, is gradually refined into a more specific definition of the sublimity of the criminal. "If it is important to be sublime in any aspect of life, then especially so in the case of evil. People spit on a little scoundrel, but it is impossible to deny a kind of respect to a great criminal: his courage astonishes you, his atrocity makes you shudder. We esteem above all his unity of character." In reading Diderot, one must not fail to take into account the rhetoric of the situation; Rameau's nephew is purposely trying to shock his interlocutor. At the same time, we note a certain tone that is scarcely present in the popular literature of the times. For here it is not merely the criminal act that fascinates, but the phenomenon of criminality as such. Moreover, the criminal is regarded with aesthetic detachment as a worthwhile object of contemplation—so much so that the narrator is distinctly perturbed by the unusual attitude of Rameau's nephew and soon concludes his story: "I began to have great difficulty in tolerating the presence of a man who discussed a horrible action, an execrable crime, in the same manner as a connois-

[5] Though written in 1762, the work was first published in Goethe's German translation of 1805. (We shall later have occasion to note how appropriate it is that Goethe should have translated this remarkable dialogue and thus introduced it to world literature.) Goethe's version was retranslated into French in 1821, but Diderot's manuscript was not recovered until 1891. I quote here from the edition by Michel Hérubel (Paris: Union Générale d'Editions, 1964), pp. 22, 79, and 83.

seur of painting or of poetry examines the beauties of a work of taste, or as a moralist or a historian extols and demonstrates the circumstances of a heroic action."

Titanism, objective detachment, and focus on the criminal mind rather than the criminal act—these are precisely the characteristics that show up in Schiller's fictionalized case study (an eighteenth-century "non-fiction novel," if you like) of Johann Friedrich Schwan, the notorious outlaw known to his time as "der Sonnenwirt." "In the entire history of man," Schiller says in introducing his tale, "no chapter is more instructive for heart and mind than the annals of his errors. In every great crime a relatively great force was in motion."[6] Men with a more sensitive understanding of human nature, he continues, will value the experience that can be obtained by contemplating this realm of criminals; they will fit it into their theory of psychology and evaluate its significance for the study of ethics. The attitudes of titanism and objective contemplation are developed consistently throughout the story. But Schiller is even more explicit than Diderot regarding the shift of emphasis from the criminal act to the criminal mind. "His thoughts are far more meaningful to us than his deeds, and the sources of these thoughts even more than the consequences of those deeds." For "that which is merely horrible is in no way instructive for the reader." Schiller is not merely commenting in passing on the phenomenon of criminality, like Rameau's nephew; he is writing a story— indeed, a "true story" that had been recounted in numerous other versions by contemporary writers who were not so contemptuous of horrible deeds. Schiller's tendency to linger on

[6] "Der Verbrecher aus verlorner Ehre; Eine wahre Geschichte." I quote from Vol. 10 of Schiller's *Sämmtliche Werke* (Stuttgart: Cotta, 1862); in this paragraph, pp. 73, 75, and 90. For the historical and biographical background of Schiller's tale, see Willi Stoess, *Die Bearbeitungen des "Verbrechers aus verlorener Ehre"* (Stuttgart: Metzler, 1913).

motivation and meaning rather than on the deeds themselves distinguishes his story from such sensational and popularizing treatments as J. F. Abel's *Tale of a Robber* (*Geschichte eines Räubers*, 1787) or G. I. Wenzel's drama *Crime from Infamy* (*Verbrechen aus Infamie*, 1788).

But in Schiller we find a new motif, one that was absent from Diderot's reflections: the thought, derived from Rousseau and the *Sturm und Drang*, that man is basically good and has been corrupted only by the forces of society. Thus, in his *Avertissement* for the first performance of his drama *Die Räuber*, Schiller outlined Karl Moor's fate as follows: "Unrestrained ardor and bad company ruined his heart— they dragged him from vice to vice. . . ." This notion, dear to the trivialized rationalism of the later eighteenth century, made its way even into the popular literature of the times. It provided the theme for Restif de la Bretonne's *Le paysan perverti* (1775) as well as for Ludwig Tieck's *William Lovell* (1793-1796). In the potboiler about "der Bayrische Hiesel" that Tieck and his preceptor Rambach wrote for the *Thaten und Feinheiten renomirter Kraft- und Kniffgenies*, we read: "through circumstances, situation, and convention a misshapen monster was formed out of such a lovely material."[7] But here it is merely a sentiment tacked onto the blood-curdling adventures of the criminal-hero.

In Schiller this rationalistic theme is announced in the title: his hero is a criminal, after all, because he has been bereft of his honor ("Der Verbrecher aus verlorner Ehre," 1786). But Schiller's version would not be of such interest to us if it restricted itself to the shallow behaviorism that under-

---

[7] Compounds with the prefix "mis-" (German *miss-*) are stylistic evidence of the general theme of the good man corrupted. Thus, at the end of *William Lovell* the evil Andreas writes to the hero: "So liess ich Dich durch alle Grade gehen, um Dich zu einer seltsamen Missgeburt umzuschaffen." ("So I had you go through all the degrees in order to recreate you into a weird abortion.")

lies most other works of the day. To be sure, it is the story of a good man corrupted by circumstances. But Schiller does not stop with external motivation. Like dozens of other heroes of rationalistic crime literature, Christian Wolf is caught poaching and sent to prison. But he is not merely damned by circumstances; he reflects on his position and consciously chooses a life of crime. "I wanted to do evil; that much I can vaguely recollect. I wanted to deserve my fate."[8] It is this decision, this shift from the act to the essence, that distinguishes Schiller's tale. "So he has chosen the worst. He had no other choice. His life is all laid out: it will be a journey to the end of misfortune. He will later write: 'I decided to be what crime made of me.' Since he cannot escape fatality, he will be his own fatality; since they have made life unlivable for him, he will live this impossibility of living as if he had created it expressly for himself, a particular ordeal reserved for him alone. He wills his destiny; he will try to love it." This quotation comes not from Schiller's story, but from Sartre's study of Jean Genêt.[9] Yet it could have been written for Schiller's "Sonnenwirt."

Christian Wolf, to be sure, is not Genêt; he repents at the end. But this striking parallel of initial motivation exhibits another characteristic that gradually emerges in the literary treatment of crime. The criminal is born uncorrupted; but once his development has been deflected from the normal path, he begins to *will* his criminality. The act of crime becomes secondary; it is merely a manifestation of a titanic impulse consecrated to evil. This is precisely the phenomenon

[8] Schiller, *Sämmtliche Werke*, x, 81.

[9] Jean-Paul Sartre, *Saint Genêt; Actor and Martyr*, trans. Bernard Frechtman (New York: Mentor Books, n.d.), pp. 60-61. This association of Schiller and Sartre is not gratuitous; see the chapter on "Schiller and Sartre: Ein Versuch zum Idealismus-Problem Schillers," in Käte Hamburger, *Philosophie des Dichters* (Stuttgart: Kohlhammer, 1966), pp. 129-77.

that Ernst Jünger noted in his *Paris Journal* after reading the first volume of the *Causes célèbres*: "The greatest crimes are based on combinations that, logically considered, are superior to the law. Moreover, the crime shifts more and more from the deed into the essence in order to attain levels at which it exists as the abstract spirit of evil in pure cognition. Finally even interest vanishes—evil is done for the sake of evil. Evil is celebrated."[10]

This set of characteristics—titanism, the good man corrupted, the will to crime, the criminal mind rather than the criminal act as a worthy object of aesthetic contemplation—is carried over into the works of romanticism whenever they are concerned with crime. Kleist's tale of *Michael Kohlhaas* and his terrible vengeance repeats the formula of Schiller's story almost exactly. But romantic *Naturphilosophie* soon imprinted its stamp on these works, distinguishing them unmistakably from the products of rationalism. For if the theories of rationalism seem to anticipate modern sociology and criminology, the attitude of Brentano's "Tale of Good Kasperl and Pretty Annerl" (1816) or of E.T.A. Hoffmann's "Fraülein von Scuderi" (1819) anticipates psychoanalysis.

Hoffmann's story, based in part on the *Causes célèbres*, is a forerunner of the detective story inasmuch as it proceeds analytically from a mysterious series of crimes, through the drama of an innocent man wrongly accused, to the solution of the mystery. But Madame de Scudéry is not so much a sleuth as a mother-confessor: she does not deduce; she is informed. The titanism of the tale is still invested wholly in the goldsmith Cardillac, a demonic figure doomed to murder and theft by powers of nature over which he has no control. It is here that the narrator's interest lies, with the innocent man whose "evil star" (a symbolic leitmotif repeated often

[10] "Das zweite Pariser Tagebuch" (October 16, 1943); in Ernst Jünger, *Werke* (Stuttgart: Ernst Klett, n.d.), III, 178-79.

throughout the work) drives him to crime. Hoffmann's theory of criminality is based on the belief that a child's character is affected by the experiences of the mother during pregnancy. Cardillac's mother, during her first month, succumbs at a court ball to the blandishments of a cavalier wearing a magnificent diamond necklace. Just as she is about to embrace him, her eyes riveted greedily on the flashing jewels, her lover collapses and falls dead on top of her. After months in bed at the point of death, she eventually recovers and gives birth to a seemingly healthy and normal son. "But the horrors of that terrible moment had affected *me*. My evil star had risen and shot off the spark that ignited within me one of the strangest and most destructive passions"— an unconquerable lust for gold and jewels.[11] This fateful proclivity leads Cardillac into the profession of goldsmith, and he becomes the most accomplished master in all France. But the criminal impulse shows up whenever he is forced to part with one of his creations: he has no rest until he is able to recover it, by theft or even by murder if necessary. In the figure of Cardillac, Hoffmann has concentrated all the characteristics of the criminal-hero that we noted in Diderot and Schiller; but by shifting responsibility for Cardillac's criminality from society to nature itself, he has given his work the characteristic twist that marks it as the product of a romantic writer.

Schiller and Hoffmann—these are the two names in German literature that meant most to Dostoevsky, who was himself inordinately fascinated with crime and criminality. This obsession, discernible even in his earliest works, was catalyzed by his experiences in the Siberian prison of Omsk, where the author gained the materials and insights that were to inform all his major works. His account of those years,

[11] E.T.A. Hoffmann, *Poetische Werke* (Berlin: Aufbau, 1958), IV, 230.

The Artist as Criminal

The House of the Dead (1862), is a document virtually unmatched in literature until the revelations of Jean Genêt. Yet though Dostoevsky's firsthand knowledge of criminals vastly exceeded that of his predecessors, it is easy to recognize traditional patterns beneath the variety of types that he records. It is symptomatic, first of all, that Dostoevsky chose to cast his memoirs in a fictional form. This device permitted him to exploit the immediacy of first-person narrative and at the same time assured him the detachment necessary for the objective contemplation of the criminal mind. As Ernest J. Simmons has pointed out, artistic selection is apparent throughout the work.[12] The effect of aesthetic unity is further enhanced by the theme stated explicitly on the last page: "After all, one must tell the whole truth; those men were exceptional men. Perhaps they were the most gifted, the strongest of our people. But their mighty energies were vainly wasted, wasted abnormally, unjustly, hopelessly."[13]

The titanic quality of the criminal, proclaimed here as a general principle worthy of Diderot or Schiller, is documented again and again by such specific cases as those of Petrov and Orlov. "I can confidently say that I have never in my life met a man of such strength, of so iron a will as he," Dostoevsky writes of the latter. "We saw in him nothing but unbounded energy, a thirst for action, a thirst for vengeance, an eagerness to attain the object he had set before him." *The House of the Dead* in itself would be sufficient evidence of the romantic conception of the criminal, that of a titanic man corrupted by external forces and now willing his evil, which places Dostoevsky in the tradition of Schiller and Hoffmann. But the real confirmation comes later, in the five great

[12] In *Dostoevsky; The Making of a Novelist* (New York: Vintage Books, 1962), p. 90.
[13] I quote from the translation of Constance Garnett, the Laurel edition (New York, 1965), pp. 351 and 86.

novels. The clearest example is *Crime and Punishment*, for in that work, as Gide noted in his lectures on Dostoevsky, the division between the thinker and the doer has not yet been established. This distinction, which produced those later heroes who regard action as a compromise of their thought, appealed greatly to Gide, Hesse, and others. Raskolnikov, however, is still a hero after the pattern of the criminals in *The House of the Dead*, a man who translates his thought into the act of murder.

Crime and Punishment represents both a critique and an ultimate deepening of the pattern established in earlier works. It is a critique to the extent that it unmasks Raskolnikov's titanic dream of Napoleonic glory, his theory of "ordinary" and "extraordinary" people, as fallacious. And Dostoevsky's belief that the criminal generates spontaneously within himself the moral demand for his own punishment amounts to a mystical intensification of the more trivial rationalistic belief in the criminal's simple repentance. To a certain extent Raskolnikov anticipates the later heroes who disdain action, for he lives to realize how miserably his own act has failed. The act itself, though rendered in meticulous detail, is reduced in importance. Dostoevsky shows us, as R. P. Blackmur has persuasively demonstrated,[14] how Raskolnikov becomes the product of his own crime. Unlike the Napoleon of his imagination, who creates his own world by his bold deeds, Raskolnikov is himself transformed by the miserable murders he commits. This is certainly what Garine, the hero of André Malraux's *The Conquerors* (1928), has in mind when he disparages the feeling of remorse so common in Russian novels. "These writers all have the failing of not having killed anyone. If their characters suffer after having

---

[14] *"Crime and Punishment*: Murder in Your Own Room," in *Eleven Essays in the European Novel* (New York: Harcourt, Brace, and World, 1964), p. 122.

killed, it is because the world has scarcely changed in their eyes." For a true assassin, Garine reasons, there are no crimes—only separate murders. The assassin's world has changed, and he sees reality from a different perspective, where the concept of crime no longer has any meaning.[15]

In Raskolnikov's case, however, the opposite occurs. Instead of changing from a man with a moral conception of crime to an assassin who refuses to acknowledge the existence of crime, he is forced to recognize the hollowness of his titanic dream and accedes to a feeling of remorse for his act. It is his act that transforms Raskolnikov, in this sense, into a criminal in his own mind. Before the murders he refused to contemplate the possibility of crime for an extraordinary man. The story of his punishment, however, is the story of the gradual growth within him of the awareness of his own guilt and his need for expiation. It is this feeling that prompts him to badger Porfiry, leading him ever closer to the fact that he is the murderer, and that finally produces his confession. In this novel, then, the romantic pattern has been preserved in its essential structure, but it has undergone a remarkable transformation in depth and meaning. The criminal-hero is suddenly charged with so much meaning, his motivation becomes so complex, that the old pattern can scarcely accommodate him. Because of Dostoevsky's dualistic vision of the world, the criminal can no longer be viewed with total objectivity; he belongs, at least in part, to the character of the author himself. And for this reason Raskolnikov awakens a different response in the reader, who views him objectively and at the same time tends to become involved in his crime. As a result of this important shift, certain writers of the next

---

[15] André Malraux, *Les Conquérants* (Paris: Grasset, 1963; Livre de Poche), p. 68. In this connection see Léon S. Roudiez, "The Literary Climate of *L'Etranger*: Samples of a Twentieth-Century Atmosphere," *Symposium*, 12 (Spring-Fall 1958), 19-35.

generation were able to see the criminal in a new light, as a metaphor for the artist himself. But the original romantic tradition continued beyond Dostoevsky into the present.

Nietzsche's wholly titanic view of the criminal was conditioned almost entirely by his reading of Dostoevsky. In his letters and works of 1887 and 1888, just after he first discovered the Russian writer, he returns again and again to *The House of the Dead*. In the notes subsequently published as *The Will to Power* he asserted that "Dostoevsky was not unjustified when he said of the inmates of those Siberian prisons that they constituted the strongest and most valuable segment of the Russian people." Then, with a characteristically Nietzschean twist, he goes on to blame contemporary civilization for its lack of titanic criminals. "If in our own times the criminal is a badly nourished and withered plant, that fact merely discredits our own social circumstances; in the days of the Renaissance the criminal thrived and won for himself his own brand of virtue—virtue *à la Renaissance, virtù*, a moral-free virtue."[16]

Toward the end of *Twilight of the Idols* (1888), again with reference to Dostoevsky, whom he calls "the only psychologist from whom I had something to learn," Nietzsche devotes a section to an analysis of the criminal. "The criminal type is the type of the strong man under unfavorable circumstances, a strong man who has been made sick." In a

[16] Nietzsche, *Werke*, ed. Karl Schlechta (Munich: Hanser, 1956), III, 619. Nietzsche was not alone, of course, in his fascination with Renaissance "criminals." Stendhal avidly read Italian chronicles of crime. Huysmans was as greatly entranced by the monster Gilles de Rais as is Durtal, the hero of *Là-bas* (1891). Walter Pater, who got some of his information about Renaissance criminals from Stendhal's *Histoire de la Peinture en Italie*, speaks in his Oxford lecture on "Raphael" (1892) of a tendency of the age: "crime, it might seem, for its own sake, a whole octave of fantastic crime"; reprinted in Kenneth Clark's edition of Pater's *The Renaissance* (Cleveland and New York: Meridian Books, 1961), p. 148.

passage reminiscent of Schiller and the Enlightenment he maintains that "it is our tame, mediocre, castrated society in which a natural man, coming from the mountains or the adventures of the sea, necessarily degenerates into a criminal."[17] The criminal shares with all great men the feeling of alienation from society; but unlike Napoleon, for instance, he has been unable to prove that he is stronger than society and hence becomes a criminal. In a letter of December 7, 1888 to Strindberg, Nietzsche remarked that the history of criminal families "inevitably can be traced back to a man who was too strong for a certain social niveau," and he went on to cite a contemporary example. "The most recent big criminal case in Paris provided a classic type: Prado exceeded his judges and even his lawyers in self-control, *esprit*, and boldness." In these passages and many others Nietzsche clearly regards the criminal as a titanic figure corrupted by society. There is a tentative identification with the genius and the artist, but since the criminal is a strong man who has failed in his aspirations, Nietzsche tends to regard him with objective detachment and sympathy rather than to identify with him.

Jean Genêt's novels and plays, and especially his autobiographical *Journal du Voleur* (1949), constitute the most powerful documents of the titanic image of the criminal in the twentieth century. "Though they may not always be handsome," Genêt announces in his opening paragraph, "men doomed to evil possess the manly virtues."[18] One could

[17] *Götzendämmerung*, Section 45; *Werke*, II, 1020-22. In Nietzsche's references to criminals the prefix "de-" (German *ent-*) has the same function as "*miss-*" in earlier writers; it denotes a deflection from or a distortion of normal development.

[18] *The Thief's Journal*, trans. Bernard Frechtman (New York: Bantam Books, 1965), p. 3. The other quotations in this paragraph are from pp. 49, 51, 5, and 243. This tradition was not dormant in France between Diderot and Genêt, of course: both Stendhal and

almost speak of life imitating art, for it is Genêt's aesthetic consciousness that endows his sordid world with its heroic dimensions.[19] This becomes particularly conspicuous when Genêt is talking about such great criminals as Stilitano, who (his homosexuality aside) bears a striking resemblance to Dostoevsky's Orlov: "Perhaps his power alone was enough for Stilitano to inspire respect without having to perform a bold deed." "Stilitano was handsome and strong, and welcome at a gathering of similar males whose authority likewise lay in their muscles and their awareness of their revolvers." The phallic imagery with which Genêt embellishes these figures—indeed, with which he endows the whole world of the criminal, including the prison buildings themselves—merely emphasizes their titanism. (Phallic imagery has been an aspect of titanism at least since Schiller.) But in Genêt the romantic titanism is carried one step further: he creates a veritable myth of criminals and criminality. Thus his book begins with a lament over the abolishment of the penal colonies in Guiana. "The end of the penal colony prevents us from attaining with our living minds the mythical underground regions." On the last page Genêt denies that he has attempted to make of his book "a work of art, an object detached from an author and the world." Yet, like *The House of the Dead*, these memoirs are vouchsafed a high degree of artistic unity by the theme that pervades them: the war between the criminal and society intensified to the level of myth.

Mérimée, for instance, were conspicuously fascinated by titanic criminals.

[19] This titanic aspect has its parallels in everyday life. John Bowers, in an article on "Big City Thieves," *Harper's* (February 1967), pp. 50-54, cites the case of a former burglar now working as a short-order cook. The ex-convict waxes rhapsodic when he recalls his days at Sing Sing: " 'I tell you they got men up there. And geniuses.' His eyes brightened." This could be called the poor man's Genêt.

As a result, the work is in no sense a simple confession, an outpouring of feeling. By mythicization and aesthetic shaping, Genêt manages to treat his own life and those of his fellow criminals with a high degree of objectivity.

In Genêt's case the initial impulse to crime came from the outside world, from society, which cast him in his role by calling him a thief. Until that point the little boy who stole had regarded his thefts as isolated acts; but society, by giving it a name, forced upon him a role which became his *raison d'être*. "If he has courage," Genêt reasons, "the guilty man decides to be what crime has made him. Finding a justification is easy; otherwise, how would he live?"[20] Hence society is necessary to the criminal; he can assert himself only by breaking its laws. "No doubt, the culprit who is proud of what he is owes his singularity to society but he must already have had it for society to recognize it and make him guilty of it. I wanted to oppose society, but it had already condemned me, punishing not so much the actual thief as the indomitable enemy whose lonely spirit it feared." For this reason Genêt the thief felt frustrated in Nazi Germany. " 'It's a race of thieves,' I thought to myself. 'If I steal here, I perform no singular deed that might fulfill me. I obey the customary order; I do not destroy it. I am not committing evil.' "

Again and again the criminal act is transmuted into a mythic deed, a gesture of evil against the morality of society. Hence the act itself is reduced in significance. The pursuit of evil becomes a goal in itself. "Toward what is known as evil, I lovingly pursued an adventure which led me to prison." In Genêt we find assembled once again all the characteristics of the genre: the titanism of the man corrupted by society, the resulting will to crime, and an interest in criminality

[20] *The Thief's Journal*, pp. 219, 220-21, and 109.

replacing that in the criminal act. The fact that he chose to translate this entire autobiography into a myth assures Genêt the final characteristic necessary for the work: a point of view which regards the criminal as an object worthy of contemplation for its own sake. He does not simply record his life. He reflects upon its deeper significance within the framework of the morality that gives it its meaning. There is a pronounced continuity of tradition in evidence here, arising with eighteenth-century rationalism and culminating in the autobiography of this twentieth-century criminal. Genêt would surely not have objected to having Schiller's words printed at the head of his works: "In the entire history of mankind no chapter is more instructive for heart and mind than the annals of his errors." And Schiller, I believe, would not have turned away from Genêt.

It should be apparent by now that the works discussed up to this point could scarcely be categorized under the heading "A Portrait of the Artist as a Criminal." The criminals that we have encountered, with the mild exception of Raskolnikov, are simply criminals and no more. That is the case even with Genêt, where we are dealing with, if anything, a portrait of the criminal as an artist. His criminality was established first, and hence antecedes his writing. Similarly, Hoffmann's Cardillac is doomed to crime by his "evil star" long before he decides to become a goldsmith (that is, an artist). It would be misleading in these cases to speak of the artist who projects himself as a criminal. For that reason it was necessary to stress, in each case, the criterion of detachment and objectivity. In all these works the criminal is regarded as an object of contemplation, rather than as a projection of the artist's own subjectivity. This criterion distinguishes these works from a substantial group of twentieth-century novels in which we can properly speak of a portrait of the artist as a criminal.

The Artist as Criminal

(3)

APART from all other differences and similarities, André Gide has this in common with Hermann Hesse and Thomas Mann: a veneration of Goethe, Dostoevsky, and Nietzsche as well as a peculiar fascination with crime and criminals. The two traits are not unrelated. We can see this if we consider three characteristic heroes of their early fiction: Gide's Michel in *The Immoralist* (1902), Thomas Mann's *Tonio Kröger* (1903), and Hesse's Sinclair in *Demian* (1917; published in 1919). All three figures are artist-intellectuals; none actually commits a crime in any legal sense. Yet the metaphor of crime leaps to their minds to express their relationship to the world about them.

Michel concludes the narrative of his spiritual rebirth by telling his friends: "I have freed myself, it's possible. But what does it matter? This objectless liberty is a burden to me. It is not, believe me, that I am tired of my crime—if you choose to call it that—but I must prove to myself that I have not overstepped my rights."[21] Similarly, Tonio Kröger regards the artistic part of his being as somehow suspect and contemptible. He tells Lisaveta Ivanovna about a banker of his acquaintance who was put into prison "for conclusive reasons" and there became conscious of his great gift for writing: "Aren't we confronted with the suspicion that his experiences are less intimately connected with the sources of his artistry than the reasons that brought him there?"[22] It is, of course, an ironic vindication of Tonio's intuition that he himself is subsequently interrogated by the police when he visits his home town, on suspicion of being an individual "of unknown parentage and unspecified means wanted by the Munich police for various shady transactions." Like Michel

[21] *L'Immoraliste*, in André Gide, *Romans*, p. 471.
[22] Thomas Mann, *GW*, VIII, 298-99.

and Tonio Kröger, Emil Sinclair is disturbed by the implications of the world, in his case the world to which he is exposed by his friend Demian. In comparison with the puritanical "light" world of his parents, it is a realm of dark powers that he often designates as "criminal." In view of the religious metaphors of the novel, it is particularly symptomatic that he chooses as models for his behavior the "criminals" of the Bible: Cain; the unrepentant thief of the cross at Golgotha; and (like Gide and Rilke before him) the Prodigal Son.

Two facts clearly set these three works apart from the others we have considered. First, they are not concerned with the criminal as an object of aesthetic or moral contemplation. Instead, the criminal becomes a metaphor for the hero, who sees himself in opposition to society. Secondly, the artist is not a criminal because he has committed any act that is technically or legally criminal. Instead, he has offended society by an attitude of mind, by what Gide would call his "immoralité supérieure," by his willingness, indeed his desperate need, to free himself from the shackles of conventional morality in order to fulfill himself as an artist. These criminals are titans of the mind, not of action. At the same time, we detect in them more than a trace of the guilty conscience of the artist that is produced, as we observed in Chapter Six, by the privileged position of timelessness from which he regards the world.[23] And it is this uneasy sense of guilt that suggests, over and over again, the metaphor of the criminal.

This attitude toward "immorality" accounts in large measure for the attraction of Goethe, the "great heathen," of whom Kierkegaard once remarked that he was only one step

[23] Walter Muschg, *Tragische Literaturgeschichte* (Bern: Francke, 1948), devotes a chapter ("Die Schuld," pp. 329-50) to the emergence of the guilty conscience of the artist in the nineteenth century. He does not, however, refer to the metaphor of the criminal.

removed from a criminal. I am referring here to the image of Goethe as it emerges in Gide's early journals, in Thomas Mann's essay on "Goethe and Tolstoy" (and, less so, in "Goethe as a Representative of Bourgeois Civilization"), and in Hesse's *The Steppenwolf* (and, less so, in Hesse's various essays on Goethe). It was particularly what they regarded as Goethe's artistic egoism that inspired them all: his Faustian willingness to submit to any experience for the sake of his development, and to cast off any human bonds that threatened to restrict him in his vocation as an artist. For this reason Gide (in an essay on Goethe in *Feuillets d'Automne*) could say that Goethe gave him confidence in his rebellion against traditional moral values. Similarly, it is a dream-interview with Goethe that sends Hesse's Harry Haller off on the psychic—and, at the end, psychedelic—investigations that result in his acknowledgment of the criminal side of his own being. ("Steppenwolf," wolf from the steppes, is the name he gives to this aspect of his personality.) Several of the scenes that Harry Haller experiences in the Magic Theater at the end of the novel involve, appropriately enough, criminal situations: killing as an *acte gratuit*, precisely in Gide's sense, and a sex murder.

Thomas Mann, in a discussion of the artist's criminality, cites a remark often attributed to Goethe: that he had never heard of any crime of which he did not feel himself capable.[24]

[24] "Dostejewski—mit Massen"; *GW*, IX, 659. After a long and fruitless search for the source of this statement, which is often quoted but never documented, I appealed to colleagues for help. I am indebted to Johannes Urzidil for proposing what strikes me as the most reasonable—and fascinating—solution to the riddle: that Goethe never made the statement in this form. What he did say, in his *Maximen und Reflexionen* (No. 1332 in the edition of Erich Trunz), is the following: "Man darf nur alt werden, um milder zu sein; ich sehe keinen Fehler begehen, den ich nicht auch begangen hätte." This is the statement that Emerson, in his essay on Goethe in *Representative Men* (1850), loosely rendered as follows, translating "Fehler" as

The Artist as Criminal

Mann calls this, admiringly, "an expression of sublime composure—a challenge to bourgeois morality." Gide was also fascinated by the same remark, which he quotes with the comment that "the greatest intelligences are also those most capable of great crimes though ordinarily they do not commit them—out of wisdom, out of love, and because they would restrict themselves by doing so."[25] It is probable, as Renée Lang observes, that Gide's vision of Goethe was "nietzschefied" to a certain extent;[26] here, in fact, we also detect clear reminiscences of Dostoevsky. Yet in a sense their intuition was correct. Certainly it is difficult to imagine Schiller saying such a thing, for Schiller, always incorruptible in his moral position, regarded the criminal as a figure whose titanic energies had been led astray. He was incapable, as we have seen, of identifying with the criminal; he wanted to study him from a distance, objectively. But an examination of Goethe's works shows that he and his heroes are indeed

---

"crime" instead of "mistake": "I have never heard of any crime which I might not have committed." Herman Grimm, who translated Emerson's essay into German in 1857, retained the error; it appears again in the final chapter of his Goethe biography (1877): "Goethe sagt einmal: von allen Verbrechen könne er sich denken, dass er sie begangen habe. . . ." (Notable here is the fact that Grimm, contrary to his usual practice, gives no source for his loose paraphrase.) Grimm's volume, which was an immense success in its original form as a lecture series in Berlin (1874-75), has remained to this day one of the most readable and popular biographies of Goethe. Whether Gide and Thomas Mann found the statement in Emerson or Grimm probably cannot be established; either is a good possibility. But it seems quite a persuasive hypothesis that the famous "quotation" goes back, as Urzidil suggests, to the retranslation of a mistranslation.

[25] André Gide, *Journal, 1889-1939* (Paris: Gallimard, 1955; Bibliothèque de la Pléiade), p. 88.

[26] Renée Lang, *André Gide et la pensée allemande* (Paris: Egloff, 1949), p. 134. This book contains the most extensive study of Gide's relation to Goethe and Nietzsche. But see also Jean Delay, *La Jeunesse d'André Gide* (Paris: Gallimard, 1957), esp. Vol. II: "Persona."

capable of using the metaphor of the criminal to express the position of the artist. (This is particularly striking in view of the infrequent occurrence of the word "crime"—*Verbrechen*—in Goethe's vocabulary.) Thus Goethe's *Torquato Tasso*, a work that the young Gide particularly admired, contains the following reflections on the part of the hero (II, 4):

> War's ein Verbrechen? Wenigstens es scheint,
> Ich bin als ein Verbrecher angesehen.
> Und, was mein Herz auch sagt, ich bin gefangen.
>
> (Was it a crime? At least it seems as though
> I am regarded as a criminal.
> Whatever my heart says, I am imprisoned.)

But Goethe was an exception in his own time. The real authority for the modern immoralists lay, rather, in the more recent figures of Dostoevsky and Nietzsche. In this connection, it was especially the Dostoevsky of the later novels— the psychologist who was intrigued by the moral ambivalence of man, his saintliness and sinfulness—who provided them with an example, and not the young admirer of titanic criminals. Thus Hesse developed his ideas on the decline of European morality and the emergence of a new and higher immorality in his essays on *The Brothers Karamazov* and *The Idiot*, which were published collectively under the title *Blick ins Chaos* (*In Sight of Chaos*, 1921). "The Karamazovs are capable of any crime, but it is only by exception that they commit one. Generally they are content merely to have conceived the crime, to have dreamed it, to have familiarized themselves with its possibility."[27] This definition of the internalization of crime is identical with that which Goethe's alleged remark inspired in Gide. With reference to Prince

[27] "Die Brüder Karamasoff oder der Untergang Europas"; in Hesse, *Gesammelte Schriften*, (Frankfurt am Main: Suhrkamp, 1957), VII, 169.

Myshkin, whose "idiocy" consists in his attempt to view all reality from a moral standpoint "beyond good and evil," Hesse notes that he is understood only by criminals and hysterics. What astonishes us is the fact that "this enemy of order, this frightful destroyer, does not make his appearance as a criminal, but as an endearing, modest man full of a child-like grace and appeal."[28] In conclusion, Hesse notes the essential fact about Dostoevsky's "criminals, hysterics, and idiots": "we regard them differently from the criminals or fools of other popular novels, we comprehend them so uncannily, we love them so strangely, we find something within ourselves that must be related and similar to these people."

The attitude of Gide's lectures on Dostoevsky (1922) and of Thomas Mann's essay on "Dostoevsky—in Moderation" (1946) is essentially identical with that of Hesse. Regarding the figures that people the later novels, Thomas Mann repeatedly uses the word "criminal" to define their attitudes and behavior; in fact, the first pages of his essay represent perhaps the finest statement on and analysis of criminality as a metaphor for the artist ever written.[29] "It seems impossible to speak of Dostoevsky's genius without having the word 'criminal' force itself upon us." He notes that Dostoevsky's conscious and subconscious senses are constantly burdened by a heavy sense of guilt, "the feeling of criminality." He points out that the Idiot, upon recovering from his attacks of epilepsy, "felt like a criminal." And he moves gradually to the more general conclusion that "every intellectual separation and alienation from bourgeois respectability, all independence and ruthlessness of thought—these are all related to the existence of the criminal and afford an empathetic insight into this existence. I find that one may even go on to say that all creative originality in general, all artistry in the broadest

---

[28] "Gedanken zu Dostojewskis *Idiot*"; *ibid.*, p. 184.
[29] *GW*, IX, esp. 656-68.

sense of the word does the same." And he cites Degas' remark to the effect that an artist must approach his work in the same frame of mind as that in which a criminal commits his deed.[30]

What matters for our purposes is not, however, the extent to which Thomas Mann and Hesse (and likewise Gide) have correctly analyzed Dostoevsky. It seems clear, certainly, that they tend to underemphasize the objective aspect of his interest in criminals in favor of his subjective identification with them—a shift of focus that is certainly justified by the dualistic vision of the later novels. But that is irrelevant. Both Hesse and Thomas Mann have used Dostoevsky as the starting point for a theory of immorality that ends with the feeling that the artist who embraces any such immorality is in effect a criminal. In other words, they themselves are so accustomed to using the metaphor of the criminal to designate the artist that they continue to do so when they write about Dostoevsky.

Nietzsche is the third of the trio to whom Thomas Mann, Gide, and Hesse appealed for authority in their positing of an artistic morality that is beyond good and evil. Nietzsche himself, as we noted, had an unmistakably titanic image of the criminal. Though fond of calling himself "the first Immoralist" in order to designate his ethical attitude, Nietzsche never used the criminal as a metaphor for his position, for the criminal is in his eyes a strong man who failed to make the grade, an *Übermensch manqué*. Thus when Thomas Mann speaks of "the loneliness of the criminal" (in his essay on "Nietzsche in the Light of our Experience") or of Nietzsche's "crime of cognition" (in the essay on Dostoevsky), he is im-

---

[30] Jacques Maritain, *The Responsibility of the Artist* (New York: Scribner's, 1960), p. 25, cites this same remark by Degas as an example of the principle that the first responsibility of the artist is toward his work—not to the good of man.

puting his own metaphorical thought to Nietzsche. Characteristically, it is not to the titanic criminals of 1887 and 1888 that
he refers, but to the section "Vom bleichen Verbrecher" ("On
the Pale Criminal") in *Thus Spake Zarathustra* (1883). For
here Nietzsche depicted a different kind of criminal: he is
"pale" because he cannot bear the burden of his crime. "He
was equal to his deed when he committed it; but he could
not endure the image when it was done. Now he always saw
himself as the doer of *one* deed. I call this insanity." In his
essay on Dostoevsky Thomas Mann remarks that he could
never read this passage without thinking of Dostoevsky; indeed,
he voices the surmise that Nietzsche himself had Dostoevsky
in mind when he wrote those words. This is impossible, since
Nietzsche first heard of Dostoevsky only four years after the
publication of *Zarathustra.* Yet it has a certain poetic truth,
for the chapter constitutes an uncannily exact portrait of
Raskolnikov, if not of Dostoevsky.

Their fascination with Goethe, Dostoevsky, and Nietzsche
(a list to which other names could of course be added) provided Gide, Hesse, and Thomas Mann with a certain authority for their theory of the immorality of the artists, which they
recorded in a number of works. It was inevitable that the
metaphor of the criminal, used tentatively and merely as
imagery in *The Immoralist, Tonio Kröger,* and *Demian,*
should precipitate itself sooner or later in the form of heroes
who are criminals in the literal sense of the word. For metaphors have a tendency—in modern literature in any case, as
we have already noted in connection with Kafka—to reify
themselves. In each man's oeuvre we do find criminal figures
who represent the conscience of the artist: the murderer
Lafcadio in *Les Caves du Vatican* (*Lafcadio's Adventures,*
1914), the embezzler Klein in Hesse's *Klein and Wagner*
(1919), and the confidence man in *Felix Krull* (begun in
1911, and published in 1954).

The Artist as Criminal

Both Lafcadio and Raskolnikov commit murder, but the similarity ends there. Raskolnikov is driven to his murders by a variety of complex motives, but his act eventually drives him to remorse and the need for expiation. Lafcadio pushes Fleurissoire out of the speeding train for no reason whatsoever, and afterwards feels not the slightest regret.[31] This murder is not a crime in any ordinary sense of the word; it does not involve any of the associations normally linked with the criminal. Rather, it is a convenient metaphor for the *acte gratuit*, the unmotivated act by which the free man demonstrates to himself that he is indeed liberated from the restraints of conventional morality.[32] It is essentially a gesture. Gide realized, of course, that there is no such thing, in reality, as a completely unmotivated act. As he noted in his remark on Goethe, the greatest intelligences usually do not commit the great crimes of which they are theoretically capable. The *acte gratuit* is more of a theoretical dream—the logical extension of what Gide called his "immoralité supérieure."[33] His fascination with criminals, however, is surely directly related to this concept of freedom. For in the gory documents of unsolved crimes that he collected and published under the title *Ne jugez pas . . .* (1930), Gide was attracted precisely by the fact that there was no discernible motive in these cases. How different this is from the gratification of Dostoevsky, when he read in the papers about a murder committed in Moscow by a young student "from nihilist mo-

[31] Jean Hytier, *André Gide* (New York: Anchor, 1962), p. 116, points out that Lafcadio is "shocked to hear himself called a *criminal*" since he feels no remorse for his deed.

[32] I have found the most helpful discussion of this often confused term in Justin O'Brien, *Portrait of André Gide* (New York: Alfred A. Knopf, 1953), pp. 186-94.

[33] *Journal, 1889-1939*, p. 55. Delay, *op.cit.*, II, 650, defines Gide's term more precisely: "moraliste ambigu et immoraliste douteux, il fut en définitive un amoraliste."

318

tives." He often boasted to his friends of this achievement of his artistic insight.[34] Dostoevsky was proud because he understood the criminal mind well enough to predict its behavior objectively. Gide, on the other hand, combed reality for evidence of the *acte gratuit*, and discovered it primarily among unsolved crimes.

Hesse's Friedrich Klein is a criminal who has embezzled a large sum of money from his employer, deserted his wife and children, and fled to the South in search of a new life and identity. For years he had suppressed part of his personality and lived the role expected of him by a domineering wife, a demanding boss, and a conformist society. He had quite literally been Klein, which means "small" in German. Now he wants to give free rein to other impulses that he feels within himself and that he acknowledges, for revealing reasons, under the pseudonym of Wagner. This name recalls to his mind not only Richard Wagner as the symbol of a supreme artistic sensibility that is indifferent to nonaesthetic values; it also refers to the principal in a famous murder case of just before the First World War. (Ernst Wagner was a psychopathic schoolteacher who murdered his wife and four children.) Here we find again the clear association of the artist and the criminal. "Wagner was the murderer and the fugitive within him; but Wagner was also the composer, the artist, the genius, the seducer, the inclination to *joie de vivre*, sensual pleasure, luxury."[35] The fact that Klein is unable to be Wagner—he rebels at the last moment in the face of a murder he is about to commit, and drowns himself—is beside the point. What is of interest is, once again, the clear instance of a criminal hero conceived purely as a metaphor for the conscience of the artist.

[34] See Simmons, *Dostoevsky*, p. 143.

[35] *Klein und Wagner*; in Hesse's *Gesammelte Dichtungen* (Suhrkamp, 1952), III, 529.

The Artist as Criminal

Felix Krull is a far less somber case. He never entertains even the slightest inclination toward murder or any serious crime. Indeed, like a true criminal in the sense of Genêt, he respects the laws of society and cleverly twists them to suit his own purposes. Yet the association of artist and criminal is no less pronounced here for all the gaiety with which it is presented. It belongs to his earliest experiences, Krull recalls at forty, as he sits in his cell writing his memoirs. His god-father Schimmelpreester taught him, at a tender age, that the sculptor Phidias was also a thief who was put into prison in Athens and who, upon ascending to Olympus, stole again and ended up in Zeus's prison. Later in the work, this same theme is repeated with reference to Hermes, the god of thieves. Krull's entire practice of deception, of the confidence game, is based on what amounts to an aesthetic theory of the absolute work of art. "Only one kind of deception has a chance of being successful and effective among people, and it in no way deserves to be called deception. It is nothing but the endowment of a vivid truth (which has not yet fully entered the realm of reality) with those material characteristics that it requires in order to be recognized and accepted by the world."[36] As critics have long recognized, and as Thomas Mann himself has pointed out,[37] Krull is another metaphor for the artist. To be sure, the metaphor is employed here for comic purposes, but its sense is no less clear. In

[36] *Bekenntnisse des Hochstaplers Felix Krull; GW*, VII, 298.

[37] See Henry Hatfield, *Thomas Mann* (rev. edn.; Norfolk, Conn.: New Directions, 1962), pp. 154-63. Also of interest in our connection is Hatfield's observation that Mann has put a number of Goethe's moral pronouncements into the mouth of his hero. Robert B. Heilman, "Variations on Picaresque (*Felix Krull*)," in *Thomas Mann: A Collection of Critical Essays*, ed. Henry Hatfield (Englewood Cliffs, N. J.: Prentice Hall, 1964), pp. 133-54, offers a brilliant interpretation of the novel as purely picaresque; but he also acknowledges certain criminal traits. And the picaresque, as we have seen, is related by lineage to the tradition of the criminal in literature.

The Artist as Criminal

Thomas Mann's mind, the artist-intellectual is inescapably bound up with associations of immorality and criminality, a theme that plays a major role in the tragic fate of Adrian Leverkühn in Mann's *Doctor Faustus*. Although the word "criminal" is not conspicuous in *The Magic Mountain*, it is clear that Hans Castorp's "aventure dans le mal" is yet another variation on the same basic theme.[38]

In the work of Rilke, finally, the metaphor, though not so clearly developed, is nonetheless present. In the Paris of his immediate experience, as we have seen, Malte thinks of himself not as a criminal, but in the milder metaphor of *Fortgeworfene*—as a castoff, a reject of life. The effect is the same, of course, for in the other works the metaphor of the criminal suggested itself not because of the criminal's evil nature, but for his alienation from society, even his ostracism. But essentially the same metaphor imposes itself as soon as Malte steps out of the present to seek the "vocables of his anguish" in "that heavy, massive, desperate age"[39] of the Renaissance—the very period whose "criminals" Nietzsche, Stendhal, Huysmans, and Pater also admired. Rilke was attracted to that age because "this century had indeed brought Heaven and Hell down to earth":[40] that is, the extremes of human behavior made themselves more radically evident than is the case in our present moderate age. "Who could be strong enough to restrain himself from murder? Who in this age did not know that the utmost is unavoidable?" And the

[38] I assume that this type of literature is implied in the Marxist attacks. Thus the article on "Kriminalroman" in *Meyers Neues Lexikon* (Leipzig: VEB Bibliographisches Institut, 1964) states that literature which glorifies crime without exposing its social causes is typical of "the imperialist period of bourgeois society." This criticism, in any case, would not be relevant to the titanic tradition, which invariably unmasks the causes of the crime, social or otherwise.

[39] *Malte*, p. 916.

[40] *Malte*, p. 912.

lives that he recounts with a strange fascination, and explicitly as metaphorical extensions of his own soul, are those of "criminals": the False Dmitri, fratricides, assassins.

A different attitude is evident, however, when we turn to Franz Kafka. In general technique *The Trial* resembles *Lafcadio's Adventures*, *Felix Krull*, and *Klein and Wagner*; like them, it is essentially the reification of a metaphor. Kafka is not telling the story of a criminal who interests him as an objective reality; rather, the trial of Josef K. is a total and absolute metaphor for his own state of mind. But we become aware of an important difference. First, the problem behind the metaphor can no longer be reduced to that of the artist and society; for Kafka, as we have seen, is thinking more generally of what he considers to be his guilt as a human being. Secondly, the case of Josef K. is so little individualized that the original metaphor becomes, in the course of the novel, a paradigm of or parable for human existence as a whole. Josef K. is not simply Franz Kafka in the sense that Felix Krull is Thomas Mann: he represents Everyman. Whereas Kafka is related to Gide, Hesse, Mann, and Rilke through his use of the criminal as a metaphor, he anticipates a different group of writers, for whom the criminal is no longer simply a specific metaphor for the immorality of the artist, but a general symbol for the guilt of mankind.

(4)

THIS distinction becomes clear if we compare Genêt's portrayal of himself as a criminal with Sartre's study of Genêt. Genêt's own work, and specifically *The Thief's Journal*, belongs to the tradition of the titanic criminal who is regarded and considered as an objective fact. Genêt defines his very existence by reference to the laws and morality of society, which he takes pleasure in violating. He stresses his difference, as a criminal, and flaunts it in our faces. His whole ambition is to force us, the readers, to accept him as he is—as a thief, a homosexual, an offense to the eyes of society, a criminal. Thus he concludes his book: "The prison—let us name that place in both the world and the mind—toward which I go offers me more joys than your honors and festivals. Nevertheless, it is these which I shall seek. I aspire to your recognition, your consecration!"

It is the central argument of Sartre's *Saint Genêt*, by contrast, that this criminal, who reveals to us the foulest abscesses of his soul, is actually the clearest mirror of our own lives. "Whatever the society that succeeds ours, his readers will continue to declare him wrong, since he opposes *all* society. But that is precisely why we are his brothers; for our age has a guilty conscience with respect to history. There have been times that were more criminal, but they cared not a rap for posterity; and others made history with a clear conscience."[41] Sartre seems to be putting his finger, here, on the difference between the titanic criminals of the Renaissance, glorified by Nietzsche and Rilke, and the more squalid criminality of modern society. But he is also highlighting an essential distinction between the criminal as a metaphor for the artist and as a symbol of society. "Genêt is we. That is why we must read him," he tells us on the last page. "Genêt holds the mirror up to us: we must look at it and see ourselves."[42]

This view of the criminal as a reflection of society differs radically from the two views we have considered, and it characterizes another group of novels that we can examine briefly.

[41] *Saint Genêt*, p. 643.

[42] This view of the criminal is to be expected from the author who wrote, in *Le Diable et le Bon Dieu* (1951): "The men of today are born as criminals. I must lay claim to my share in their crimes if I wish a part of their love and their virtues."

The Artist as Criminal

Who are *Les Faux-Monnayeurs* of Gide's novel (1926)? On a literal level, of course, the title refers to the gang of real counterfeiters whose story Gide clipped from *Figaro* in 1906. But on a symbolic level the counterfeit coins passed off by the schoolboys refer to the counterfeit values of an entire society: the phony though successful novels of Passavant, whom Edouard detests; the hypocrisy of the parents of the errant students; the false ideas accepted, out of convenience or in the name of tradition, by a society unwilling to face reality.[43] These are the ideas that Edouard outlines in his theory of the novel (Part II, Chapter 3). The whole problem of writing, he says, boils down to "how to express the general by the particular—how to make the particular express the general." But this is precisely what a symbol does, and it emphasizes the difference between the criminality of *Lafcadio's Adventures* and that of *The Counterfeiters*. Lafcadio's murder is virtually an intellectual exercise; if anything, it is the attempt to express a theory by its projection into reality. It has little to say about society as a whole, and merely renders Gide's theory of liberty and the *acte gratuit*. The counterfeiters have a very real existence in the novel; at the same time they symbolize the entire artificial attitude of the world represented in the novel.

We have seen that Döblin had a professional interest in criminology and psychiatry. As a result he attempted to make his characterization of Franz Biberkopf as realistic and plausible as possible. At the same time, Biberkopf represents more than the "physique and character" of a criminal. "Years ago I had an observation station for criminals," Döblin re-

[43] The symbolism of counterfeiting has been much discussed in Gide criticism. See Hytier, *André Gide*, pp. 212-13, or Harold March, *Gide and the Hound of Heaven* (Philadelphia: University of Pennsylvania Press, 1952), pp. 276ff.

324

called. "That gave me much that is interesting and worth recording. And whenever I encountered these people and others
like them out there in the world, I got a strange image of
our own society: that there is no rigid and definable boundary between criminals and non-criminals, that at every conceivable point society—or better, the part of it that I saw—
was undermined by criminality. That in itself was a unique
perspective."[44] Clearly, Franz Biberkopf is not a metaphor
for the artist or intellectual. He does, to be sure, bear a certain superficial resemblance to the titanic criminal, a good
man destroyed by the powers of society. Yet he is considerably more. The entire structure of the novel, with its montages of the contemporary world, concentrates upon and in
Franz Biberkopf all the currents of modern society, to which
he responds and which his own behavior reflects. The author
repeatedly stresses his typological significance, as we have
noted. It is this view of Biberkopf as a symbolic figure that
permits Döblin to conclude his novel with the paean to freedom, in which he expresses his confidence (which we can
now regard only with a strong irony) that the world is about
to emerge from its depths and rise toward a better society.
But to the extent that Franz is representative, during most
of the novel he reflects in his person the very criminality that
Döblin perceived in the entire society of his time.

In Chapter 32 of *Huguenau* Broch sets forth a theory of
the criminal that corresponds closely to that outlined by
Genêt. The criminal should not be confused with the rebel,
he argues, for the rebel protests against existing society in
an attempt to change it. The criminal, on the other hand—
like Genêt in Nazi Germany—feels distinctly uncomfortable
without the framework of the conventional social structure.

[44] "Mein Buch *Berlin Alexanderplatz*," reprinted in Muschg's edition of *BA*, p. 505.

The Artist as Criminal

The thief and the counterfeiter (Broch writes almost as though he had Genêt and Gide in mind)[45] would have little interest in the proclamations of communism. "The burglar who sneaks out of an evening on silent rubber soles to practice his trade is an artisan like any other. He is a conservative, like all artisans, and even the profession of the murderer —who with a knife between his teeth clambers up the unaccommodating wall—is not directed against the whole community but is merely a personal affair that the murderer has to settle with his victim. There is no attempt to upset the existing order."[46]

Huguenau, according to Broch, is neither a criminal nor a rebel; or rather, he is something of both. As a "deserter" he neither rebels nor conforms: he simply ignores the rules of society. Yet in his behavior during the six months following his desertion Huguenau behaves fully like a criminal: he threatens, cheats, blackmails, rapes, and murders. At the same time, this is the man whom Broch calls "the truly 'value-free' man and hence the adequate child of his time."[47] Of the possible responses to a period of disintegrating values, Pasenow and Esch, by attempting to escape present reality rather than face it, choose false ones. Instead of freeing themselves from the archaic systems of the past, they drag ethics down with them into the realm of the instinctive. This

[45] He could not, of course, have known Genêt; but he refers repeatedly during these years to Gide's work, and the volume itself reveals the influence of *The Counterfeiters*.

[46] *Schlafwandler*, p. 445. Ernst Jünger, one of the most subtle theoreticians of criminality, makes a similar distinction in his essay on nihilism, "Über die Linie" (1950); *Werke*, v, 264. "The nihilist is not a criminal in the conventional sense, for in that case there would still have to be a valid order. For the same reason, however, crime plays no role for him; it moves from the moral context into the automatic." This sounds very much like a description of Huguenau during his "value-free" stage.

[47] In a letter of July 19, 1930; *Briefe*, p. 26.

is what Broch calls the archetype of tragic guilt. "The avenger for this guilt—externally favored by the crisis of 1918—necessarily arises in the 'value-free' objective man (symbolized by an almost criminal type) who simply lives his childhood dreams naïvely to their end in reality: Huguenau."[48]

For Broch, one might almost say, the criminal is more than the symbol of an existing society: he virtually becomes a model for the inaugurator of a future society, a society in which men, relinquishing the useless ideals of the past, will gradually create a new ethical mode realistically adapted to the exigencies of the times. For this reason Broch is able to maintain that the epilogue hints at the possibility of "a returning ethos, the Platonic freedom that alone matters."[49] Huguenau does not reach this state; like a true sleepwalker, he relapses into a convenient set of partial values when his "vacation" is over. Yet he represents the objective "value-free" man who must necessarily precede any new society based on an ethos of earthly values. Whether Huguenau is descriptive or prescriptive, whether his criminality is partially conditioned by his rebellion and his desertion, in the novel he functions neither as an objective titanic figure nor as a portrait of the artist, but as a symbol of society as a whole.

The murderer Moosbrugger is one of the most important characters in Robert Musil's novel *The Man without Qualities*. In the absence of a critical edition of Musil's gigantic fragment, any conclusions regarding the meaning of this unquestionably symbolic figure must be hedged in by a number of cautious reservations. Musil's preoccupation with his elephantine work extended over a period of some forty years; his conceptions changed—often rather radically—as he worked. Stages of the composition are preserved in various manu-

---

[48] Letter of April 10, 1930; *Briefe*, p. 18.
[49] *Briefe*, p. 18; cf. *Briefe*, pp. 25-26.

scripts, from which we learn that the hero was first called Achilles, then Anders, and finally Ulrich. The first two volumes, which Musil himself published in 1931 and 1933, represent more or less his own plan for the novel at that particular stage. But even here the manuscript has not been totally integrated, and certain passages are comprehensible only with reference to earlier plans. After Musil's death in 1942, his widow published further portions of the novel. Finally, in 1952, a "standard" edition of the entire novel was brought out by Adolf Frisé; it is at present the only edition of the complete work available. It now seems clear that Frisé's edition is quite unreliable for critical purposes. On his own initiative Frisé incorporated early versions into the later manuscript, changing the names and making whatever alterations were necessary in order to preserve a superficial appearance of continuity. But the edition almost totally disregards certain important changes in conception. This fact affects the figure of Moosbrugger specifically. In the light of recent investigations, however, it is possible to make a few tentative observations on his probable significance.[50]

Moosbrugger is a dominant figure in the first half of the novel. Guilty of the brutal murder of a prostitute (shades of *Berlin Alexanderplatz*), he is tried for the crime and becomes literally a *cause célèbre* occupying the attention of all the other characters in the novel. As an objective case of criminality he affords the author occasion for essayistic speculations on the subject of criminal law and on the ambiguities

---

[50] I refer particularly to Ernst Kaiser and Eithne Wilkins, *Robert Musil: Eine Einführung in das Werk* (Stuttgart: Kohlhammer, 1962), esp. pp. 48-60 and 151-94; and Wilhelm Bausinger, *Studien zu einer historisch-kritischen Ausgabe von Robert Musils Roman "Der Mann ohne Eigenschaften"* (Hamburg: Rowohlt, 1964), esp. pp. 72-93. In this connection see Hildegard Emmel, *Das Gericht in der deutschen Literatur des 20. Jahrhunderts* (Bern and Munich: Francke, 1963), esp. pp. 56-81: "Das Problem des Verbrechers: Hermann Broch und Robert Musil."

involved in law and psychiatry (e.g., was Moosbrugger in possession of his faculties when he committed the murder), and even for a passage on Musil's favorite topic: the relativism of possible opinions that can be held on a given subject.

At the same time, Moosbrugger is definitely more than an object of aesthetic contemplation, for it is clear that he has a deeper grip on Ulrich, the hero of the novel. "For some unknown reason Moosbrugger concerned him more immediately than his own life that he led; he seized him like an obscure poem in which everything is slightly distorted and twisted, revealing a meaning that drifts, dismembered, in the depths of his heart."[51] Moosbrugger, this sexual offender with the good-natured face, represents saint and sinner in one. (His forename, by the way, is "Christian.") The influence of Nietzsche and Dostoevsky is apparent in the ambivalence of this figure, in whom, as in the Renaissance criminals whose stories Malte recounts, the forces of irrationalism manifest themselves in extreme form. Musil's notes make it clear that this particular theme of the intellectual-murderer *Doppelgänger* belongs to the earliest conception of the novel. In several of the first versions, in fact, the two aspects were to be combined in one and the same figure (Achilles). On a second level of composition (where the hero was called Anders), the dual personality was broken down into two figures: but Anders was to undertake to help Moosbrugger escape from confinement. This seems to indicate that the young Musil shared with Gide, Hesse, and Thomas Mann the conception of the criminal as a metaphor for the artist, as a a projection of the irrational side of his being.

Gradually, however, Musil's ideas changed. According to all indications Moosbrugger was to vanish from sight after the first part of the novel; and Ulrich's interest in him was to

[51] *Der Mann ohne Eigenschaften* (Hamburg: Rowohlt, 1952), p. 124.

be refined into a more critical contemplation, without the metaphoric extension of personal involvement. Instead, Moosbrugger was to represent exclusively a reflection of the sexuality, aggressiveness, and madness that Musil observed in contemporary society. This accounts for the obsession with Moosbrugger in the public imagination. Every conversation returns ultimately to this criminal; every woman dreams of Moosbrugger. And Ulrich is led to observe that "if humanity as a whole could dream, Moosbrugger would have to be the product."[52] If it was Musil's intention to shift the emphasis in this way, then we would have a parallel to Gide's shift from *The Immoralist* to *The Counterfeiters*, from the criminal as a metaphor for the artist to the criminal as a mirror of society.

This final shift is not, of course, limited to writers. It seems to be a general characteristic of contemporary society, reflecting as it were an almost mythic sense of guilt. "Perversions are not actually deviations," Ernst Jünger noted in his *Paris Journal*; "they are liberated elements that are present and active in all of us. . . . Hence the terrible sense of excitement that comes over a metropolis when it is faced with the fact of a sex murder. Then each individual feels the rattling of the bolts in his own underworld."[53] And Sartre says the same at the end of *Saint Genêt*: "To be sure, he wants to impute to us mistakes that we have not committed, that we have not even dreamed of committing. But what does that matter? Wait a bit until you are accused: the techniques

[52] *Der Mann ohne Eigenschaften*, p. 78.

[53] "Das erste Pariser Tagebuch" (October 6, 1942); *Werke*, II, 414. If we accept this reasoning, by the way, then a fondness for detective stories would have to be explained, by analogy, as a sort of spiritual masochism: we admire the cerebrations of the sleuth, but writhe with the apprehended criminal, in whom we recognize ourselves. The ultimate trivialization of this attitude is evident in the film *Bonnie and Clyde* (1967), which depicts a ruthless gangster and his floozy as though they were simply the lovable boy and girl from next door, out on a spree.

have been perfected, you will make a full confession. *There-fore*, you will be guilty."[54]

The phenomenon that Musil presented creatively in the figure of Moosbrugger and that Jünger and Sartre have analyzed critically is precisely the one that led many journalists, both in this country and abroad, to speculate on the more sinister implications of President Kennedy's assassination. For many commentators (and I do not mean, of course, those who suspected a conspiracy involving more than one man) were impelled to ask themselves what sort of society could have bred a man like Lee Harvey Oswald. Can an act of that sort be regarded as an isolated incident, or is it rather the manifestation of a deeper social disorder? The implications of this line of reasoning are so terrible that it has produced what might almost be called a collective nervous breakdown, which is reflected in the literature of the times. For in most recent literary developments, the figure of the criminal has given way to that of the madman as the only "adequate child of our time."[55]

[54] W. H. Auden, "The Guilty Vicarage," in *The Dyer's Hand and Other Essays* (New York: Random House, 1962), pp. 146-58, seems to imply the same conception. According to his theological analysis of detective stories, the main interest lies in "the dialectic of innocence and guilt," while the reader identifies wholly with the detective as a representative of society and order. "If one thinks of a work of art which deals with murder," by contrast, "its effect on the reader is to compel an identification with the murderer which he would prefer not to recognize. The identification of fantasy is always an attempt to avoid one's own suffering: the identification of art is a sharing in the suffering of another." Auden adduces *The Trial* at this point to illustrate the difference between a work of art and the detective story.

[55] I take it that this is what Northrup Frye has in mind (*Anatomy of Criticism*, p. 48) when he speaks of the shift from "an ironic comedy addressed to the people who realize that murderous violence is less an attack on a virtuous society by a malignant individual than a symptom of that society's own viciousness" to the "comedy of manners" in which "the hero is regarded as a fool or worse by the fictional society, and yet impresses the real audience as having something more valuable than his society has."

331

chapter ten

The View from the Madhouse

(1)

WHEN we venture into the realm of recent German fiction, we expose ourselves to the laws of a topsy-turvy world, a fairy-tale kingdom in which normal restrictions are invalid and everyday conditions annulled. It is a land of insanity, abnormality, and absurdity without parallel. In this world people suddenly make up their minds to deform themselves in order to remain children and to play their *Tin Drum*. Sadistic *Giant Dwarfs*—from the title of a prize-winning novel —set upon their parents in bed, tying them together so that they can observe the act of procreation at their lascivious leisure. Gigantic soldiers wander through a *Landscape in Concrete*—another novel-title—where they have the most improbable picaresque adventures and finally kill their girl friends by biting them in the jugular vein. It is a world where the *Opinions of a Clown*—and this does not imply the realistic reminiscences of an Emmet Kelley or a Marcel Marceau —are considered worthy of enumeration. In this world hitherto normal people, rejecting their true identity, suddenly say *Call Me Gantenbein* and put on the yellow armband and the dark glasses of the blind, in order to view the world henceforth from this new point of view.

It is unnecessary to cite further titles, for these five best sellers by well-known and representative writers[1] should suf-

---

[1] In the order mentioned: Günter Grass, *Die Blechtrommel* (1959); Gisela Elsner, *Die Riesenzwerge* (1964); Jakov Lind, *Landschaft in Beton* (1963); Heinrich Böll, *Ansichten eines Clowns* (1963); Max Frisch, *Mein Name sei Gantenbein* (1964). Gisela Elsner does not belong in the same class as the others; she is mentioned here only because her novel, which won the international Prix Formentor, had such a *succès de scandale*.

332

fice to illustrate a characteristic phenomenon in German fiction between 1959 and 1965.[2] We note first that the typical hero of the German novel in the early sixties presents himself as a pronounced caricature or distortion of human nature. These heroes are not rounded characters, but exaggerations, to the point of absurdity, of certain traits—lust, sadism, irresponsibility, cutting frankness, and so forth—that are usually suppressed or at least balanced by other elements of the personality.

This leads us immediately to a second observation. The fictional world that is created in these novels is regularly presented from a distorted perspective. In most cases we are dealing with first-person narratives: the dwarf, the giant, the clown, or the supposedly blind man tells us his own story and thus offers us his own point of view as the only proper one. In the cases when there is a third-person narrator, the latter identifies himself so closely with his hero, after the fashion of Kafka, that absolutely no discrepancy is apparent between the views of the fictional figure and those of the narrator, who might otherwise put the world back into its customary perspective. It is, in other words, a deformed world that is offered to us. For this reason we have moved an important step beyond the criminal of the preceding chapter: the criminal occurred as a metaphor or symbol, but he did not determine the point of view of the narrative. (Even Genêt accepted the framework of conventional morality.) Here, however, we have more than the simple metaphor of insanity: we are asked to share this view from the madhouse.

Finally, the typical mood of this world is a grotesque and often macabre gallows humor, which unmasks the absurdity of everyday reality and gives the novel its tone.

[2] Every reader can easily supply additional examples of his own from German and American literature: Arno Schmidt, Friedrich Dürrenmatt, Reinhard Lettau; John Barth, Joseph Heller, Bruce Jay Friedman, John Updike.

View From the Madhouse

Characteristics of this sort distinguish the most recent fiction from the typical novel of the first postwar years. The representative hero of the period 1945-1955 was a returning veteran to whom the world at home had become alien—an outsider, but not a caricature. His perspective was slightly off-center, but still related to the whole. Very often he appeared in the guise of his typological ancestor Odysseus, possibly the first returning veteran in world literature.[3] Like Beckmann in Wolfgang Borchert's *Outside at the Door* (*Draussen vor der Tür*, 1947), like the sober, lyrical "I" in the poems of Günter Eich, like the melancholy soldiers in Heinrich Böll's early stories, he could not identify fully with the prevailing reality of the postwar world, yet he did not deny its existence. In contrast to the often scurrilous exuberance of much recent prose, the tone of those first novels was consciously restrained and low-keyed.

In his book on postwar German literature Marcel Reich-Ranicki[4] coined a number of suggestive designations for those first representative authors: Hans Erich Nossack he called "the sober visionary"; Alfred Andersch "the vanquished revolutionary"; Siegfried Lenz "the calm accessory." Note the adjectives: sober, vanquished, calm. They characterize quite precisely the tone of most German prose up until about 1955. These writers distrusted any kind of stylistic bravura, dismissing it contemptuously as "calligraphy." But the nouns of the epithets—visionary, revolutionary, accessory—point to future developments, for they indicate an awareness and tension that produces an inner conflict. The sober hero who calmly criticizes society will permit himself to be good-naturedly humored, tolerantly shrugged off, or rejected with shocked as-

[3] See my article "The Odysseus Theme in Recent German Fiction," *Comparative Literature*, 14 (1962), 225-41.

[4] *Deutsche Literatur in West und Ost: Prosa seit 1945* (Munich: Piper, 1963).

tonishment for only so long. Finally he assumes the role that society forces upon him: the role of the fool, the court jester, the blind man, the abortion. If you treat a writer as a clown long enough, then he will finally appear as a clown. We have here an almost classic case of the collective reification of a metaphor. Perhaps in this role, the writer thinks, he can jolt society into attention, if it refuses to heed sober admonition.

This radical displacement of the fictional perspective can nowhere be seen more clearly than in the proliferation of insanity in recent German literature. It is a veritable bedlam of madmen. Think of the three international theatrical successes from Germany: Friedrich Dürrenmatt's *The Physicists* (*Die Physiker*, 1962), Karl Wittlinger's *Do You Know the Milky Way?* (*Kennen Sie die Milchstrasse*, 1955), and Peter Weiss's *Marat/Sade* (*Die Verfolgung und Ermordung von Jean Paul Marat*, 1964) all take place in a madhouse. Insanity, so to speak, represents the final stage of a process: it is the ultimate intensification of the role of the outsider who is rejected by society or who himself rejects society—alternatives which in the last analysis produce the same effect. In order to understand the implications of this development, as well as the dangers inherent in it, let us consider a few typical examples. The first is Ernst Kreuder's delightful fantasy *Enter without Knocking* (*Herein ohne anzuklopfen*, 1954).

(2)

THE SCENE of the action in Kreuder's novel is a neurological clinic. In the first chapter the hero leaps out of a speeding train, clambers up the wall, and jumps down into the courtyard of the asylum, where he remains until the end of the novel as a voluntary paying guest. In this sanatorium everything is inverted. The patients are completely in possession of their senses; only the chief psychiatrist is mad. For

View From the Madhouse

Kreuder the madhouse has become a place of refuge, where normal people can withdraw in the face of the ostensible insanity of everyday reality. Kreuder's hero, who is nameless for the first half of the book, expresses this unambiguously in the second chapter of his story:

> Anyone who looks around in the world today, among the people in his neighborhood, and has not completely lost his senses—any such person is horrified by the unimaginable ugliness, the detestable ugliness that manifests itself wherever 'healthy common sense' prevails unhindered. . . . Anyone who is repelled by ugliness because he knows that beauty is reality, uncorrupted reality, distrusts the machinations of that 'healthy common sense' which is so well adapted to exploiting the starving and protecting the prosperous from any discomfort; so well suited to justifying heartlessness and to making a life-task of public and planned deception. The calculation is simple: the much-vaunted common sense excludes the most human capacity, sympathy, and thereby it breaks the contact with all that is animate, with reality.

Kreuder supplies us with a typical case of the displacement of perspective, for in his novel the equation is absolutely equal: normal is insane and insane is normal. Genuine human understanding, which treasures the good and the beautiful, thrives in the madhouse; the outside world is in a state of madness. The occupants of the sanatorium live in complete freedom, for they may be just as they wish, without being compelled to play roles forced on them by society. Outside, by contrast, life is ruled by what Kreuder calls the "Summer Schedule of the Strait-Jacket Life" or the "Official Timetable for Human Age," and freedom is merely an illusion.

But Kreuder's fantasy remains completely unproblematic, for the two worlds hardly come into conflict. The inmates are able to found their League of Brotherliness without hindrance, for they have no difficulty duping their demented doctor. Otherwise the outside world cannot touch them. Kreuder is concerned solely with depicting this model of a world in reverse. He cares neither for the realization of his vision nor for the problematic confrontation of the two worlds. At most, he is interested in the paradigmatic antithesis: we see life and the ideal, reality and the absolute. Because the two realms remain separated by the walls of the asylum, no crises are produced. The whole remains a charming and even instructive fantasy, for Kreuder's concern is aesthetic rather than ethical.

But Kreuder's successors go beyond this pure contrast. In his novel *Billiards at Half-past Nine* (*Billard um halbzehn*, 1959) Heinrich Böll carries the theme a step further by translating the confrontation of the two worlds into moral terms. For Böll the madhouse still possesses the value of the absolute, but this novelist is so deeply committed to the present that he is not content with a flight from reality. The madhouse has become a place of respite, of regaining inner composure, from which one ultimately returns to act in the world outside.

Böll's novel portrays a family that has stubbornly refused to take part in the ugly reality of a Germany gone mad. As in Kreuder's novel, each of the three main figures has created for himself a refuge from detested reality. The grandfather, Heinrich Fähmel, conceived in his youth the social role that he intended to play in life, and by blindly acting out this role for fifty years has succeeded in disconnecting himself from reality; in his innermost being he does not feel affected by the world outside. His son Robert protects himself from the assault of the world by translating all external reality immediately into aesthetic abstractions: for him life takes place on the billiard table or in the mathe-

337

matical formulae that he dreams up for his amusement. But the grandmother, Johanna, has acted most consistently: she has fled to the madhouse.

Johanna's ostensible "insanity" revealed itself quite early. In 1917 she was impelled by her antipathy toward the First World War publicly to label its instigator an "imperial fool" —a case of *lèse-majesté* that was excused at the time as due to an intellectual infirmity attributable to her pregnancy. (Here already we see that Kreuder's formula is still valid: the person who sees the truth clearly is dismissed as mad.) Johanna's intellectual "infirmity" manifests itself again during the Second World War, when she refuses to accept from the family's rural properties any foods to which she is not legally entitled. Instead, she hands out bread, butter, and honey to strangers who are less favored. Her Christian love for her fellow men, which she not only affirms in principle, but also puts into action, is again held to be insanity. Finally, her remarkable behavior, which also takes the form of criticism of the government, comes to the attention of the authorities, and there is only one possible way for her to save herself. In 1942 she has herself declared insane and withdraws into the madhouse. But even sixteen years later, in 1958 (the year in which the novel takes place), Johanna still prefers her life in the madhouse to everyday life in the Federal Republic of Germany, and her explanation clearly reminds us of Kreuder's lovable madmen. "I can't step back into the magic circle again," she says. "I am afraid. Much more than before. You have obviously gotten used to the faces, but I am beginning to long for my harmless idiots." The asylum is again the place of brotherly love and true humanity, in contrast to the false and inhuman reality of the ostensibly healthy world of reason.

This reverse symbolism is brought out even more clearly in the course of the novel through the introduction of parallel

338

figures. For instance, Böll mentions a parish priest whom the church authorities have hidden away in a remote village because of his mad ideas:

> There he preaches away over the heads of the peasants, the heads of the school children. They do not hate him, they simply don't understand him. They even venerate him, in their fashion, as a lovable fool. Does he really tell them that all men are brothers? They know better and secretly think: "Isn't he a communist, after all?"

We are still dealing with the same displacement of perspective that we noted in Kreuder's novel. The view from the madhouse is actually the view with which the author identifies—and along with him, naturally, the reader—while the everyday world remains mad and in need of redemption. But Böll adds a fuse to this potentially explosive situation when, unlike Kreuder, he allows the two worlds to come into contact.

The novel takes place on various temporal levels. On the one hand, the reader learns, through frequent flashbacks, how it happened in the course of fifty years that grandfather, grandmother, and son of the Fähmel family came to shut themselves off from the prevailing reality. On the other hand, the level of the present action culminates in a moment of decision. This is what matters to Böll: not the mere representation of the model situation, but the moment of decision and action. On this September day of 1958 all three main characters suddenly realize that it is not sufficient to stand apart from life, looking on with aesthetic detachment; it is necessary to intercede actively. In other words, one must return from the secure idyll of the madhouse into the chaos of the everyday world if one wishes to assert oneself as a free individual. At this point Böll goes beyond Kreuder's aesthetic antithesis of real and ideal. But the confrontation of the absolute ethos of the madhouse with the relativized reality of the world presents difficult problems.

Mother Fähmel decides to make an energetic protest against the false life of the present, where the very men who occupied important offices in the Nazi government are still in positions of high authority. She returns to reality and, with a pistol that she has stolen, shoots at a minister of state—a man who once again threatens to set Germany on the same fateful path that led it into two world wars. She does not shoot for revenge, she says, but in order to prevent any future evil. She calls the minister "the murderer of my grandson," and she says that she is committing "not murder of a tyrant, but murder of a man who claims to be decent." Her shot is the symbol of her protest against the deceitful respectability of a generation that has forgotten an evil scarcely past, and it shatters the protective shells in which the members of the family have lived for years. Here, at the end of the novel, both the grandfather and son decide to return to reality (from which each had retreated at age twenty-nine!) and take an active part in life. The minister has escaped with a light wound; Johanna appeals to Paragraph 51 of the penal code (mental incompetence)[5] and is returned to her madhouse, where she feels most at home in any case. Everything has seemingly been resolved. As far as the family is concerned, the symbolic shot unquestionably has a beneficial effect: Heinrich and Robert will no longer be satisfied to observe the world condescendingly from their aesthetic distance. They will attempt, each in his own way, to alleviate the visible ills of the world.

But are we not left with a sense of nagging uneasiness?

[5] This is the same Paragraph 51 under which Franz Biberkopf (*Berlin Alexanderplatz*, p. 491) was admitted to the sanatorium some thirty years earlier. The German *Strafgesetzbuch* has been in effect since 1871.

What if the minister had died? Has not Böll evaded here a certain thorny dilemma? For if in this novel the perspective of insanity is the one with which we are expected to identify, then does the madman actually have the moral right to commit murder? And if so, is not the symbolic effect of the protest immediately canceled out by the appeal to Paragraph 51, to mental incompetence? We can take a protest seriously only if the one who protests is prepared to lay his or her own life on the line, to accept the consequences of the protest. Is it not logically inconsistent that the moral attitude for which the author has enlisted our sympathy should turn out, in the end, to be "incompetent"?

To put the question in this way is, naturally, purposely crude and somewhat unfair to Böll. In the first place, the minister does not die; in the second place, Mother Fähmel is not the most representative figure of the novel. But Böll's novel reveals the difficulties that arise if one attempts to confront madness, as a model of absolute good, with the reality of everyday life. The madhouse as a symbol of truth is valid only as long as it remains hermetically sealed off, as it does in Kreuder's novel. As soon as the absolute begins to intercede in the world, certain moral dilemmas not easily disposed of unavoidably arise. Böll's novel merely hints gently at this problem.

Thomas Valentin's first novel sounds virtually like an answer to Böll's implicit question. In *Hell for Children* (*Hölle für Kinder*, 1961) the discrepancy between absolute truth and action has been intensified to the utmost extreme. Once again, it is an action in the present that is glaringly illuminated by a series of flashbacks. The traveling salesman Ernst Klewitz is introduced as a man who had a miserable childhood, a circumstance that has led him to the bitter conclusion that life is nothing but hell for children. This conviction, irrespective of its validity, develops in the case of Klewitz into a real psychosis and finally brings about a nervous breakdown. Around this time he becomes acquainted with a boy whose unhappy existence reminds him of his own childhood. He decides, like Böll's Mother Fähmel, to act. In order to save the child from his drunken parents, he attempts to flee with him. When the police catch up with the two of them at the border, Klewitz decides to kill the boy rather than to expose him again to the beatings of his brutal parents.

We see that Valentin has here stretched to the very limit the moral dilemma that is merely suggested implicitly by Böll. To be sure, Klewitz' conviction, his view from the madhouse, is in an absolute sense as correct as Johanna Fähmel's. But he succeeds in carrying out the murder that she botches, and the reader, who up to this unexpected turning point has identified with Klewitz, suddenly recoils in horror. Does Klewitz' view, however right it may be, entitle him to extinguish a human life? And here at the very end we come upon a surprising twist. Klewitz' lawyer tries to persuade him to appeal to the aforementioned Paragraph 51, but Klewitz refuses to accept what he regards as a cheap way out. "How is it that suddenly, in the middle of my life, I am mentally incompetent for a week? I don't accept the gift! I don't understand why they open this door to me, this door to the freedom to be temporarily insane. I understand absolutely nothing but one thing: they cannot take the responsibility away from me! I don't want their revolting sympathy."

Valentin is pleading just as passionately as Böll for a change in the world. For him, also, the view from the madhouse is a view of the truth. But he proceeds to the final consequence of this attitude. If circumstances are completely reversed, then the obligation for moral responsibility now rests with the madman. He may no longer withdraw, under the protection of Paragraph 51, into the idyllic world of the madhouse; he must submit to justice. The absolute is valid only in the madhouse; in life one must compromise. So the model remains—but it is only a model.

This is perhaps the ultimate explanation for the surprising turn of events that electrifies the reader at the end of these two novels. The authors apply their whole skill to winning us over to the reversed perspective—and then shock us with the dilemma that arises as soon as one attempts to apply this truth in life itself. This is thus the final ironic meaning of these novels: that a world in which such moral dead ends can exist is in dire need of change. From under the mask of the madman peers the revolutionary, who no longer expresses his opinions so soberly and calmly. He makes us accomplices in the crimes and murders that are committed—a lesson learned, by the way, from Dostoevsky. And the reader, who has allowed himself to be caught up in the enticing perspective of "insanity," can no longer evade the moral responsibility imposed at the end. This constitutes the cleverest manipulation of *littérature engagée*. The sober veteran, who fifteen years earlier was still standing "outside at the door," now grins at us from the portals of the madhouse.

(3)

THIS obsession with insanity is of course not unique in postwar literature. Scholars have long been aware of the prevalence of the theme of insanity in the works of German romanticism,[6] and it is no accident that the phenomenon occurs at this particular time. For insanity was not in fact defined in its present sense until the end of the eighteenth century.

[6] See Hermann A. Korff, *Geist der Goethezeit* (3rd edn.; Leipzig: Koehler und Amelang, 1959), III (*Frühromantik*), pp. 162 and 222; and Albrecht Schöne, "Interpretationen zur dichterischen Gestaltung des Wahnsinns in der deutschen Literatur" (Dissertation: Münster, 1952). For the more general background, see Michel Foucault, *Madness and Civilization; A History of Insanity in the Age of Reason*, trans. Richard Howard (New York: Pantheon, 1966).

View From the Madhouse

The word for insanity (*Wahnsinn*) had existed in German at least since Martin Luther's translation of the Bible in the middle of the sixteenth century, but the concept had entirely different associations for Renaissance man: madness was viewed as a spiritual affliction to be revered, not as a mental aberration to be understood and healed. It was only when the notion of madness was secularized, some two hundred years later, that the word entered into common usage as the designation for a state of mental illness. This semantic fact is related to a curious historical circumstance. Even during the Age of Reason men did not yet make clear distinctions between insanity and other forms of behavior arbitrarily lumped together as irrational. The great places of confinement for which the seventeenth and eighteenth centuries are notorious were used indiscriminately for the mad, the criminal, and the impoverished. Insane asylums for the specific care of the mad came into being only after the French Revolution. Michel Foucault dates the modern attitude toward madness from 1794, the year when the inmates of Bicêtre were released from their chains. From this time on, insanity was regarded with a new sympathy and a new interest. A similar symbolic date might be established for Germany as well.

In 1796 Christian Heinrich Spiess published a collection of *Biographies of Madmen* that responded to public demand much as did the *Causes célèbres* in the case of criminality.[7] The preface even contains a similar rationalizing justification:

> Insanity is terrible, but it is even more terrible that one can so easily become a victim of it. Overstrained and violent passion, deceived hope, forlorn prospects, often merely imagined danger can deprive us of the most precious gift

[7] *Biographien der Wahnsinnigen* (Leipzig, 1796). I find it equally symptomatic of the times, by the way, that this volume was recently reprinted in a splendid new edition by the publisher of Günter Grass's works (Neuwied and Berlin: Luchterhand, 1966).

of our Creator: our reason. And who among mortals can boast that he was not once in a similar position, hence in a similar danger? If I recount to you the biographies of these unhappy persons, I do not wish merely to awaken your sympathy, but to demonstrate to you above all that each of them was the author of his misfortune, hence that it lies in our power to prevent a similar misfortune.

The literature of the period contains many figures who dance precariously along the edge of the abyss of insanity. We recall the despairing harp-player in Goethe's *Wilhelm Meister's Apprenticeship* (1795-1796), the poet Balder in Ludwig Tieck's *William Lovell* (1793-1796), the fury-ridden night watchman of the anonymous *Vigils of Bonaventura* (*Die Nachtwachen des Bonaventura*, 1805), the mysterious *Doppelgänger* in E.T.A. Hoffmann's *The Devil's Elixirs* (*Die Elixiere des Teufels*, 1815-1816), or the composer Johannes Kreisler, who figures in several works by Hoffmann. Generally speaking, these and the other frequent cases can be reduced to a common denominator. These figures, all of them brilliant, expose the perils of a romantic subjectivism that has been exaggerated to the point of solipsism. These near-madmen are, in other words, the caricature of an age that had surrendered heart and soul to the philosophy of Fichte and Schelling. This is most clearly expressed in the raving speech of the ducal tutor Schoppe in Jean Paul's novel *Titan* (1800-1803):

"Sir, anyone who has read Fichte and his General-Vicar and Brain-Servant Schelling as often as I for pleasure, finally becomes serious about it. The Ego posits Itself and the finite Ego along with that remnant that some people call the world. . . . The Ego thinks Itself, therefore it is an 'As-if' Subject and at the same time the depot for both—the devil! there is an empirical Ego and a pure Ego. . . . I can

345

tolerate everything but the Me, the pure, intellectual Me, the God of Gods—How often have I not changed my name like my cousin-in-name-and-deeds Scioppius or Schoppe, becoming a different person annually, but the pure Ego still pursues me perceptibly."[8]

It is a delightful exercise to trace this parodied Fichteanism through the works of romanticism, but the result remains everywhere the same. Insanity is considered a condition of pathologically exaggerated sensibility, of subjectivism carried to an absurd extreme. Sometimes this subjectivism is the object of persiflage (as in Jean Paul); sometimes it is rendered as a grave warning (as in Tieck); sometimes it is represented as a means of cognition (as in Hoffmann). But in contrast to the characteristic conception of insanity in contemporary literature, we can detect the following differences. First, these cases have no typological value; they are exceptions (often artists or men with artistic proclivities) who possess a deeper insight into the secrets of nature than the ordinary citizen. Thus the hero of *Heinrich von Ofterdingen* (1802), according to Novalis' paralipomena, was supposed at one point to assume a "voluntary madness" in order to "divine the meaning of the world." Yet their cognition in no sense invalidates the meaning of the everyday world, but merely transcends and intensifies that meaning. Secondly, these madmen are concerned solely with metaphysical and transcendental matters; their madness leads them into no conflict with the prevailing reality. The two worlds, then, are not contradictory but complementary: two levels of the same organic unity that constituted nature in the eyes of the romantics.

If we bypass the lovable eccentrics of Gottfried Keller, Theodor Storm, and Wilhelm Raabe—they are usually mere-

---

[8] *Titan*, 33rd "Jobelperiode," 132nd "Zykel." The language of the original is just as idiosyncratic as that of my translation.

ly idiosyncratic, with no hint of real insanity—then it is not until the early twentieth century that we again encounter a pronounced fascination with the phenomenon of madness.[9] In the major novels of the twenties and thirties insanity once again plays an important symbolic role: we think, for instance, of the murderer Moosbrugger in Musil's *The Man without Qualities*, the stonemason Gödicke in Broch's *The Sleepwalkers*, and Franz Biberkopf during the last book of *Berlin Alexanderplatz*. In this connection we also recall Georg Heym's stories, the visions of insanity in the poems of Georg Trakl, or the miserable end of Adrian Leverkühn in Thomas Mann's *Doctor Faustus*. Examples from the works of the period can easily be multiplied.

But times have changed. Here insanity fulfills an entirely different function from that it assumed in romanticism or in contemporary fiction. In the first place, these figures—Leverkühn, Heym's madman (in "Der Irre"), Gödicke, Moosbrugger, and Biberkopf—are without exception clinical cases of true insanity: they represent neither an exaggerated subjectivism nor the "correct" point of view. The psychiatric interest of a generation schooled in Freud reveals itself both in the careful motivation and in the factual description of the psychosis.[10] In the second place, these cases of insanity symbolize an entire civilization that is shot through with insanity. Ludwig Gödicke, who according to Broch has suffered a total breakdown and must now painfully reassemble "the

[9] One significant exception, which in many respects anticipates the twentieth century, is Georg Büchner's powerful novella *Lenz* (written in 1835), which portrays the madness of the dramatist Reinhold Lenz. Büchner was himself a trained physiologist with a particular interest in the nervous system.

[10] It is worth noting that these same years produced a variety of studies by psychiatrists with a literary bent, both on the relationship between genius and insanity and on literature as a source of documentation for cases of insanity.

components of his ego," corresponds to a pluralistic age that has lost its unifying center of values. And the symbolic parallel between Adrian Leverkühn's insanity and the decline of Germany during the Nazi period has often been pointed out.

Döblin noted in 1927, while he was finishing *Berlin Alexanderplatz*, that he had learned something very important during his days as a resident physician in the neurological clinics: "I discovered that I can tolerate only two categories of people along with plants, animals, and stars: children and madmen."[11] This statement is obviously a rhetorical exaggeration, but it helps to explain both the tenderness and the clinical detail with which he depicts Franz Biberkopf's weeks in the sanatorium at Buch. Needless to say, to the extent that Biberkopf is a representative man, his paranoia must also be regarded as symbolic of the condition of the age as a whole, a collective illness that Döblin hoped might be cured by greater self-awareness, by sacrifice, and by cognition of death.

Musil's Moosbrugger, finally, is not only a criminal; he is also a madman who has been in and out of several asylums before his trial for the murder of a prostitute. Musil seems to separate these two functions. Moosbrugger's lawyers, it is reported, "made little use of the most obvious explanation: that it was a case of mental illness. . . . It looked as though they were still hesitating to give up their villain and to release the incident from their own world into that of the sick—a matter in which they agreed with the psychiatrists, who had declared him healthy as often as they had declared him men-

[11] In the essay "Arzt und Dichter"; *Aufsätze zur Literatur*, p. 362. In this essay Döblin speaks of the relationship between his profession as doctor and his vocation as writer.

tally incompetent."[12] Even Moosbrugger himself plays the game, using French and Latin expressions that he has picked up in various prisons and madhouses. "Moosbrugger did not let a single opportunity pass to demonstrate, in the public trial, his superiority over the psychiatrists and to unmask them as pompous simpletons and swindlers who were totally ignorant and ought to accept him into the madhouse, when he simulates, rather than sending him to prison where he belongs." Despite the vacillation between crime and insanity, between insanity and moral responsibility, it is clear that Moosbrugger symbolizes the collective psychosis of an entire society.

In all these cases, then, we are dealing with insanity in the strict sense of the word—that is, with a genuine psychosis—and this insanity is held up as the mirror of an insane age. This differs quite radically from the literary function that we noted earlier. For in the works of Böll, Kreuder, and Valentin the madness is in no sense, or at least not primarily, a psychiatric condition, but a moral one. And it does not reflect its age, but is presented in dialectical contrast to the prevailing reality.

(4)

MADNESS as a literary symbol has a long and venerable history, a history that reaches back to the *poeta vates* of antiquity and to which *Don Quixote* as well as Dostoevsky's *The Idiot* belong. But the meaning of the symbol changes with the times. It is a convenient framework into which each generation places its own values. In his study of the eccentric in German literature Herman Meyer observes that the eccentric, who occurs so frequently in literature of the eighteenth

---

[12] *Der Mann ohne Eigenschaften*, p. 70; quotation below, p. 74.

and nineteenth centuries and who is closely related to the madman, virtually disappears with the emergence of naturalism.[13] Meyer attributes this phenomenon to the rise of positivism; for the eccentric, as a type, is dependent upon the belief in the metaphysical freedom of man: eccentricity interests us as a possibility of life for the completely free man. (This is the same justification that our own hippies claim for themselves in the mid-sixties.) Positivism, by contrast, regards man simply as a random intersection of certain biological and sociological conditions. The eccentric no longer has any value as a valid potentiality of human existence and human development, but is considered as nothing more than a pathological exception, having at most a certain clinical interest.

So we can probably conclude that the reappearance of symbolic eccentrics and madmen in our own age indicates the presence of a philosophical foundation in which, once again, freedom occupies a central position. It is just such a philosophical basis, indeed, that we find in the various trends of existentialism, under whose banner so many postwar novelists have written. As in so many other cases, Nietzsche is one of the important sources of this contemporary phenomenon. In the preface to *Thus Spake Zarathustra* (1883) the prophet expresses his disappointment that people do not want to hear the message he has brought back from his ten years in the mountains. "Not a single shepherd and *one* herd!" he exclaims. "Everyone wants the same thing, everyone is alike: whoever feels otherwise goes voluntarily into the madhouse." Here, seventy years before Kreuder, we find precisely the same symbol used in precisely the same way: the madhouse as the refuge of true understanding, in contrast to an uncomprehending world.

Nietzsche had elucidated the basis for his image in *The*

[13] Herman Meyer, *Der Typus des Sonderlings in der deutschen Literatur* (Amsterdam: H. J. Paris, 1943), esp. Chap. 8, pp. 223ff.

View From the Madhouse

Dawn (*Die Morgenröte*, 1881), his speculations on moral prejudices. In a section entitled "The Meaning of Insanity in the History of Morality"[14] Nietzsche praises "madness" as the force that breaks through the bonds of conventional morality to new ideas and values. "Almost everywhere it is madness that paves the way for new thoughts, that breaks the spell of venerated customs and superstitions." He even goes a step further, claiming that "all those superior men, who felt an irresistible urge to break the yoke of some false morality and to establish new laws, had no alternative—*if they were not really insane*—but to become insane or to pretend to be so." And this holds true, Nietzsche claims, for innovators in every area, not merely in religion and politics. Nietzsche comes back to this image, in one form or another, repeatedly. Thus he suggests that the Good, the Beautiful, and the Mighty need to keep a court jester if they want to hear the truth; for the court jester is "a being with the prerogative of the madman, not to be able to adapt himself."[15] On the whole, Nietzsche's use of the symbol of madness, like almost everything else about him, was in distinct opposition to the prevailing notions of positivism, which (like the old professors in *Berlin Alexanderplatz*) regarded insanity merely as a physiological condition to be cured by sweatbaths.

Among the writers of the twenties and thirties who shared Nietzsche's conception of madness, none is more conspicuous than Hermann Hesse, who asked himself in all seriousness

[14] Book I, Paragraph 14: "Bedeutung des Wahnsinns in der Geschichte der Moralität"; *Werke*, ed. Karl Schlechta, I, 1022-24.

[15] Book V, Paragraph 451: "Wem ein Hofnarr nötig ist"; *Werke*, I, 1230. See also Günter Grass, "Vom mangelnden Selbstvertrauen der schreibenden Hofnarren unter Berücksichtigung nicht vorhandener Höfe," *Akzente*, 13 (1966), 194-99. Though Grass does not mention Nietzsche, he speaks of the glaring conflict between the compromises necessary in reality and the uncompromising nature of true art— much like Böll or Valentin.

whether, under certain cultural circumstances, it is not "more dignified, nobler, more proper to become a psychopath than to adapt oneself to the present conditions at the expense of all one's ideals."[16] (It is symptomatic that Hesse, in 1919, outlined his beliefs in a major essay entitled "Zarathustra's Return.") In *The Steppenwolf* (1927) madness is the symbolic form that Hesse's belief in Magical Thinking takes. This belief, outlined particularly in his essay on Dostoevsky's *The Idiot*, holds that true reality consists of an acceptance of all aspects of the world, and not merely of that half that is arbitrarily called good or right by conventional bourgeois morality.[17] Harry Haller, the "Steppenwolf," sees himself at the beginning of the novel as a rather schizophrenic personality who belongs in part to the bourgeois world and in part to the wilderness of the steppes. The two fallacies of his thought are: first, that he regards these two parts of his personality as contradictory rather than complementary; and second, that he has oversimplified the totality of the world into this simple dualism.

The mysterious tract that he obtains at the beginning of his adventures bears the motto "Only for Madmen." It outlines the development that he must undergo in order to become a full human being: he must accept all the impulses of his nature that he has hitherto repressed so carefully. A short time later, when he meets the prostitute Hermine, he tells her: "Don't scold! I already know that I am mad." He is amazed when Hermine, the prophetess of his humanization, replies: "You're not at all mad, Herr Professor. In fact, you're far too little mad to suit me!" Haller's entire reeducation toward an acknowledgment of his personality, then, is seen under

[16] *Kurgast*; in Hesse, *Gesammelte Dichtungen* (Suhrkamp, 1952), IV, 57.

[17] "Gedanken zu Dostojewskis *Idiot*" (1919); *Gesammelte Schriften*, VII, 178-86.

the aspect of madness. Consistently, before he enters the Magic Theater toward the end of the novel, as he approaches the culmination of his spiritual odyssey, he receives the warning: "Only for Madmen. The Price of Admission is Your Reason."

In *The Steppenwolf*, then, the meaning of insanity differs completely from the meaning that it carries in other contemporary works: *The Man without Qualities, Berlin Alexanderplatz, The Sleepwalkers*. For Hesse, as for Nietzsche, the values have been reversed: the madman sees the truth that is hidden from the "rationality" of the everyday, bourgeois world. The madhouse is the refuge where man can discover his individuality in total freedom.

Nietzsche and Hesse are the direct precursors of the philosophical freedom that we find again in *Enter without Knocking*. Kreuder's madmen also seek in the sanatorium above all a place of freedom where they can be themselves, without being forced to fulfill false roles thrust upon them by society. But very specific limits are imposed upon this existential freedom. On the one hand, man has the absolute freedom to determine his own being. He is at liberty to be "mad." But on the other hand, his freedom ceases the moment it threatens to encroach upon the freedom of his fellow man. Man possesses, so to speak, a negative freedom: the freedom to rebel, to protest against the prevailing reality, to be philosophically mad; but this implies in no way the absolute freedom to act. For this reason Kreuder keeps his madman carefully segregated from the world outside; Zarathustra is most at home among the eagles on his mountain, far from the "herds" below. And Harry Haller is truly free only in the psychedelic visions of the Magic Theater; at the end of the novel he returns once more to reality. Böll and Valentin, by contrast, show the serious dangers that arise when the free man seeks to act in accordance with his "mad" convictions. With the remarkable prescience of first-rate writers they anticipate the moral issues and ambiguities that, in the course of this decade, have been shifted from literature to the front page of every newspaper by the civil rights movement, the debate concerning Vietnam, and the student rebellions.

(5)

THERE are only two avenues of escape from the dilemma posed by the radical confrontation of reality and the absolute. The first is the way of tragedy, in which man comes into conflict with the laws of ethics through his acts. This is probably the deeper meaning of the novels by Böll and Valentin: as long as the world is not changed, the free man must either remain in the madhouse or perish. For if a man insists on asserting his absolute values in reality, he transgresses the legitimate boundaries of his own freedom.

Second, there remains the escape of humor. But if this humor arises from a perspective that, as we have seen, is in itself perverted or mad, then it can easily degenerate into the grotesque.[18] The result is the novels of Günter Grass, Gisela Elsner, Jakov Lind, and others. The grotesque has one immeasurable advantage: it makes possible a nontragic action, since it no longer operates through the antithesis of reality and the absolute. Instead it takes place in an intermediate realm where the madman can do anything he likes: remain a child and play his tin drum; overpower his parents and tie them together in bed; bite his beloved to death; play the role

[18] See Wolfgang Kayser, *Das Groteske; Seine Gestaltung in Malerei und Dichtung* (Oldenburg and Hamburg: Gerhard Stalling, 1957). I am not using the word precisely in Kayser's sense, but these contemporary grotesques display several of the characteristics that Kayser defines (pp. 193-203). Kayser stresses the grotesque perspective, which presents an alienated world as an expression of the id in various manifestations of the absurd.

of a blind man or a clown. The radical confrontation is avoided from the start by the displacement of the perspective of the entire work. The reader knows immediately that he is not dealing with conventional reality, but with a realm of the imagination where normal rules no longer apply.

Recent German literature is rooted, for the most part, in an existential experience of the dualism of self and world, in which the individual seeks desperately to preserve his own freedom in the face of a detested reality. Since 1945 this awareness has passed through three stages or degrees of intensity. In the first stage, everyday reality still dominates the foreground, and the lonely individual is forced to the side with his protests. (This is the general pattern followed by the early postwar literature, which focused on the experiences of returning veterans.) On the second level, the position of the outsider has become absolute: reality and truth confront one another as outside world and madhouse. (This is the pattern of the madhouse novels of Kreuder, Böll, and Valentin.)[19] In the third stage, finally, reality has been completely vanquished: we are left with a realm of the imagination shaped and controlled wholly by the view from the madhouse.

---

[19] The same pattern can be observed, by the way, in the many closed-scene dramas of the period, in which the place of action is symbolically shut off from the world: e.g., the prison in Siegfried Lenz's *The Time of the Innocent* (*Die Zeit der Schuldlosen*, 1961) and in Hermann Moers's *At the Time of the Thistle Blossom* (*Zur Zeit der Distelblüte*, 1959). In both of these plays the theme is not so much criminality as madness in the sense in which we have discussed it. For the same reason, moreover, Thoreau's famous remark in his essay on "Civil Disobedience" belongs in this category: "Under a government which imprisons any unjustly, the true place for a just man is also a prison." For Thoreau is concerned with justice, not with evil as the symbol of a titanic hero. One feels reasonably sure that Thoreau would not have been comfortable with Genêt, or Dostoevsky's Orlov, or even with Schiller's Christian Wolf. But he would have been right at home in Kreuder's madhouse or with Böll's Mother Fähmel.

(This is the pattern of the grotesques of Grass, Lind, Elsner, and others.)

At this point German literature reached the final limit in the displacement of perspective. It could not be pushed any further. In one of his best known essays Ortega y Gasset claimed that the distortion of perspective has led to the "dehumanization of art" in the twentieth century.[20] Ortega was thinking particularly of abstract painting, but his conclusions apply equally well to recent literary developments. For the danger existed—and still exists—that the most recent prose writers, by making the distorted perspective into an absolute point of view, might gradually lose all contact with human values if they do not return to the level of human reality. The last chapter of Günter Grass's *The Tin Drum* vividly demonstrates how difficult it is to get back to reality from the realm of fantasy.

We recall that Oskar Matzerath, that obscene and infantile dwarf, is writing his memoirs during a two-year period of custody in a mental institution. His life up to this point has taken place on the level of fantasy, where it was unnecessary to assume any moral responsibility. From this level he fled—by way of transition, so to speak—into the madhouse, where he is still secure from the onslaught of reality. On his thirtieth birthday he learns that he is now going to be released. He must return to the outside world, or, to put it more precisely: for the first time in his life he must submit to reality and its ethical system. For his entire previous life has taken place in the fairy-tale world of fantasy, where questions of guilt and innocence do not become acute.

What I have feared for years, ever since my flight, announces itself today on my thirtieth birthday: they

[20] In *The Dehumanization of Art, and Other Writings on Art and Culture*, trans. Helene Weyl and others (New York: Anchor Books, 1956).

have found the true guilty man, they re-open the case, ac-
quit me, release me from the nursing home, take away
my sweet bed, put me out into the cold street which is exposed to all the elements, and compel a thirty-year-old
Oskar to collect disciples around himself and his drum.

Like Valentin's hero, Oskar Matzerath realizes that Paragraph 51 is merely a temporary solution: ultimately a man
must take upon himself the responsibility for his own deeds.
Life, if it is to have any meaning, must finally return from
the realm of the imagination and the madhouse into reality.
Grass, in a brilliant move, has reversed the historical process:
his hero moves symbolically back from the world of the
grotesque through the madhouse to the everyday world.

What is valid as the theme of a novel, however, also has
a certain validity as an aesthetic principle. The flight into
the grotesque is only a temporary solution, which cannot satisfy us in the long run. The theme of insanity, with its radical
confrontation, shows that the humanly interesting problems
take place in the border zone where reality and the absolute
collide. This is the territory where literature has always produced its greatest works. The radical displacement of perspective from this border zone is a characteristic of postwar
German literature—and not only of German literature, of
course. Black humor in England and America as well as the
theater of the absurd tend in the same direction. This attitude has produced some fascinating and unforgettable works
that often cast an unexpected light on life and glaringly illuminate its absurdities. But how far from the center can the
perspective be displaced?

By 1965 German literature had reached a precarious point.
The flight into the grotesque, as effective as it may be at
times, could no longer satisfy, for it ultimately became an
aesthetic evasion of the burden, indeed, of the duty of taking

an ethical position. In the hands of mere trivializers it had become an amoral and hence inhuman form of art. Moreover, the grotesque degenerated to such an extent during the years of its popularity that it became an empty routine, no longer bringing forth the desired effect of aesthetic alienation, but at most the yawn of *déjà vu*. The grotesque arose initially as the response to a reality that writers considered so absurd that it could be treated only by absurd distortion. But when everybody is insane, then the rational man again comes into his own.

THE HISTORY of literature can be read, from one point of view, as the continuing struggle of rationality against irrationality, of control against excess, of subject against object. Every Rousseau has his Voltaire. Classicism inevitably summons forth the romantic revolt. In postwar Germany—and elsewhere too, I believe—the total displacement of perspective into the madhouse has produced a reaction to the other extreme. This has been conspicuously the case in the theater, where the documentary drama has recently taken precedence over the theater of the absurd. The case of Peter Weiss is paradigmatic: he had his first international success with a madhouse play (*Marat/Sade*), but he followed it up, only a year later, with *The Investigation* (*Die Ermittlung*, 1965), an "oratorio" lifted verbatim from the records of the Auschwitz trials. Two other notable successes have been Rolf Hochhuth's *The Deputy* (*Der Stellvertreter*, 1963), a heavily documented attack on Pope Pius XII for his dealings with the Nazis; and Heinar Kipphardt's *The Affair of J. Robert Oppenheimer* (*In der Sache J. Robert Oppenheimer*, 1964), based on the hearings of the Atomic Energy Commission in 1954.

In the novel a similar phenomenon can be observed both in the United States and abroad. Truman Capote's "non-fiction novel" *In Cold Blood* (1965) has been one of the most successful books of the sixties; but the question of literary merit aside, it unquestionably represents a reaction against the novel of the absurd and against the black humor that dominated the literary scene for a number of years. In France certain practitioners of the *roman nouveau* have attempted to create a novel in which the perspective is wrested away from any narrator, mad or otherwise, and handed over to the objects of the everyday world. Alain Robbe-Grillet has provided a theoretical basis for fiction of this kind in his essays *Pour un nouveau roman* (1963). For our purposes it suffices to note that both the "non-fiction novel" and the *roman nouveau* reveal a disenchantment with the trend that, in its ultimate excrescence, produced the madhouse novel and the grotesque.[21]

Critics in Germany have made subtle distinctions between the various trends that have emerged there in the past few years; critics have to make a living, too. But from a broader, international perspective, most of these movements can be grouped together generally as a collective reaction against the grotesque with its emphasis on distortion and subjective idiosyncrasy. In Dortmund, for instance, a group of young writers who call themselves *Gruppe 61* have begun drawing their subject matter, according to the title of their recent anthology, from *The World of Work*. Several other novelists, who have become known as exponents of "Cologne Realism," have produced a type of narrative, often more programmatic

[21] The debate regarding "Document or Literature" has become so urgent that it provided the theme for the seventh conference of German and French writers, held in Bourges (December, 1967) and sponsored by the International Office for Communication and Documentation. For a stimulating discussion of recent developments in the German, French, and English novel see Hector-Jan Loreis, *Nieuwe Roman=Nieuwe Filosofie; Van de nouveau roman naar de nouveau nouveau roman* (Brussel and Den Haag: Manteau, 1967).

359

than aesthetically effective, in which the author disclaims any psychological insight and attempts to withdraw with coy self-effacement behind the objects of his fictional world. And in general, the most recent generation of German writers has devoted itself (with more earnestness than success) to various adaptations of the *nouveau roman*. The outsider, after his stay in the madhouse, now suffers under the delusion that he is a camera or a tape recorder.

This unresolved tension between subject and object, between man and the world, characterizes much of the writing in Germany today. The novels produced by the adherents of the new realism are no more likely to endure than the more irresponsible effusions of the grotesque. Many contemporaries seem to have forgotten a basic aesthetic principle that Friedrich Schlegel perceived over a century and a half ago. In his notebooks for 1797 Schlegel observed that the lyric form is purely subjective, while dramatic form is purely objective. "As form, the epic obviously has precedence: it is subjective-objective." And ten years later he noted that "epic poetry is the root of the whole and the exact middle between the wholly interior lyrical and the wholly exterior dramatic poetry."[22] This is a principle that the major novelists seem to have followed instinctively. Kafka knew that objectivity of form applied to a world of objects produced a dull, pedantic gravity; hence he focused his objective view on human actions. Rilke knew that subjectivity of form applied to the human subject produced an unbridled, idiosyncratic whimsy; hence he focused his subjective view on the world of things. In both cases the tension between subject and object was resolved harmoniously by means of a unity of aesthetic design or mythic action. But in novels where the subject is allowed

[22] Friedrich Schlegel, *Literary Notebooks, 1797-1801*, ed. Hans Eichner (Toronto: University of Toronto Press, 1957), pp. 48 and 238.

to rampage, uncontrolled by an objective view, there can be no unity of form; and in those where the object prevails, untempered by subjective feeling, there can be no meaning.[23] The finest novelists in Germany today, such as Heinrich Böll and Günter Grass, seek a delicate balance between the two extremes in their attempt to do justice both to reality and to the individual with his sense of the absurd: Böll through a selective totality within a symbolic model, and Grass through the totality of multiplicity within a mythic action.

If it is possible to derive any consolation from literary history, we can recall that the most impressive works have usually represented a synthesis of antithetical attitudes: *The Magic Mountain*, whose hero is man, the "Lord of the Antinomies"; *The Sleepwalkers*, where the total rationality of the essay is balanced by the utter irrationality of the lyrical outcry; *Berlin Alexanderplatz*, in which the chaos of the city is restrained by the structure of classical tragedy. The greatest poets and novelists have always been those whose profound commitment to the world was matched by an unflinching dedication to the human soul. Rilke, in any case, was such. And such, too, was Kafka.

---

[23] A similar situation exists in poetry as well: at one extreme the often formless and highly propagandistic poetry of action; at the other, the essentially meaningless, ideographic forms of "concrete" poetry.

Index

Index

Index

289-95; will to, in Schiller and Genêt, 299-300; mythicized by Genêt, 308-9 criminal, and rebel contrasted, 292n., 325-26; shift of interest to detective, 292-94; different literary treatments of, 295; romantic view as titan, 297; Dostoevsky's view, 301-5; as metaphor of artist in Gide, Hesse, Mann, Rilke, 310-22; as symbol of society for Broch, Musil, Döblin, Sartre, Jünger, 322-31

Curschmann, Michael, 271n.

Dali, Salvador, 187
Dante Alighieri, 69, 262
Darwin, Charles, 192
death, modern obsession with, 215-17; pre-modern attitudes toward, 217-18; sublimation of through art, 218-19; modern view of as immanent in life, 219-22; four factors determining modern view of, 222-28; in *The Notebooks*, 232-35; Mann's view of, 235-38; Broch's view of, 241-47; and mysticism in fiction, 247-53; Kafka's view of, 253-57; treatment of in novel of thirty-year-old, 278-80
Degas, Edgar, 316
Dehmel, Richard, 105
Delay, Jean, *La jeunesse d'André Gide*, 313n., 318n.
Descartes, René, 192
detective, replaces criminal as hero, 292-94
Detektivroman, 293

"Deutscher Michel," as hero, 113, 126, 135
Dickens, Charles, *Bleak House*, 293
Diderot, Denis, 295; *Neveu de Rameau*, 296-97, 298, 301, 302, 306n.
Dilthey, Wilhelm, *Das Erlebnis und die Dichtung*, 226
Döblin, Alfred
  general: his obsession with facts, 102-3; his life, 104-6; his view of simultaneous experience, 205; interest in criminals, 324-25; sympathy for madmen, 348; and *passim*
    works: *Manas*, 103, 112; *The Three Leaps of Wang-Lun*, 103, 105, 123n.; "Discourses with Calypso," 105; *Lydia und Mäxchen*, 105; *The Murder of a Marigold*, 105; *German Masquerade Ball*, 106; "Self over Nature," 106
  Berlin Alexanderplatz: contrasted with *The Magic Mountain*, 99-100, 137; three functions of weather reports, 99-101; role of narrator, 100, 110: montage, 100-2, 207; compared with Dos Passos and Joyce, 107-8; role of city, 107-9; vertical and horizontal simultaneity, 108-9; productive role of language, 110; Biberkopf as exemplary hero, 111, 136, 286; conflict between chaos and order, 113-16; leitmotifs, 114-16; Biberkopf analyzed according to Kretschmer, 117-19; theme of sacrifice, 119-20, 240;

Index

Index

Index

Index

Index

Index